CAMBRIDGE STUDIES IN PHILOSOPHY

Portraying analogy

CAMBRIDGE STUDIES IN PHILOSOPHY

General editor D. H. MELLOR

Advisory editors J. E. J. ALTHAM, SIMON BLACKBURN,
DANIEL DENNETT, MARTIN HOLLIS, FRANK JACKSON,
JONATHAN LEAR, T. J. SMILEY, BARRY STROUD

Portraying analogy

J. F. Ross

Professor of Philosophy
University of Pennsylvania

Cambridge University Press

CAMBRIDGE
LONDON   NEW YORK   NEW ROCHELLE
MELBOURNE   SYDNEY

Published by the Press Syndicate of the University of Cambridge
The Pitt Building, Trumpington Street, Cambridge CB2 1RP
32 East 57th Street, New York, NY 10022, USA
296 Beaconsfield Parade, Middle Park, Melbourne 3206, Australia

First published 1981

Printed in Great Britain by
Redwood Burn Limited
Trowbridge, Wiltshire

Library of Congress catalogue card number: 81–15463

British Library Cataloguing in Publication Data

Ross, James F.
Portraying analogy.–(Cambridge studies in
philosophy)
1. Analogy
I. Title
169   BD190

ISBN 0 521 23805 6

Contents

v

*I dedicate this work to Kathleen
and our children, Seamus, Ellen, Richard and Therese.
In recognition of their great love.*

Preface

The same word often has different but related meanings (e.g. *catch*/fish; *catch*/ball). Some philosophers have proposed that shades and kinds of such differences can be explained systematically. Aristotle and Aquinas developed theories of analogy to account for such phenomena, theories they applied to the philosophy of language, metaphysics, philosophy of science, philosophy of nature, theology and ethics, and that distinctively characterized their philosophical styles and even their products, such as analogous definitions.

After investigating the analogy doctrines historically, (Ross 1958, 1961, 1962a and b) and applying them to religious discourse (1970b), I began to examine whether the 'classical account', the account developed from Plato and Aristotle through Aquinas and Cajetan (1498), approximates the truth or points toward truths about meaning with similarly comprehensive consequences for contemporary philosophy.

By 1970 it emerged that the analogy phenomena have to be comprehensively redescribed because the classical theory suffers from limitations of scope and perspective (see chapter 1) and is based upon false premises, chiefly: (1) that word meanings are ideas-(concepts-, thoughts-) in-the-mind-signified-by-conventional-sounds; (2) that sentence meaning is the molecular sum (syncategorematically computed) of the atomic meanings of the component words; (3) that different meanings for the same word are formally *caused* by differences in the referents, differences that are reflected in the conceptions, formed by abstraction, that *are* the meanings of the words; and (4) that only some words are analogical, equivocal, and the like.

In fact, the key assumptions and metaphors of the classical story about analogy were exhausted, as far as fruitful theoretical elaboration is concerned, by the time Cajetan produced *De Nominum Analogia* in 1498, the last systematic explanation of analogy of meaning since the middle ages.

And so, over the last decade I have undertaken a new investigation, exploiting Aristotle's, Aquinas' and Cajetan's insights into the analogy phenomena and into the profound consequences of such phenomena for philosophy, to identify an explanatory structure inherent in natural language and to trace some of its ramifications for philosophical analysis. At least to a first approximation, I have found an explanation for analogy of meaning, both denominative and proportional, and have identified some very important consequences for philosophy.

I thank the many people who have influenced this work, especially Roderick M. Chisholm, a model of philosophical excellence, who suggested my inquiring into analogy in 1957 and is surely an originating cause.

Felix Alluntis, O.F.M., first introduced me, as an undergraduate, to Duns Scotus in 1951 and emphasized the importance of understanding the analogy debate. Arthur T. Geoghegan, another teacher and friend for thirty years, taught me as a teenager that a good thinker develops positions of his own, enriched with historical perspective – something also encouraged by the late Francis P. Clarke, my friend and predecessor at the University of Pennsylvania. A number of friends helped by their obvious respect for the idea that contemporary thought can be enriched with distillations from medieval achievements, among them my colleagues Charles Kahn and Elizabeth Flower, Norris Clarke, S.J., Mary T. Clark, C.S.S.J., Alan Wolter, O.F.M. and Ronald Santoni and his colleagues at Dennison University.

I particularly thank the generous philosophers who examined my work in their papers – George Mavrodes, William Rowe, David Burrell, L. S. Lyons, Tobias Chapman, D. Griffin, Charles J. Kelley, Kai Nielsen, John Donnelley, James J. Heaney, Norris Clarke, Edwin Curley, Edward Weirenga, Robert Oakes and John Hick.

I have had only one discussant in depth on these matters, my friend Margaret Wilson, who astutely noted my lapses from promised explanations and diagnosed some counterintuitive classifications of examples, while steadfastly nourishing my confidence. She recommended that I find some form of publication before I killed interest in the material by baroque elaboration. For her faith that something worthwhile would eventuate, and for other things, I cannot express thanks enough.

Otto Springer, Vartan Gregorian and Claude Welsh (an exemplar of a friend) and David Goddard brought the resources of the University of Pennsylvania to my assistance for leaves of absence when help was indispensible. Similarly, I thank Morton White who supported my 1975–6 year at The Institute for Advanced Study,* Princeton, where I thought about analogy while inquiring into the relationship between natural rights and natural law (results forthcoming in due time).

I particularly acknowledge Nelson Goodman's *Languages of Art*, (1968) that made my world partially the product of his art and discourse. Phillip Quinn discussed a version of this material, responding with written suggestions that, along with the remarks of other members of the 1977 NEH Summer Seminar at Brown (Faith, Meaning and Religious Knowledge)† led to a substantial rewriting of the book. Chris Bache, a self-styled stowaway at the mentioned Seminar, disputed me persistently and developed the opinion that analogy is the coral reef of dead metaphors. Some of the many contributions of seminar members are mentioned from time to time in text and notes.

Many secretaries helped. Janet Wolff did the first major typing, followed by Sherri Jones. Duane Williams, a philosopher with more important things to do, set up the basic typescript that has since gone through several rewritings. My daughter, Ellen, typed directly from my henscratch in 1977 and collated drafts of the footnotes in six different manuscripts. Diane Stillwell and Lore Silverberg typed the antepenultimate draft. And the penultimate retyping was done by Kathy McClendon, Mrs Ruth Hugo, Marie Cannon, Margaret Rose Steeg, and Sandy Natson. The final typescript was prepared by Sandy Natson.

* My research at the Institute for Advanced Study was supported by an N.E.H. Grant to the Institute, no.FC 10503.
† N.E.H. Grant award no.FA-26537-77-163 to Brown University.

Introduction

Why look for a systematic account of the meaning relationships different tokens of the same word[1] have to one another (*drop*/stitch, *drop*/friend, *drop*/hint) when hardly anyone seems to have missed having one for five hundred years?

First, something with comprehensive philosophical consequences may have been overlooked. Both Aristotle's and the medieval Aristotelean writers' accounts of analogy (of diverse but related same-word meaning) affected the whole of those philosophies.

Secondly, the linguistic phenomena are pretty much as the classical writers said they were, though their explanation is not right. Such extensive data fairly beg us to probe for the hard bone of law underlying 'focal meaning', 'family resembling terms', 'systematically ambiguous expressions' and the panorama of verbal proportionality, metaphor, denomination and paronymy, remarked by philosophers of all epochs and persuasions.

Thirdly, there is no competitor for the classical account, despite its false foundations, mentioned in the Preface, and its limitations of scope and perspective, described in chapter 1. We need a competing portrayal, preferably one that construes the superficially chaotic data as the logical outcome of simple linguistic universals.

Fourthly, the analogy phenomena require revisions in the philosophy of language and probably in the philosophy of mind as well. A systematic study of same words refutes the assumptions that sentence meanings are the syncategorematic 'sum' of independent word/morpheme meanings (like a wall assembled out of varied stones) and that an ideal dictionary would have an entry for every meaning of every word in the language. Instead, the analogy phenomena and the 'software' that creates them support 'infinite polysemy' hypotheses (cf. Weinreich 1971: 322, and Lyons 1977: §13.4, 550f) and establish that one expression affects the meaning of others concatenated with it.[2] Further, the analogy phenomena disconfirm that sentences have truth conditions that are their senses,

1

and that knowing its truth condition is necessary for knowing the sense of a sentence, and so require a reassessment of the objectives and capabilities of truth-conditional analysis (see chapter 8).

Moreover, opinions about the relationships of thought to language – like the revived Ockhamist 'language of thought' idea (Fodor 1975) – that suppose meaning to be affixed to inscriptions and sounds by their relationship(s) to something *else* (whether 'sentence-like mental representations', thoughts, or denoted things) will fail, as the medieval 'concept' theory of meaning did, to explain the analogy phenomena.

Instead, we have to work from the premise that *linguistic* meaning is intrinsic to acceptable expressions in natural language. It is not some extrinsic relationship of the parts, one by one or all together, to thoughts or other things, but is the contrasting combinatorial acceptability *among* the distinct words of the language.

Lastly, if analogy of meaning is even substantially as I construe it, there are consequences for what philosophical analysis can do; for instance, a philosopher cannot provide a single truth-conditional analysis of what 'being a cause', 'knowing', 'being thought' (and most of the other things philosophers want to know about) *really* is. Yet we can refine a practicable relationship between analysis and analysandum and we can find a place in philosophy again for fashioning 'analogous' definitions. So there are important incentives for reopening this old topic.

Although I use the classical account (summarized variously at pp. 17–19, 164–5, below) to identify and initially classify the data that need an explanation, I do not absorb it into the present theory. That is because it assumes, wrongly, that same-word meaning relationships do not result from linguistic structure, but from the relationships of thought to things. Yet, without the classical observations and hypotheses, I doubt that I would have found the phenomena coherent enough to demand explaining (after all, Wittgenstein's identifying family resembling terms did not stir demands for their explanation) or have realized how much rethinking about linguistic meaning philosophers still have to do. So, I frequently mention what Aristotle, Aquinas and Cajetan said, not as 'scholarly boilerplate' but because their perspective upon the issues is still revealing.

2

This is a typical explanation, one that (i) conceptually aligns and classifies observed phenomena and (ii) identifies an underlying structure that (iii) logically (or causally) determines the observed phenomena to be as they are (in the relevant respects needing the explanation). As far as it is practicable, I describe the explanatory structure in terms of the broadest explanatory factors known in the area of inquiry.

It is not explanation in the sense of finding the (efficient) cause of a happening – e.g. explaining someone's being taken sick or how an accident or fire happened; this is a structural explanation of a *kind* of happening, like an explanation of what hepatitis is in terms of what the liver is and how it functions.

I call it a 'portrayal' because the explanation's key predicates are metaphorically extended from other realms of discourse and are not yet naturalized citizens in talk about meaning, the way 'attraction' and 'force' became long ago in physics. The metaphor, as Aristotle remarked, 'puts the matter before the eyes' (*Rhetoric*, III, ch. 2 and ch. 11). It reveals the presence of law where before there appeared only disorder, just as a certain profusion of dots with the right perceptual set causes the faces of the Presidents or various animals to emerge. Thus, 'dominance', 'resistance', 'adaptation', 'contagion', 'intransigence', 'linguistic inertia' and 'linguistic force' are used metaphorically to draw a new picture of analogy.

The most important question for evaluating a new portrayal, I think, is this: What does it make us see in its subject that was not accessible to us before? In the present case it is that analogy of meaning (all the analogy phenomena including mere equivocation) is the consequence of an underlying synchronic structure, composed of (i) *linguistic inertia* (that words recur in the same meanings if nothing differentiates them) and (ii) *linguistic force* (that words resist concatenating into unacceptable expressions by making step-wise meaning-adaptations, comparatively to other occurrences, to avoid doing so.)

The judgment that one portrayal is better than another is not justified exclusively by the narrower considerations that apply to whether, *within*, say, a Kantian portrayal of knowledge, one account is 'a better explanation than another'. For, as in painting, comprehensiveness, inventiveness, discipline and an inexhaustible revelation (in the representation) of what is represented have more to do with significance and preferability than item by item truth. 'Science . . . is willing to accept a theory that vastly outreaches its evidential basis if that theory promises to exhibit an underlying order, a system of deep and simple connections among what had previously been a mass of disparate and multifarious facts.' (Carl Hempel 1966: 132.) Besides being as embracing as the classical account, I think this portrayal of analogy meets two conditions for being preferable: (i) the more you understand the portrayal, the more the phenomena *appear* as portrayed; (Goodman 1968: 33, reports someone's telling Picasso that his portrait of Gertrude Stein did not look like her; Picasso replied 'It will'); (ii) the more extensively this picture is compared with the classical one, the more the phenomena appear to be as portrayed here *rather than* as in that account.

Some of the layers in this account have involved project-bound decisions about the predicate scheme model (to be explained in chapter 3), about how to characterize predicate modes and about how extensively to use explicit definitions as a means of conceptual alignment; these are all matters that might have been handled differently, or more successfully, without much change in the overall observations or explanation. So, one has to distinguish the details that are incidental, temporary, dispensible and entangling, from the underlying insight into differentiation, its causes, and the systematic identification and distinction of analogy, simple metaphor, mere equivocation, denomination and paronymy. These things can survive a rather considerable reformulation of the whole explanation.

2 THE GENERIC PHENOMENON

Everyone who speaks one of the relevant natural languages (the living Indo-European ones, at least), from the youngest speaking children through the least intelligent persons capable of coherent discourse and the most sophisticated masters of the language, characteristically and automatically uses the same words in different meanings, sometimes related (*see*/light, *see*/point; *collect*/books, *collect*/friends, *collect*/debts, *collect*/barnacles), and sometimes unrelated (*charge*/enemy, *charge*/battery, *charge*/account).

4

The *Merrill Linguistic Readers* (Fries 1966), widely used for beginning reading, employ common words like 'fix' in multiple senses to achieve variety of expression within a beginner's vocabulary: 'Daddy will *fix* you', '*Fix* my wagon', '*Fix* my pants', '*Fix* my dinner', '*make* a bed', '*make* a sandwich', '*make* a mistake', '*make* time for', '*make* a plane', '*make* an appointment', and so on. It is *easier* for a small child to comprehend the same word with multiple meanings than it is for him to distinguish the same number of visible word forms. So the child has *already* mastered response to some semantic structure by which distinct senses for the same word are determined in context. What is that structure?

Further, the multiple English entries for a single Italian word in an English–Italian dictionary (J. Grassi 1933) illustrate its variety of meanings: '*levare*' means 'to raise, lift up, take away, remove, carry, take off, raise up, lift, get out, buy (a large quantity), prohibit, levy.' (In English the words 'raise' and 'lift' pretty much divide the senses of the Italian word between them). And '*dare*' means 'to give, hand, grant, permit, commit, appoint, announce, produce, yield, show, tell, stroke, dart, incline to, sell, buy . . .' Certainly native speakers know what '*dare*' means, so something determines which sense the word has. What is it?

Other dictionaries – French, Polish, Spanish, German – yield consonant results, as do dictionaries employed in reverse to give multiple foreign-word equivalents for English words. Which meaning a word has in a given occurrence is neither random nor haphazard, and yet what determines which meaning it has cannot be the speaker's *intentions* about what the words are to mean, either. For who, except perhaps a poet, has embracing intentions as to what individual *words* are to mean? And who knows how by *intention* to determine what a word means (except to stipulate or to distinguish)? It cannot be done by intention alone. For a string of words can mean exactly what we intended them *not* to. We are looking, instead, for a universal linguistic force – some ubiquitous causation – that is present throughout the language (as inertia and gravitation are present throughout the universe) and is variously manifested by identifiable phenomena in all extended discourse.

Aristotle and Aquinas, as I said, recognized that the meaning relationships among same words are regular, classifiable (as mere equivocation, analogy of proportionality, metaphor, or denomination) and systematically explainable; (their explanation was a

5

theory of concept-generation). But no succeeding mainstream philosophers, except for Locke's interest in denomination (*Essay* III, III, 171 VI, 9 and III ch.25, 2–7), paid serious attention to accounting for same-word meanings, not even Wittgenstein after he turned up 'family resembling terms' while digging for other things.

The search for what determines which meaning a word has in a given context, and what accounts for its differences from one occurrence to another, gains the prospect of success once we notice that *all* the regular cases of a word's having diverse meanings have a common feature. (That doesn't include, of course, the *initial* cases of direct borrowing from another language and of stipulation and misuse – what Boethius, and then Cajetan, called 'equivocation *a casu*' (by chance) in contrast to 'equivocation *a consilio*' (by convention.) That common feature is *differentiation* (contrasting adaptation to context), *fit* to diversity of linguistic environment. Sections of chapter 3 illustrate it and show how it is caused by 'dominance' (see below). Here I stress that differentiation has both homonymy and polysemy as outcomes. The classical writers, by failing to identify anything common to mere equivocation and analogy, missed uncovering the structual 'software' that generates the whole range of analogy phenomena and diachronically develops the expressive capacities of the language. (See sections 4 and 5 below.)

3   THE SPECIFIC ANALOGY PHENOMENA

There are five meaning relationships explained in this book. For now, I will provide examples and brief descriptions with the warning that these descriptions skip essential qualifications offered later, and that the 'examples' (e.g. *charge*/account) are shorthand for examples in complete discourse environments. In general, I ask the reader to interpret the examples as if they were in complete environments that disambiguate them as I construe them.

(a) *Mere equivocation* Examples: *charge*/account, *charge*/enemy; *watch* (time), *watch* (duty crew); *pen* (writing), *pen* (enclosure); *bank* (verge), *bank* (depository). Description: same words (the same from the point of view of spelling and sound) that are *unrelated* in meaning. As will be shown, no near synonym of the one instance is also a near synonym of the other, unless it, too, occurs merely equivocally.

(b) *Analogy of proportionality* Examples: *collect*/pension, *collect*/books; *create*/time, *create*/trouble; *establish* (verify), *establish* (demonstrate). Description: same words, taken in pairs, that differ but are related in meaning. Some near synonyms, (say 'picked up' and 'received' for 'collect', 'make' for 'create', and 'prove' for 'establish'), of the one instance are also near synonyms for the other. Further, the difference in their meanings is marked by a difference in the group of meaning-related *other* words that can be substituted for the two instances. (I circumscribe the conditions for being meaning-related and for being substitutable later on). For now, it is enough to note that if we listed the near synonyms, the contraries, hyponyms, determinables, determinates, and the like, for each instance, they would differ, even though there would be a definite overlap of common words. I call such a difference a 'predicative' difference and model it (chapter 3) with predicate schemes.

(c) *Simple metaphor* Examples: *sow*/seeds, *sow*/dissension; *creep*/child, *creep*/disease; *flow*/water, *flow*/conversation. Description: same words, taken in pairs, that differ but are related in meaning, that satisfy the analogy conditions in (b) above, and also satisfy an additional condition of *asymmetry*. Roughly, certain meaning-related words substitutable for the non-metaphorical occurrence are not substitutable for the metaphorical occurrence, even though other words 'implied' by those very words *are* substitutable and are part of what is meant.

There is really no single statement adequate to convey this asymmetry until one sees it mapped out with examples (chapter 4). In any case, metaphorical occurrences are probably the most easily identifiable of the analogy phenomena, and meaning asymmetry with non-metaphorical instances is obvious even to persons who have not yet found a way to describe it.

(d) *Denominative analogy* Examples: *brilliant*/book, *brilliant*/writer; *play piano* (habit), *play piano* (ability); *hat* (object), *hat* (picture); *plow* (tool), *plow* (activity). Description: same words, taken in pairs, that differ but are related in meaning, and (whether or not they differ in ways already mentioned, predicatively), differ in predicate *mode*. That is, they differ in so far as what is predicated *inheres* in what it is predicated of. For instance, 'He plays the piano' can *attribute* a pro-

7

clivity, an ability or an occupation, and so forth. Because this sort of differentiation involves the mode of attribution, sometimes it is called 'analogy of *attribution*', (e.g. by Aquinas, Cajetan and others).

These phenomena are based upon 'relational naming' (denomination), characterizing something by way of relationships it bears to other things: *Victorian*/manners; *brilliant*/book, *judge*, *husband*. The denominative phenomena are astonishingly varied, ranging from interdefinable pairs, analogous by attribution (*brilliant*/book; *brilliant*/man) to 'representative analogy' where the representation gets the differentiated name of what is represented: 'the appellant' (his lawyer), 'the court' (the judge), 'the United States' (its ambassador) and 'the hat' (portion of a picture). (Cf. Plato, *Par.*, 131; *Rep.*, 596a; and Aristotle *N.E.*, 1096a, 17ff; *Meta.*, 1003a 33–1003b, 10; *Cat.*, 1a ff).

Comprehended within these four classes of same-word relationships are countless millions of same words, taken in pairs, in the contemporary corpus of the relevant natural language(s). Yet there is still another class of words, as impressively large as these, the morphological variants of one another: paronyms.

(e) *Paronyms* Examples: *healthy/healthful*; *explain/explanation*; *conceal/concealment*; *smoke/smoker*. Description: paronyms are not same words but are variants upon the same root with meaning differences that correlate in a law-like way with the morphological variation. The meaning relationships among paronyms parallel the analogy phenomena among same words and are explained in the same ways.

That is to be expected, because analogy in one language (*sana medicina*, *sana complexio*) may be paronymy in a cognate language (*healthful*/medicine; *healthy*/complexion).

The predicates of the analogy theory {is merely equivocal/is analogous by proportionality/is metaphorical/is analogous denominatively} differentiate, by analogy of proportionality, to encompass paronyms. 'Is univocal' drops out of the classification.

That enormously extends the theory's descriptive power, in effect, to *all* occurrences, taken in pairs, that are not distinct words, and powerfully demonstrates the *truth* of the theory's key premise: (roughly) that words take on different presuppositions (different affinities and oppositions to other words) depending upon what words you combine with them. For the key words of the analogy

8

theory itself, when applied to paronyms, automatically adjust and no longer presuppose that the things classified are same words, but now presuppose on the contrary that the things classified are morphologically *variants* of one another. (Chapter 8 shows that differentiation does not, as a rule, generate a *disjunctive* meaning, as one might at first suspect.)

4   SOME BROAD BACKGROUND CONSIDERATIONS

Words differentiate because some words dominate others. One's interchanging contrasting completion expressions (say, the words *'eyes'* and *'paint can'* printed on little cards) in the same sentence frame (printed with an appropriate blank space) – 'She *dropped* her . . .' – will show that. No word dominates all other words and all words are dominated some of the time. Some words are dominated in a great variety of ways, especially common words like 'make', completed with 'time/trouble/way/appointment/bed/ money/merry/haste/cake/dinner/love/war'.

Dominance and indifference, illustrated extensively in chapters 2 and 4, are the observable, generic causes of the specific analogy phenomena (sketched in section 3 above) that are modeled and distinguished in chapters 4 and 5. Explanation at greater depth, though more conjectural and metaphorical, postulates that universal forces are manifested by the whole range of analogy phenomena. I describe that briefly, and then explain the principle that linguistic meaning determines the expressive capacity of sentences, that relative meaning (see p. 14 below) is logically antecedent to absolute meaning and that changes in absolute meaning can come about only through changes in relative meaning.

(a) *Inertia and linguistic force* A word, recurring in the contemporary corpus of the language, without regard for time order, has the same meaning as any other given token unless something differentiates them. That is *linguistic inertia*.

Nevertheless, the undeniable fact – the one to be explained – is that the same word, far more often than one would initially expect, has different meanings when it recurs. For instance, recall the many meanings of the Italian *dare* listed above and the corresponding ranges for the English 'give' and 'take'.

A second fact: the meaning differences among *distinct* words

9

supervene upon their differences of combinatorial possibility, with the logical consequence that not all grammatically complete and correct strings of words are acceptable in a given environment, and almost every (perhaps every) such string is unacceptable in some environment.

Generally, *words resist combining unacceptably in the linguistic environment, until forced to*. That is *linguistic force*. In other words grammatical strings will not go together unacceptably (as 'not English') if there is any step-wise adaptation of word meanings (comparatively to their other occurrences in the corpus) which would result in an acceptable utterance and is not prevented by the environment. And those step-wise adaptations are the specific kinds of differentiation described in this book: analogy of proportionality, metaphor, denominative analogy, and mere equivocation. (Paronymy simply replicates those relations for morphological variants of one another.)

For the time being, think of contrasting adaptations as involving the suppression of affinities and oppositions to *other words*, relations that, if maintained, would make the resulting string unacceptable. Think of it as the suppression of which ones, among other words, are its synonyms, opposites (etc.). For example, 'collect' in 'collect/pension' and 'collect/garbage' suppresses some affinity in each, for 'received as owed' and 'was paid' are near synonyms of the former and not of the latter. Suppressing affinity and opposition to some words is typically equivalent to acquiring such relations to still other words.

Diachronically, linguistic force has dramatic manifestations in continuously new senses of words as new combinations, new patterns of dominance, happen to occur. The automatic differentiation of the analogy predicates, when I applied the classification to paronyms, illustrates that.

The resistance I speak of is not all of the same kind and strength. Sometimes, when the concatenated meaning is inaccessible – such as 'Night sings posts', 'He lubricated his fallacies' – the string is unacceptable in a given environment and sometimes not, as with 'Cone No.6 doffed its tip in the peephole' (Updike 1980: 191) and 'I image December's thorn screwed in a brow of holly' (Dylan Thomas 1934). Unacceptability, then, has various bases, and concomitantly, *unacceptability variously based is variously resisted*.

Although I do not investigate the bases of unacceptability or the diversity of resistance in this book, I estimate that chiefly and ubiquitously words resist failure to achieve an overall meaning. That happens when a word (or more) is simultaneously dominated to be both duck and rabbit; that is, in one meaning (and *not* the other) to hook up with what precedes and in another (and *not* the former) to hook up with what follows: 'Saturday followed Mary' for instance can be environmentally dominated so as to require 'followed' to be temporal (and *not* physical) in order to hook up with 'Saturday' (the day), and to be physical (and *not* temporal) to hook up with 'Mary'. Such conflicting dominance prevents the overall concatenation that 'Friday followed Crusoe' achieves in *Robinson Crusoe*.

The lesser resistances, varying with the kind of discourse and the community of speakers, include weak resistance to commonplace falsehood, especially to those concatenations that deny the empirical beliefs incorporated into the word meanings that compose the sentence itself. So, 'cats are *invisible*', does not disambiguate to mean 'too small to see', as in 'atoms are *invisible*', unless dominant expressions in the environment *force* it to. (See Churchland 1979, on empirical belief elements of word meanings.)

This is a 'weak force', reflecting our collective experience with the world. It is undeniably much weaker than (and gives way to) resistance to 'no hook up at all', but it is still a driving energy modifying dominance. Its single effects are localized, reflecting particular portions of experience, but like the force that deflects neutrinos, it is, in the cosmos of discourse, a starbuilder.

And so, with various resistances to variously based unacceptability, *sentences make what sense they can*. That trivial truth, like 'apples fall', realizes universal law: inertia and resistance to unacceptability. Its synchronic manifestations are the species of analogy and equivocation, described in this book, and its diachronic manifestation is continuous evolution of expressive capacity.

(b) *Intrinsic meaning, expressive capacity and media of thought*
There simply could not be phenomena of the kinds I have described, which manifest an inertia–resistance structure that generates endless expansion of expressive capacity, and which depend only upon how words happen to be combined, if *linguistic meaning* were not something intrinsic to the language and distinct from speaker-meaning, referential meaning, ideas in the mind, and sense-meaning (Lewis 1962). Linguistic meaning either is, or is the cause of, contrastive

expressive capacity. I suspect that contrastive expessive capacity is realized by (but is not the same as) the contrasting combinatorial possibilities of distinct expressions, and that linguistic meaning is prior to use the way capacity is prior to function.

Contrasts of linguistic meaning could be described as contrasts of semantic features of distinct expressions (Fodor and Katz 1964; and Katz 1966, 1972) if we could identify a rich enough set of features and if we were to adapt the semantic-feature analysis to deal with infinite polysemy. Even more congenial to my account is Lyons' (1977: 512–70) idea that the lexicon consists of patterns of affinities and oppositions of meaning. For a general account of meaning (and thought) that can accommodate the analogy phenomena has to explain how 'horse' and 'husband' differ *within the language*, apart from what they stand for and apart from what horse-concept or husband-concept, or idea, someone thinks he has. For if they occurred in an undeciphered language, the symbols would still have contrasting linguistic meaning, even if in our culture we had no use for such words or no corresponding ideas.

Obviously any natural expression has limited expressive capacity. Limits can be altered by altering the component words and by altering the meaning of a component word; for example, by causing 'sober' in 'The captain was sober today' to alter, by dominance, from 'not ebullient' to 'not intoxicated'. Difference of words correlates with difference of expressive capacity. 'Snow is white' *can't* express, as distinct from 'encode', what 'God is one' does (though no one has yet satisfactorily said why). And that difference is independent of what you or I *think* the words stand for or mean or what 'idea' we think we have. An adequate account of meaning has to explain what it is to have linguistic meaning and how it controls expressive capacity.

Because meaning determines expressive capacity, the *words* of an analysandum affect the formulation of the analysis (as I explain in chapter 8). Besides, I call attention to the dependence of expressive capacity upon inherent linguistic meaning because thought *in* words subsists in, and is limited by, the expressive capacity of interacting words.

Expressing oneself in one's natural language(s) is a *medium of thought*. Some of our thoughts subsist in their verbal expression the way a Wyeth painting subsists in egg tempera on board, having no existence apart from it and yet not being made *out* of it, as a chair is made out of wood, but being made *in* it, as joy can *be*, not merely be exhibited, in a dancer's movement.

Words, of course, are not the only media of thought. There are sketchings, and makings, and doings, and imaginings, and patternings in which we judge, question, assert, doubt, associate and draw conclusions. But only some of those are media for *expression*. A medium for expression is a means of communication through discriminable, inherent, contrastive possibilities for articulation.

Just how contrasting possibilities within a medium take on *expressive* actuality, I cannot even guess at present. But I do know that what can be thought in words, like what can be said, is limited to the expressive capacity of the symbols. And, as we now know, the expressive capacity of words can be modulated by new collocations of words – that is, by differentiation. In fact, poets and other creative writers arrange words to exploit evolving expressive capacity with new thoughts.

Philosophical theories that treat thoughts as independent of words and words as independent of one another are doomed to fail to explain the analogy phenomena and doomed to misapprehend what meaning is. The combinatorial differences of different words are the basis for their contrasting relative meanings, and the contrasts among such words are the foundation for the distinct relative meanings of same words. Put simply, the different meanings of the same word correspond to combinations of different words; and the distinct meanings of different words are founded upon the difference between the acceptable combinations of the one and those of the others. And so, for there to be contrasting combinatorial possibilities for two different words, some combinations that fit the grammar have to be unacceptable, either absolutely or environmentally, (otherwise there would be no difference of acceptable combinations and thus no basis for linguistic meaning difference). But unlike artificial languages, expressions in natural languages *resist* unacceptable new collocations by *surrendering* affinities and oppositions to other words and acquiring new ones. Differentiation of meaning and evolving expressive capacity are the logical consequence.

The combinatorial differences that I sketched above logically precede (and sometimes determine) application of the symbols to classify (represent) a world (realm) into arrays of referents, just as limited spelling and sound combinations (e.g. 'order counts') logi-

13

cally precede arrangements of letters into words. Because the combination of words can alter the meanings of the combined words (creating new combinatorial possibilities), it can and does alter the realms and ranges of reference.

5 ABSOLUTE AND RELATIVE MEANING

This book is about relations of relative meaning. I do not show how symbols got the first meanings they ever had, or how they came to have the meanings they have now, nor do I trace the differentiations, diachronically, from one meaning to another. We already know that linguistic force (resistance to unacceptability by step-wise suppression of affinities and oppositions to other words that would be unacceptable in the environment) will generate new meanings, both analogous and merely equivocal, as words happen in new configurations. We don't need to trace chains of individual differentiations to prove that. Theories that explain *what* meaning is and how symbols acquire it, and particularly, how symbols are related both to things in the world and to thought, I call theories of absolute meaning.

My hypotheses are about sameness and difference of same-word meaning and how they come about and how they are related to the combinatorial possibilities of distinct words. I refrain from more than initial and tentative conjectures about absolute meaning (see 4b, above) because I am certain that something is fundamentally wrong with all the theories of absolute meaning I have ever heard of. They do not account for (and usually do not recognize) the analogy phenomena; they provide no account of 'linguistic meaning' – meaning *internal* to the language; they provide no account of the fact that utterances and inscriptions can express (not merely encode) thoughts, and no account of the fact that we (often) think *in* words (as a painter thinks in shapes, contrasts and color) and not merely with words, as with tools. I venture that absolute meaning is to a far greater extent dependent upon antecedent relative meaning (internally acceptable combinatorial patterns) than the reverse, and that the idea that primitive humans endowed grunts and twitters with ranges of referents (and subsequently with rules of combination) is pure superstition.

One can dismiss these broad speculations and still understand my description of the analogy phenomena and appreciate their signifi-

14

cance for philosophy. One does not have to be willing to revamp philosophy of language and philosophy of mind to find this material useful.

Limitations of the classical account and the relationship of analogy to verbal proportionalities (like the 'verbal analogies' tests for college students) are explained in chapter 1. Then, differentiation and dominance are explained and illustrated (chapter 2). The predicate scheme model is developed (chapter 3), to allow for a more rigorous statement of dominance claims and to ground the 'near-synonym' shorthand for predicate-scheme relations, (I have already used that shorthand in section 2, above). Chapter 4 distinguishes, by means of predicate schemes, mere equivocation, analogy of proportionality, and simple metaphor and explains how analogy produces clustered meanings of words, how linguistic abstraction differs from metaphor, and what categorial contrast of meaning consists in. An interesting outcome is that a *categorial* contrast of contexts differentiates all common completion words, but not all of them merely equivocally. (That is important, as Aristotle realized, for metaphysics.)

The many kinds of denominative analogy are explored in the first half of chapter 5 where I speculate about 'inherence' to clarify 'predicate modes'. In the second half, I extend the analogy theory to paronyms, as already mentioned. Then in chapter 6, to support the hypothesis that relationships among same words are adequately encompassed by the five-fold classification already mentioned, I explore figures of speech and figurative discourse. It turns out that figurative or 'heightened' discourse is typically sprinkled with words whose shortest hypothetical sequence of step-wise differentiations (from typical instances *outside* such heightened discourse) involve *both* simple metaphor and another kind of analogy. Thus, I say that figurative discourse is characterized, semantically, by 'double differentiation'.

The account of analogy is applied, in chapters 7 and 8, particularly to explaining the embedding of craftbound discourse in unbound discourse and to a scrutiny of truth-conditional analysis. Certain disputes about the cognitive content of religious and metaphysical discourse can be resolved simply by applying the analogy information. Chapter 7 concentrates upon the cognitivity issue for religious discourse, with collateral attention to legal discourse. The same strategy can be (and should be) adapted to showing meaning continuities between 'theoretical' and 'observation' predicates in science and to displaying the cognitive pathway from discourse about the 'manifest image' of the world to discourse about 'the scientific reality'.

Chapter 8, assessing the objectives and capabilities of truth-conditional analysis, rejects the position that to know what a sentence means one has to know its truth conditions. I argue that one cannot fix the sense of expressions under analysis or determine the scope of similar expressions that have to satisfy its truth conditions, without a benchmark[3] occurrence in actual discourse.

Concerning whether the analysis has to be substitutable for the analysandum, or mean the same thing, or be merely equivalent to it, and so forth, I conclude that any articulation of what is meant that makes a cognitive advance can be satisfactory, while analyses that state *meaning-relevant* truth conditions are especially useful. (A condition is meaning-relevant just in case one of the words in the analysandum would have had a different meaning if that condition had not been necessary for the truth of what the analysandum is used to state.) Further, there cannot be a single truth-conditional analysis of 'knowing', 'believing', or practically anything else philosophers want to know about, because such predicates are projected analogously. Lastly, I illustrate analogous projection of predicates from legal discourse and demonstrate that there cannot be disjunctive definitions of analogous words.[4]

For a brief overview, one can read: chapter 2: section 1, 5 and 7; chapter 3: sections 5, 6, and 7; chapter 4: three, or so, pages opening each of the five sections; chapter 5: section 2; chapter 7: section 5; chapter 8: section 3(b).

When we compare the words used in science, metaphysics and religion with the same words in commonsense talk about the world, we notice how many common words are used analogously (as I explain that relation). There are not equally apt and specific words for us to apply univocally instead of the analogous ones; nor can we invent them. The philosophical significance of that matter has gone too long unexplored.

16

1

The limitations of classical analogy theory and the Miller's Analogies transition

The classical theory of analogy of meaning, *analogia nominum*, explained how same words are partly the same and partly different in meaning, ultimately and fundamentally, by appeal to relevant sameness and difference in the sorts of *things* to which the words are applied.[1]

Analogous terms differ from merely equivocal terms (which are also to some degree and in some respects partly the same in meaning) because the sameness and the difference in the analogous meanings are not merely coincidental, not merely haphazard, *a casu*, but are *a consilio*, conventional. In a law-like way they reflect metaphysical similarities and differences of the referents, that are preserved as similarities and differences in the concepts abstracted from such things.[2] Those similar but differing concepts *are* the meanings of the words that are analogous.[3]

The classical account of analogy involved several distinct inquiries, only the first of which will be pursued here. To use medieval Latin terms, there is *analogia nominum*, 'analogy of names' or 'analogy of meaning', a phenomenon I take to be ubiquitous, indigenous and characteristic in natural languages. It is an obvious characteristic by which natural languages differ from artificial languages and the most evident strength through which natural languages expand to incorporate new ideas and by which the language performs some of our thinking for us.[4] It is the phenomenon investigated and explained in this book.

There is also *analogia rationis*, 'analogy of reason', analogous thinking or reasoning; and there is *analogia entis*, 'analogy of being', analogy among things. To varying degrees, Plato, Aristotle, Aquinas, John of St. Thomas and Cajetan explored aspects of these issues as well. (See the extensive citations provided by Lyttkens 1952.)

17

With respect to *analogia rationis* there are three main lines of inquiry: the logical, the psychological and the epistemological. The former concerns whether reasoning involving analogous *terms* has any validity, any degree of reliability either deductively or inductively (Bochenski 1948; Palmer 1973). The psychological problems concern how we recognize analogy among words and things, construct analogous reasoning and learn to employ natural language analogously. The epistemological aspects concern the justification of judgments that situations are analogous or that the same predicate applies analogously to contrasting situations, and how, in general, we come to know that things are analogous.

The *analogia entis* embraces all the ontological or metaphysical issues about whether things are *really* analogous to one another and if so, what makes them so, and all the other questions about the existence of mind-independent similarities among things, similarities that cannot be reduced to specific identities describable in words that apply univocally to the objects under discussion (Bochenski 1956). Plato, Aristotle and Aquinas (as well as many others) seem to have felt certain that not all similarities are founded upon identities that can be characterized with univocal predicates.

Occasionally recent philosophers have tried to resolve one or another of these issues; e.g. Bochenski (1948) attempted to provide a model of formal validity for analogous reasonings and inquired provocatively about 'sameness' and 'identity' (1956), and Palmer (1973) attempted to demonstrate the invalidity of all such reasoning about God.[5] But as long as analogy of meaning has not been sufficiently explained, satisfactory progress on the other issues is unlikely.

The objectives of a contemporary analogy theory, namely, to describe, distinguish and explain analogy, equivocation, metaphor, denomination, paronymy and figurative discourse, and to apply the explanation to the resolution of certain cognitivity disputes and to a more articulate understanding of philosophical analysis, differ very little from those of the classical theory. But the locus of the account, almost exclusively in linguistic regularities and without an 'idea in the mind' model for linguistic meaning, is entirely different.

Aquinas and Aristotle apparently thought that the natural language so closely reflects reality that the final step in explaining any meaning relationship must always lie in some entitative relationship. They did not look to the language for the explanation of the meaning relationships (analogy, mere equivocation and meta-phor), but looked *through* the language, to what they regarded as ultimate.

Without begging the questions as to whether the 'final' expla-nation for analogy, equivocation and metaphor is to be sought in metaphysics, psychology, or physiology, and without begging questions as to the relationships of *analogia nominum* to *analogia rationis* and *analogia entis*, I provide an initial explanatory pattern that locates these meaning relationships *within* natural language itself. Four particular limitations of the classical theory are dis-cussed below.

1 LIMITATIONS OF CLASSICAL ANALOGY THEORY

The classical theory (1) gravely and implicitly misappraised the uni-versality of differentiation for same words; (2) it provided only an inchoate and misdirected explanation, hardly more than an initial description of the phenomena; (3) it was a hybrid of synchronic and diachronic hypotheses; (4) it had so heavy a metaphysical and psychological bias as not really to be a linguistic theory at all. As Henry Hiz (1967:74) pointed out, criticizing Chomsky, there is an important question that must be answered *linguistically*: 'How does it happen that an ambiguous sentence ceases to be ambiguous when placed in the context of other sentences?' This book provides a partial answer.

I further agree with Hiz when he says, 'But it should be easier to explain why we assign such-and-such a structure to a sentence by pointing out how this sentence changes the readings of neighboring sentences than by referring to innate universal ideas and mental reality' (1967:74).

(a) *The extensiveness of the phenomenon*

As Aristotle noticed, things are said *to be*, no matter of what sort they are; and yet, not all are said to be, in the same sense. 'Some think "being" and "one" mean the same thing, while others solve the argument of Zeno and Parmenides by asserting that "being" and "one" are used in a number of senses.' (*Soph. Ref.*, ch. 2, 182b–25) And *Metaphysics*, IV. ch.4, 1030a–33:

19

For it must be either by an equivocation that we say these *are* [substances and the things of the other categories] or by adding to and taking from the meaning of 'are' (in the way in which that which is not known is said to be known) – the truth being that we use the word neither ambiguously nor in the same sense, but just as we apply the word 'medical' by virtue of *reference* to one and the same thing, not *meaning* one and the same thing, nor yet speaking ambiguously; for a patient and an operation and an instrument are called medical neither by an ambiguity nor with a single meaning but with reference to a common end [italics added].

Aristotle also says (at 1003b, 6–10):

So too, there are many senses in which a thing is said to be, but all refer to one starting point; some things are said to be because they are substances, others because there are affections of substance, others because they are a process towards substance, or destructions or privations or qualities of substance, or productive or generative of substance or of things which are relative to substance, or negations of one of these things or of substance itself. It is for this reason that we say even of non-being that it *is* non-being. (See Aquinas' explanation, *In Met.*, IV, 1, n.539.)

'To be' differs in meaning according to the category of the things that are said to be and is univocal only for things of the same category, (*N.E.*, 1096a, 10–29.) Aristotle also recognized that other words, 'cause', 'principle', 'good', 'material', 'form', and *many* others (note his continual attention in *Metaphysics* to diverse senses of same terms) differ in meaning according to their general discourse contexts.[6] So he inquired into the meaning relationships of same words and distinguished the univocal, the equivocal, and the meaning relationships that are intermediate, the analogous.[7]

Aristotle did not discuss whether intermediate relationships of meaning are the rule or the exception. So, he did not postulate that *all* noun phrases and verb phrases and modifying expressions exhibit differences of meaning as their contexts are varied and that there must be a *general* explanation of that fact.

Similarly, Aquinas treated analogy of meaning as being characteristic of religious, scientific and philosophical discourse and, like Aristotle, used many examples from ordinary discourse. But he, too, failed to grasp that the underlying phenomenon is *differentiation*, and thereby left out the large-scale background against which the other limitations of the classical account would have appeared anomalous. Would they have continued to classify words, e.g. 'sharp', 'obscure', as 'equivocal' (as if all words were not), once they noticed that (a) every word has (or can have) merely equivocal

20

occurrences, (b) every term has analogous occurrences and (c) every sortal has or can have metaphorical occurrences?

The classical analogy theory purported to account for scientific (philosophical) words that differ in meaning but do not differ as 'simple equivocals', e.g. 'to be' in various existential claims, 'thing', 'something', 'one', 'good', 'true', applied to all things no matter of what sort, 'knows', 'understands', 'loves', and 'wills' as applied to rational animals and to intelligent beings essentially distinct, (Aquinas, *Summa, Ia,* 13), the application of 'matter', 'form', 'accident', 'substance', etc. to quite different things.

Although the examples were varied, the classical theory was applied to escape theological and metaphysical difficulties that arise, on the one hand from considering that such pairs, applied to categorically contrasting things, mean exactly the same thing and, on the other hand, from considering that such terms are totally unrelated in meaning. The metaphysical and theological applications smothered the analogy theory by confusing and concealing the generic nature and the ubiquity of differentiation. Particularly, the behavior of simple (mere) equivocals was not noticed to be generically related to analogous and metaphorical terms and was not thought to require a similar explanation.

Even if one is asking the right questions, the nature of the phenomenon is still elusive. For instance, asking what is common to all cases of analogy, I replied earlier with full confidence (even after considerable reflective inquiry) 'meaning *derivation*', something by which analogy seems to differ from mere equivocation. I concluded therefore (Ross 1970a and b) that to construct a new analogy theory one needs primarily to find the regularities underlying derivation and, having found them, to apply such regularities to resolving the cognitivity puzzles over religious and theoretical discourse. Moreover, the idea that analogous meanings were differentiated because of the *categorial* contrast of their completion expressions (Ross 1970b) seemed persuasive because (a) it was illustrative of the emerging dominance phenomenon, (b) categorial contrasts were so important to Aquinas and Aristotle and (c) the *kinds* of analogy that most often interest philosophers involve words used for experienced things and in religion, metaphysics and science, for things categorially different. Even by 1971 it still had not become clear that analogy that involves categorial contrasts is only a sub-case of analogy in general and that 'derivative meaning'

21

is a misleading and inefficient conception of the overall phenomenon of analogy. A few years later, the importance of explaining the *generic* phenomenon, differentiation, finally emerged and eventually lead to the inertia-resistance structure underlying dominance.

The right way to begin description is not to consider analogy as *derived* meaning, but rather to consider analogy as a species of a common phenomenon that includes mere equivocation and is characteristic of natural languages and inevitable in the absence of semantic regularities that prevent it: namely, *words differentiate in suitably contrasting environments*. Satisfactory explanation for that must, logically, precede an account of derivative meanings.

Some may think 'analogy of meaning' should not be treated as a species of differentiation because analogy, at least etymologically and by custom, connotes some sort of *derivation* ('*per prius et posterius*'), particularly some relation of similarity among the designata of the terms. But that would not prevent analogy from being a kind of differentiation. Furthermore, similarity of meaning is not the foundational characteristic of analogy of meaning; relatedness of meaning is (see chapter 4): mere equivocation is differentiation without relatedness; analogy is differentiation *with* relatedness.

(b) *Limited explanation*

The classical writers counted as 'explanations', hypotheses that were too limited in scope, erroneous in assumption and in some respects plainly irrelevant. They appealed to the ontology of the things referred to, and the heart of their account was an attempt to connect features of the *world* (similarity of things) with features of *words* (similarity of meaning) by hypotheses concerning the way in which *concepts* are formed (similarity of concepts). The classical theorists did not discuss the factors that determine *which* sense (or meaning) of a merely equivocal word ('pen') belongs to a given occurrence. That is because they considered linguistic meaning to be in the *mind* and to be the result of abstraction and not to be *inherent* in the written and spoken words.

My general picture is different. Meaning is inherently in the sentences just as law-like regularity is in nature. *Grasping* the meaning is a mental or quasi-mental phenomenon; *having meaning* is an inherent property of well-formed and acceptable expressions. Writing and speech are not encodings of one another or of something in the mind. Words are not signs of meanings (e.g. ideas), they *mean* (contrastively symbolize and combinatorially have expressive possibilities, actuality and limitations).

The fact that things of different categories differ, and yet are similar in their kinds of being and give rise to similar but differing concepts (as Aristotle and Aquinas supposed), explains why 'to be' and 'exists' differentiate when applied to such things only on the assumption that those similar but related concepts *are* the meanings. But the theory of concept formation does not account for the fact that the *same* word differentiates instead of being replaced with a distinct word having a similar meaning.

The classical psychology of concept formation does not explain adequately why we form the concepts that we do form rather than others in the presence of perceivable objects or why we have the words we do have and not others. Apparently it did not occur to the classical writers to investigate why we attach 'similar' concepts to different occurrences of the same word when we often also attach equally 'similar' concepts to distinct words. Yet there must be an explanation and one that relies not merely upon the supposed intentions (or purposes) of speakers or upon the supposed analogies among things. Why is there not a common word for 'pounce', 'bone' and 'spine' (Aristotle, *Post. An.*, 98a, 20f and Cajetan 1498, ch.11, no. 117), when there is a common word for gravitational, chemically and electrically caused motion – 'attraction'? Do the former have less in common than the latter?

Even if the classical theory did succeed in explaining partial *carry-over* of meaning by overlap of concepts, that still leaves it unexplained that the same word is used in different but related meanings rather than different words.

The classical theory is *inextricable* from its commitment that the meaning of a word is an accompanying concept in the mind. The implausibility of that underlying account of meaning makes it impossible to repair the classical theory. Further, the classical theory, especially in Cajetan's exposition, (1498: ch.11, no. 123), makes assumptions about the *priority* of meanings over one another that can be supported only on doubtful metaphysical premises, for instance, that 'exists', applied to God, is 'prior' in meaning to 'exists', applied to creatures because the being of God is ontologically prior to that of creatures (Aquinas, *In. I Sent.*, 22,1,2 c.)

And there are also false assumptions about psychological and epistemic priority. For instance, that the sense in which a person is healthy is chronologically, psychologically or epistemologically prior to the sense in which his medicine or complexion is healthy. After all, the order of learning can be reversed, and even the order of the definitions can. At every crucial stage, the functioning of language is 'explained' by appeal to non-linguistic phenomena whose role as a meaning *determinant* is insufficiently justified.

Finally, the traditional theory cannot answer internal questions it generates, for instance: what characterizes the difference between a *false* statement involving an analogous predicate and a metaphor? What *exactly* is the difference between simple equivocation and analogy of meaning? How does analogy differ from metaphor? What accounts for the fact that the same word has different meanings when combined in diverse ways with certain other terms (*law case*/*case law*)? And if two terms T^1 and T^2, are analogous to one another and T^3 is analogous to T^2, is it analogous to T^1 and if not, why not?

A defender of the traditional theory might rejoin that I unfairly criticize it after having generalized the phenomenon to be explained far beyond Aristotle's and Aquinas pretensions. They considered cases of *derivative* meaning, but I have claimed that the phenomenon first to be explained is *differentiation*, a much larger class of linguistic relationships. I reply that one cannot explain derivation synchronically until we have accounted for differentiation. For, we cannot say what 'derivation' consists in, what causes it, what determines the order among derivative meanings or what the meaning relationships among various derivatives might be.

'Healthy' in 'Fido's complexion is healthy' is 'derived' from the sense of 'healthy' in 'Fido is healthy'. That certainly does *not* mean, or even entail, that one must learn the one by first learning the other or that the second occurred before the other in someone's experience. The same holds for the statement that 'wise' in 'God is wise' is derived from 'wise' in 'Socrates is wise'. What does 'derived' mean here? Does it mean that we learned to talk about Socrates before God? Of course not. Nor does it mean that no one could learn that one meaning without first learning the other or that the word in one use is definitionally prior to the word in another use, in such a way that the order could not be reversed.

Aquinas' observations (*In I Sent.*, 22, 1, 2, c; Cajetan 1498: ch. 11, no. 123) about psychological and ontological order among concepts are in effect misleading because they conflate the account of analogy of meaning with *analogia rationis*. 'For the order of the term follows the order of knowledge ... but because we know that power through its effects, we name it from its effect' (*C.G.*, 1,34.) The whole analysis of meaning relatedness as a relation *per prius et posterius* involves a confusion that persisted from Plato and Aritotle right into our time. There are such meaning relationships, but they are not the explanation of analogy or metaphor; rather, they are a *result* of analogy of meaning.

(c) *Synchronic and diachronic phenomena*

The classical theory is not explicit on whether analogy of meaning is, in its explanation, a synchronic or a diachronic phenomenon, though in my opinion its dominant thrust, with small lapses, is synchronic. Those elements that concern the relationship of words to their referents, via concepts reflecting the differences among referents, seem to treat analogy as synchronic, as the result of a constant and time-invariant causal structure. And the observations about psychological and epistemic priority and the order of abstraction seem to posit general causal mechanisms, not, of course, mechanisms controlling the evolution of languages but to explain the origin of and distinction among concepts.

Differentiation is *observable* within a static corpus of discourse; so its basic explanation ought to be by way of a time-invariant structure, just as Aristotle and Aquinas supposed. But because the theory of meaning is different, so will be the locus of explanation: 'Being analogous in meaning' is a relationship that holds pairwise among same words regardless of their temporal relationships, provided only that it is reasonable to regard the pairs as belonging to the same corpus of the language. (There are, of course, diachronic analogy phenomena, but they are results of and manifestations of synchronic linguistic structures.)

(d) *Metaphysical bias*

The classical theory of analogy was metaphysically biased because crucial elements of the theory were justified merely as applications of metaphysics. In fact, the theological, metaphysical, psychological and epistemological applications of the theory subordinated the elements of the philosophy of language.

Historically, it has been common to answer questions about meaning through metaphysics; Plato, Locke and Berkeley, paradigmatically, did so; and some contemporary nominalists, Goodman (1968), Quine (1960) and even a 'Cartesian' linguist, Chomsky (1972), have followed suit. But in formulating a new theory, I do not account for a difference in the meaning of 'intelligent' in the sentences 'God is intelligent', and 'Socrates is intelligent', by talking about the metaphysical difference between God and Socrates, but rather by talking only about the linguistic differences between 'God' and 'Socrates' and the linguistic environments of the utterances. No doubt the separation of purely linguistic and referential considerations cannot be perfect; issues about acceptability of sentences shade into issues about commonplace falsehood. Yet as far as possible, this form of explanation is to be pursued.

Some philosophers think we cannot escape appealing to properties of referred-to-things to account for differentiation because of the uniqueness of some referential expressions. Mavrodes (1970:747–55), for instance, argued that, on my premise (which he did not share), if 'intelligent' differs in meaning in the two cases above mentioned, 'intelligent' should also differ in meaning depending upon whether the utterance, 'The person St. Francis loved best is intelligent', *refers* to Francis' mother or to God. But, he argued, if the latter is true, then the theory cannot be developed without dependence upon the metaphysical differences of the referents. He argued, further, that if the term 'intelligent' does *not* alter its meaning on account of a change of the referent, we will encounter an anomaly because this syllogism, 'The person St. Francis loved best is intelligent; St Francis loved God best; therefore God is intelligent', has a conclusion where 'intelligent' differs in meaning from its use in 'St. Francis' mother was intelligent' but where the difference of meaning is not accounted for by anything.

Mavrodes vividly illustrated the difference between explaining differentiation by appeal to semantic *dominance*, e.g. by appealing to 'his mother' in the second premise of the one syllogism and to 'God' in the other, and explaining differentiation by appeal to differences in the *things* referred to. The classical analogy theory characteristically reasoned as Mavrodes illustrated, with metaphysical considerations, e.g. that God is transcendent, unperceivable, not in any space, incomprehensible, etc., while Socrates' intelligence is limited, confined to experiences arising in space and time. There is

26

no need to explain such differences of meaning by invoking hypotheses about differences in the referents, as the sequel will show.

2   MILLER'S ANALOGIES: A TRANSITION

(a)   *Proportionalities and analogy of meaning*

In an improbable source, the College Board Tests (*Miller's Analogies Test*, 1969), I find a convenient transition from classical to contemporary theories of analogy, a transition that illuminates Aristotle's and Aquinas' otherwise puzzling correlation of quasi-mathematical proportionalities with analogy of meaning.[8]

In my first expositions of Aquinas (1958 and 1961) I did not appreciate the connection between analogy of meaning and verbal proportionalities expressed in quasi-mathematical form (a form of expression frequently employed by those writers): 'A is to B as C is to D'. And neither did Mascall (1949), Penido (1931), Emmet (1946) and Garrigou-Lagrange (1947–8, 5th ed.), though all tried to illustrate it. But it is now clear enough, including interchanging expressions to create metaphors, which Aristotle illustrated in *Poetics*, 1457b, 16–30.

Consider the proportionality: '*Warden is to guard as doctor is to* (A) nurse; (B) patient; (C) surgeon; (D) ward?' The test-makers offer 'nurse' as the answer, indicating that one should formulate the relationship in which the first pair stands and then find the answer that will establish the 'same relationship' between a second pair and will not hold for any other pair. For instance, 'supervise a person administratively subordinate' would characterize the warden–guard relationship and also indicate 'nurse' as the missing fourth element, while excluding each of the others.

'Supervises' might also characterize the relationship of doctor to patient; but the *sense* of 'supervises' would not be univocal with (the same as) 'supervises' in 'The warden supervises the guards'. Presumably, *ceteris paribus, univocally* designated common relationships are to be preferred to equivocally designated ones and analogously or metaphorically designated common relationships are to be preferred to merely equivocally designated ones.

Verbal proportionalities (verbal analogies) can be based upon implicit predication that is non-univocal but not merely equivocal (as   Aristotle   and   Aquinas   observed):   'Dentist:cavity:

:doctor:disease'. 'Treats', 'cures', and the like, are related in meaning, but not univocal in the corresponding explicit predications. So too with 'Asylum:refugee::destination:traveler'.

'*A horse is to a herd as a mountain is to a range.*' The common relation may be 'usually belongs to'. Do the sentences, 'A horse usually belongs to a herd', and 'A mountain usually belongs to a range' employ 'usually belongs to' equivocally? I think so. Does the fact that 'The horse stopped belonging to its herd' is acceptable, non-figuratively, but 'The mountain stopped belonging to its range' is not, show that the phrase 'belongs to' has different contraries in its two occurrences and, thus, is equivocal? I think so. Does the fact that 'usually' has different meanings in the two cases show that 'usually belongs to' has different meanings? Certainly. That is, 'a horse *usually* belongs to a herd' means 'in nature, apart from husbandry', whereas 'usually' with respect to mountains concerns frequency of distribution geographically. That verbal proportionality turns upon a common relational predicate that occurs equivocally.

The point of the classical quasi-mathematical talk about 'analogy of proper proportionality' was that proportionalities typically presuppose predicates analogous in meaning. Some relationships, say, between man and his activities, are proportionally similar to other relationships, say, between God and his activities ('Socrates is to philosophy as God is to the world': 'understands it') and the common words that especially aptly characterize the relations are *non-univocal*, as we find in many *Miller's Analogies* examples (see illustrations below).

Aristotle, *Topics*, I, 17, 108a, 7–11, said: 'Likeness should be studied, first, in the case of things belonging to different genera, the formula being: "A:B::C:D" (e.g. as sight is in the eye, so is reason in the soul and as calm is in the sea, so is windlessness in the air.)'

The classical explanation why a term in related but different senses (meanings) may be the most apt common predicate presupposed by true proportionality, and why there is no comparably specific univocal term that is apt, is that the relations that are only proportionally similar give rise, via abstraction, to concepts that are not the *same* but are related to one another by priority–posteriority (*per prius et posterius*) and that although different, they attach, by their similarity, to one word rather than many. The key step, not satisfactorily explained, is why *not* distinct words when distinct words are also similar in meaning, e.g. 'saw' and 'viewed'?

The classical writers did not assert that we always have an apt analogous term to apply to a true verbal proportionality; in fact, Aristotle remarked that we do not (*Post. An.*, II, 14, 98a, 20f) and Cajetan (*De Nom. Anal.*, ch. 11, no. 117) agreed: '*unity or diversity of name should be considered accidental*' [italics added].

For instance, although a squid's pounce, a bone and a spine do not have one name, they are no less analogously similar than if they had one name. Nor would they be more similar if they had one name. Nevertheless, if they were called *bones* by a common name in such a way that through lack of words or because of their proportional similarity the name *bone* were extended to the others, we would believe bones, squid's pounce and spine to be of the same nature and notion. Especially, because, as was explained above, certain proportions flow from things which are proportionally the same as if they had one nature. (See also Cajetan 1509:4*.)

No matter how small the vocabulary, provided it has relation terms and permits the formation of verbal proportionalities, there is always some word that is at least as apt as any other within the vocabulary to characterize the common relation in a true proportionality. Yet it is not necessary that there be one word *more* apt than any other, though for relations that are only proportionally similar, no word applied univocally is as apt and specific as some word applied non-univocally. In fact, *the expressions involved may make it impossible for any word to apply univocally because they dominate and differentiate any common word that preserves the truth and the sense of the original verbal proportionality.* That is the position I will explain and defend. And that, I think, is also the classical position as to God, metaphysics and theoretical science, in so far as common predicates from the vocabularies for 'ordinary experience' are applied to such subjects.

For all we know at the outset, the reason why there are analogous predicates for certain true verbal proportionalities and not distinct words, may be something like this: relatively to our vocabulary, (i) the contrasts implied by any *pair* of *distinct* words are greater than (comparatively to other classifications) the case warrants, and fail to represent the discernible *relatedness* of the cases; and (ii) the two cases are more like other cases with the same name, e.g. of 'usually belongs to' ('Two white knights usually belong to a chess set'), than they are like anything characterized by a contrasting name that either excludes, or otherwise displaces this name, 'belonging to'; and (iii) the two cases are more like one another than they are like any pair of things aptly characterized only by distinct words and not aptly characterized by meaning-related same words.

So, I suggest we look at the way we classify things under a limited label scheme (vocabulary) without, at the outset, explaining our verbal behavior with hypotheses about the things we classify.

(b)   *Verbal analogies based upon non-univocal predication*

We can indicate a proportionality without naming the common relationship, where, were the relationship named with one word, it would be named equivocally (but not merely equivocally): 'Philosophy is to insincerity as love is to slavery.'

Metaphors are sometimes created by substituting one word of a proportionality for another: as 'knowing is to the object known, so is sensation to the object sensed'; and thus, one is sometimes described metaphorically as '*sensing* that it is so'. Aristotle pointed out (*Poet.* 1457b) that metaphors can be created from proportionalities by *denomination*: 'if A:B::C:D, then in a sentence D is substituted for B'. (He does not give an explanation of why not all such sentences are acceptable.) 'As old age (D) is to life (C) so is evening (B) to day (A). One will accordingly describe evening (B) as "The old age of the day", (D&A) ... and old age (D) as the evening or sunset of life (B&C)' *Poet.* 1457b, 23–25. (Aristotle illustrated the reversibility that is common in metaphors supported by proportionalities but that has never been explained.)

Aristotle also indicated that where A:B::C:D and there is a *name* for the C:D relation but there is no name for the relation A:B, we *transfer* the name of the C:D relation to name the A:B relation. That indeed is metaphorical proportionality and it is '*improper*' (to use Aquinas' phrase, Ia, 13, 3 ad 3; *De Ver.*, 7, 2c; I *In De An.*, 10, n. 160) because the relation signified by 'CRD' is *only* by similarity, relatively to the vocabulary, the same as the relation signified by 'ARB'. In fact, 'ARB', *except* as considered to be proportionally similar to 'CRD', is evidently false: that is, underlying this kind of metaphor is a commonplace falsehood. 'The boiling sun sowed flames in all the fields.' That is why it is improper proportionality (Aquinas, *In I Sent.*, 23, 1, 1 and 2c, and 2 ad 1; *Ia*, 13,6).

In the *Miller's Analogies* tests, besides cases where the relationship is purely mathematical, e.g. 'double' in '4 is to 2 as 8 is to 4' or merely grammatical, e.g. 'is the plural of', or metalinguistic, e.g. 'is more specific than', 'is spelled backwards', and 'is included in the spelling of', there are many cases where the *common relational word* would (if expressed) *not be used univocally*. For instance:

brunch:lunch::smog:haze. The test-makers think 'is a *combination of*...' is the key idea, brunch being a combination of breakfast and lunch and smog being a combination of haze and exhausts. Skipping other difficulties now, 'is a combination of x and y' does not apply to brunch and smog in the same sense; that is, 'is a chemical suspension of' may apply in the one case and not in the other. So too, with the senses of 'is opposed to' that might apply in the 'philosophy . . . slavery' example above.

The analogy of proper proportionality that Aquinas talked about is of this sort: the presupposed common word is not univocal but is not merely equivocal either. (Aristotle noted that such terms as 'is the same as' and 'is commensurable with' differentiate depending upon the kind of things compared; *Phys.*, VII, ch. 3, 248b, 1–27 and 249a, 1–24 and see *Top.*, II, ch. 17, 108a, 7–10.)

For the *Miller's Analogies* examples, there is always more than one word to name the same relationship. Apart from a theory of the sort to be offered, it would be difficult to determine that there is not always some *univocal* common word for the relationship. We can conjecture, from the way verbal proportionalities were employed by classical philosophers, that in relation to a limited vocabulary, there are similarities of relations aptly described with analogous terms for which no univocal term is appropriate. And none can be devised.

In my theory the absence of such univocal predicates is explained by the fact that if one formulates first the verbal proportionality, Socrates:philosophy::Fido:his master, and then creates corresponding sentences that express the relation, 'Socrates *loves* philosophy' and 'Fido *loves* his master', the mere concatenation of the common predicate, *'loves'*, with the contrasting sentence frames, 'Socrates . . . philosophy' and 'Fido . . . his master', differentiates the common word. There *can be no univocal* common term of the same level of specificity as an analogous term that aptly names the relation presupposed.

Another example: Even numbers:odd numbers::elephants:mice. Someone proposes: 'Every even number is larger than some odd number (one) just as every elephant is larger than some mouse'. Concatenation of 'is larger than' with 'number' in contrast to 'elephant' sufficiently differentiates 'is larger than'. One *cannot* say the same thing by merely substituting a common univocal predicate for 'is larger than'. And that has nothing to do with the metaphysical re-

31

lationships of numbers and elephants or with your or my beliefs about them; that is simply a result of the linguistic relations of the words involved. A consonant consequence is that a near synonym of an analogous pair, when substituted, will also be analogous.

The test question is 'Law:citizen:: (a) democracy:communism, (b) weapon:peace, (c) reins:horses, (d) gangster:policeman'? The answer is (c). I suppose such terms as 'guides', 'restrains', or 'directs' might name the common relationship. But if 'restrains' is accepted as more specific and more apt than 'guides', then the common word differentiates in 'Law *restrains* the citizen' and 'Reins *restrain* the horse'; it is *metaphorical* in the first case in comparison to the second. (Why the first case should be metaphorical in relation to the second and not the other way around, and how we can explain metaphor without recourse to talk of 'priority' of occurrences in time and 'literalness' are discussed in chapter 4.)

Here are some other proportionalities where an apt common word in the corresponding explicit relational statements would be metaphorical. (1) The farmer:seeds::sun:flames (*sows*); (2) Thief:money::age:beauty (*steals*); (3) baby:locomotion::time:worry (*creeps*); (4) leaf:fire::shy:person: (*shrivels, burns*); (5) road:mountains::argument:objection (*twists, turns, surmounts*). Once the pattern is exhibited, one can construct lists at will. And one can then construct further metaphors by *denominative interchange* (see ch. 4, denominative metaphor): e.g. of A for C, or D for B or vice versa, 'beauty's thief', 'the leaves of loneliness', 'autumn of inquiry'.

My hypothesis is that if the common word does *not* occur univocally in the sentences articulating a true verbal proportionality, then it differentiates because of the semantic features of the other words involved (or implied). Thus, we travel from the medieval doctrine of analogy of proper proportionality among *referents* to a contemporary doctrine of *semantic contagion* as the fundamental feature underlying analogy, metaphor and mere equivocation.

2

The genus:
meaning differentiation

1 MEANING DIFFERENTIATION

Words in English and other Indo-European languages, in suitably contrasting contexts, differentiate. For example, 'She *dropped* a stitch', 'She *dropped* her hem-line', 'She *dropped* her book', 'She *dropped* a friend', 'She *dropped* her courses'. The meanings of 'dropped' are appropriate, *fitted* to the completion words and, so, differ. That is the generic linguistic phenomenon that includes mere equivocation, analogy and metaphor.

Words also adapt in *predicate mode* (e.g. to whether what is ascribed is ascribed as an action, state, proclivity, ability, etc.: 'Jones plays golf', 'Smith plays the piano', and to whether it is ascribed as a cause, effect, symptom, state, etc.) and to contrasts of *ascription*: to contrasting implied vantages, e.g. of agent or observer. Predicate mode and ascriptive differentiation are explained in chapter 5.

The meaning of *any* word, whether it be as common as the nouns, 'chair' and 'ball', or the verbs, 'fix', 'strain' and 'look', or whether it be statistically less common, like 'investigator', 'interlocutor', 'expect', or 'anticipate', differentiates relatively to some of its other occurrences. Consider the sets:

(1) The junk men *took* the *chair*.
(2) The chairman of the board *took* the *chair*.
(3) He dropped the *ball* on his first catch.
(4) He skipped the *ball* because of the late hour.
(5) He *fixed* the leak in the pipe.
(6) He *fixed* the time of the appointment.
(7) He *fixed* the race.
(8) He *strained* the soup before serving it.
(9) He *strained* his back lifting.
(10) He *strained* his eyes to catch a glimpse of her.
(11) He *looked* over the plant.
(12) He *looked* over the fence.
(13) The *investigator* was retained by the police.
(14) The *investigator* does not necessarily publish his results.

33

(15) He *anticipated* the response.
(16) He went there because he *anticipated* her.

Even syncategorematic words differentiate. 'That's *the* way to town', '*The* whale is a mammal', '*The* trouble is . . .', and '*The* man died'. Prepositions differentiate (e.g. '*in* the house', '*in* the book') and articles do as well, 'I have *an* idea', 'I'll have *a* cookie', 'I have *a* brother, too'; 'have' differentiates as well.

Enumerative induction will not show that *every* word differentiates; but I think experiment will convince fluent speakers that fit to context is evident and universal. The versatility of Latin and French words is perhaps obvious to us because we notice how many distinct English words we need to translate a single foreign word. (See Introduction above.) Yet, that all terms differentiate can be *proved* only after the phenomenon has been explained.

Fit to context is necessary but not sufficient for differentiation; there have to be *contrasting* adjustments (fits) to produce *diversity* of meaning. The contrast between 'door' and 'eyes' in 'He closed his door' and 'He closed his eyes', or 'stitch', 'friend', 'book', in 'She dropped her (noun phrase)', causes the differentiation of 'closed' and 'dropped', when those differing direct objects are substituted (the rest of the sentence frame remaining constant). Otherwise, there would be no linguistic cause of differentiation.

2 SAME WORDS

We have to adopt a criterion for different occurrences of the same word. Roughly, they are the same if spelled and sounded the same; more formally:

Def. II–1: Same terms: The class of allograph/allophone tokens, indifferently substitutable for one another (on grounds of spelling and sound) in every context in which any one of the class occurs meaningfully, is the class of same-term occurrences, with respect to a given inscription or sound which occurs meaningfully in some given context.

'Substitutable', for purposes of this definition, does *not* mean either of the things it means later (see senses 2 and 3) but means (1) 'can be put in place of one another without creating a different word or sentence or bringing it about that the meaning of any component word is different from what it was before the substitution'. It corresponds to Lyons' idea (1966:73) that 'two expressions are in contrast if the substitution of one for the other in the same context produces a different word or sentence; otherwise they are in free variation'. Thus all tokens of the same type are freely variant (spelled and sounded 'the same').

(2) The second kind of substitutability is 'with preservation of *acceptability* and of consistency/inconsistency with the original' – that is required for members of paradigmatic sets and, therefore, of predicate schemes in chapters 3 and 4, but not here.

(3) The third is the substitutability of near synonyms, that is substitutability 'to produce a replacement sentence approximately the same in meaning as the original'. This notion is explained in chapter 4.

I understand that a properly spelled word cannot, sometimes, be substituted for an improperly spelled occurrence; that is provided for by the requirement of 'meaningful' occurrence, to eliminate 'material supposition', often called 'mere mention' (see below). And that explains why the formal definition (II–1) is so complicated.

'Look out', and 'look over' in some contexts count as whole terms *not* made up of the constituent terms 'look' and the preposition 'out' or 'over' functioning adverbially. I use 'same term' and 'same word' interchangeably even though the former expression is broader because expressions like 'in English' and 'come on' and 'look out' count as single terms in some contexts where we would not count them as single words. 'Term' has a formality that makes sentences harder to understand than does 'word', so I frequently use the latter where the former is technically more accurate.

In 'Scrooge was mean' and 'He tried to tell us what "incongruous" and "blithe" mean,' 'mean' (meaning 'parsimonious') and 'mean' (meaning 'to convey') are occurrences of the same word, being allograph–allophones of one another. So also: 'The cat *caught* the mouse at once', 'The student *caught* the teacher's likeness in his sketch', 'The man *caught* the train after lunch', 'The boy *caught* the fish for lunch'. 'Caught' differentiates across a set of sentence frames of the same surface grammar: noun phrase (composed of definite article and common noun) and verb phrase (third person, singular, past tense verb, with direct object) and adverbial phrase. The verb 'caught' is the same word, having multiple occurrences in these sentences, despite differences of meaning. No significance is to be attached to the suggestion that there is some sort of meaning *derivation* in the 'caught' cases and no derivation in the 'mean' cases, so

35

that 'caught' is a single word with multiple occurrences while 'mean' is an allograph for two different words. For there is no derivation in the 'caught' cases either. 'Derivation' is a false scent left by the classical theory of analogy.

Tokens of the same word may be spelled differently (misspelled or alternately spelled). The misspellings and alternate spellings are allographs of the standard spelling by a normative 'allograph' criterion that correlates the deviant spellings with a preferred allograph type. The same is true of deviant phonemes. Usually, whatever would count, for a distributional linguist, as a set of same-term occurrences will be acceptable for the theory I am developing (Lyons 1968). Thus the members of the correlated allograph/allophone class form an equivalence class distributionally but need not be equiform appearances or indistinguishable sounds.

Because homonyms are phonemically equivalent but do not always have allographic inscriptions, not *any* two tokens that are phonemically equivalent are occurrences of the same word, only the ones that are both said and spelled the same way: e.g. 'He made it *home*', uttered in baseball talk and about the efforts of a sick man to reach his home, but not 'sail' and 'sale'.

Sometimes we say that tokens that are spelled the same way and are pronounced the same way are, nevertheless, two different words or two different terms, as 'direct' in 'direct delivery to one's home' and 'direct an orchestra'. But that concept of 'different terms' and 'different words', otherwise perfectly acceptable, requires, for its application, a *comparison* of both the syntactic role and the contextually determined meanings of the pair. It involves a distinction needed for some theoretical purposes but inefficient here.

The criterion I employ does not suppose that we do not know the meanings of the words. But it is independent of a *comparison* of the particular meanings, allowing us to establish that we have same-word occurrences on sound and spelling alone, before making any judgment about their comparative meanings.

We do not need to compare the meanings, e.g. of homonyms, to one *another* in order to determine the orthographic or orthophonic type of each token and, thus, to determine whether they are tokens of the same word. In 'The fifth sentence on the page contains the symbol "means"', 'means' occurs in the latter *without* a meaning, since it occurs, as the medievals said, in 'material supposition', merely mentioned but not used. But 'means' still belongs to a class

36

of allophone–allograph tokens each of which is substitutable for any other in any context of *meaningful* occurrence.

Discourse context: there is a discourse context for a word whenever it occurs (physically), as used, within an uttered or written complete sentential expression, and there is a distinct occurrence of a word as often as it occurs within a complete sentential expression.

'Complete sentential context' is an idealization. Most 'sentences' in colloquial speech are incomplete or grammatically incorrect (or both) and questions, commands etc., are perhaps as common as declarations. Further, declarations have no monopoly on statements. Nevertheless, let the declarations be representative, and let an utterance *count* as complete when a corresponding complete expression can, with reasonable certitude, be constructed from the context given. That way, we can count such a context as 'complete' for our purposes, as well. I regard complete sentences as 'contexts' and 'broader units of discourse', including gestures, references and other utterances on the same or related subjects, as the 'environment'. (Sometimes other writers regard the sentence as the environment and the discourse background as the context.)

3   DIFFERENCE OF MEANING FOR SAME WORDS

Same words have the same meaning unless the opposite is both caused and indicated. This is the inertia principle. There would be nothing gained from premising that same words can differ in meaning when nothing linguistic indicates it or causes it.

Indicators of difference of *sentence* meaning are not alone sufficient to indicate difference of word meaning because, when sentences involving a common word differ, the explanation of the difference of meaning could lie in something other than a difference of meaning in the common terms, e.g. in contrasting surrounding terms or in the wider discourse environment, including gestures and prior references or assumptions (see Haack 1968). And, obviously, a pair of sentences with a univocal common word can differ in meaning: 'I *saw* the cat'; 'I *saw* the dog.'

Sometimes sentences with the very same words (in the same order) differ in meaning: (a) 'That's my view' and (b) 'That's my view.' Can we tell whether the common word 'view' has the same or different meanings? Not by anything explicitly given within the sentences.

To determine whether there is a difference of sentence meaning (as would be indicated by a difference of entailments), we need already to know whether 'view' differs, (Haack 1968: 64, and Lehrer 1974b). Suppose (a) is employed in an environment that indicates that one is expressing one's controverted opinion. Suppose (b) is uttered with a gesture indicating the panorama visible from one's lawn. The two could as well be reversed. Whatever determines the particular meaning is outside the sentence itself and is environmental rather than sentential or contextual.

One cannot in this case, therefore, determine whether the two sentences differ in entailments, in paraphrases, in which objections or qualifications would be semantically appropriate (e.g. 'Oh, but you have a better one in back') until one has already determined whether the two tokens of the word 'view' have the same meaning.

That is frequently true: applying tests to indicate differences of meaning between sentences presupposes that we already know whether words, occurring in both, have or do not have the same meaning. So, tests for difference of sentence meaning may (and sometimes will) beg the question as to whether common terms have the same meaning.

What, then, can be employed to test for difference of meaning for individual words in sentence frames that differ in other respects? For instance, (a) 'Smith *stopped payment* on his check before it had cleared the bank'; (b) 'Jones *stopped payment* on his car after the third month.' These involve different senses of 'stopped payment' (e.g. the contrast of stopping paying (b), and stopping *being paid* (a)), but that difference in the *particular expression*, 'stopped payment', will not necessarily be located by the differing entailments, paraphrases, grammatical transformations, objections, or qualifications appropriate to the two sentences. Those differences might just as well be attributed to the other features in which the sentences or environments differ.

Tests for sameness of meaning for *different* words, tests for synonymy, cannot be effective for my purpose, either, because they all involve the *substitution* of one expression for the other and a subsequent application of tests for difference of sentence-meaning to the resulting sentences. Lyons' earlier account (1968: 428) – 'two (or more) items are synonymous if the sentences which result from the substitution of one for the other have the same meaning' – has the incongruous result that merely equivocal words are always synonymous! (That has an important consequence, see below.)

Substitution cannot be effective for same words, as is illustrated with simple equivocals, 'pen' and 'pen'. *For every pair of same words is substitutable, salva veritate, regardless of differentiation.* That is one of the most significant pieces of evidence that the dominance hypothesis (which lies at the foundation of the present theory) has to be true. Substitution tests work only on the condition that the meaning attached to the substituted inscription resists adaptation to the full extent that it differs from the original word. Though such resistance may obtain in the case of inscriptions for different words, it *never* obtains in the case of inscriptions for the same word.

If we took the token, 'caught', from the sentence 'He caught a fish' and physically transferred it (by interchanging the very printing) to the sentence 'He caught a cold', putting it in place of that occurrence of 'caught', the resulting sentence would have exactly the same meaning as did the former. This is an important indication of the *law-likeness* of the adaptation regularities being investigated: the generalizations to be offered support appropriate counterfactual statements.

Tests for sameness of meaning for *same* words have to be carried out through *comparisons* of their meanings. That does not, as I mentioned, beg the question as to whether we know the meanings to be the *same* or not; for one thing, even if they are different, we may not have noticed or characterized the difference. (Aristotle, as did Wittgenstein later, remarked (in *Top.* I, 18, 108a, 17–36) upon the treachery of unanalysed terms.)

Many of my claims about analogy depend upon the premise that an *n*-tuple of occurrences of a particular word differ in meaning. Sometimes the truth of such assertions is not apparent and there ought to be a way of resolving doubts, at least for enough cases to support the rest of the theory, as, for instance, about the *Miller's Analogies* examples in chapter 1. Moreover, many philosophers, Duns Scotus, Ockham, Quine, Cartwright and Mavrodes for instance, have expressed doubt that 'exists' differs in meaning when applied to numbers, sets, Socrates and God; and some people have said that 'caught' does not differ in meaning in the examples mentioned in section 2, above, in this chapter.

Meaning-difference tests will help to resolve such disagreements, though, in the long run, whether a given test, even adjusted to our experience, is adequate to reveal difference of same-word meaning depends upon whether it identifies such differences compatibly with our intuitions – not necessarily with all our individual intuitions, but rather with the general pattern of our intuitions, which will, no doubt, become adjusted themselves after we find tests that are serviceable: a kind of reflective equilibrium reached through the feedback adjustments of both tests and intuitions. So the tests I begin with are no more refined than the linguistic intuitions (insights) I use to adjust them.

Aristotle remarked, *Topics* (I, 15, 107a, 14), 'the same term does not bear the same meaning in all its applications' and provided us with an initial battery of tests for difference of meaning for same words, in *Topics* (I, 15, 106a–107b), offering fifteen observations upon marks of difference of meaning.[1] I present them here, with some alterations to apply to the kinds of cases I am discussing, to serve as patterns upon which further tests may be invented as they are needed.

4 ARISTOTLE'S TESTS FOR DIFFERENCES OF MEANING AMONG SAME-TERM OCCURRENCES

(a) *Disparity of contraries* If there are distinct contraries for a word, then the word bears several meanings: 'dull' and 'flat' are distinct contraries of 'sharp'. Also, 'fine' as applied to a picture may have 'ugly' as its contrary, but as applied to a house, 'ramshackle'; so, 'fine' is an equivocal term. (Aristotle apparently did not realize that all words are, or can be used equivocally.) Some of Aristotle's examples, of course, depend upon oppositions peculiar to classical Greek; but there are in each case modern counterparts: e.g. 'true' which has 'false' and 'out of plumb' and 'off pitch' as contraries.

(b) *Homonymous contraries* Even when the contraries bear the same name, e.g. 'blurry' as contrary to 'clear', used both for color and for sound, they may be homonymous, and therefore different. So, 'clear' is equivocal.

Aristotle suggested that the difference in the sensory mode by which the judgments of obscurity (blurriness) are warranted indicates a difference of meaning. Similarly, with 'sharp' and 'dull' in regard to flavors and solid edges. 'Blurry' applied to visual images and to thoughts, also manifests a difference in its appropriate contraries: 'well-focused', 'intelligible', etc. Although Aristotle's interpretation of this test relies upon the epistemic disparity in the conditions for applying the common contrary, 'blurry', nowadays we can restrict our interpretation to semantic factors, e.g. to disparity of the near synonyms or further contraries (e.g. 'blurry'/'clear').

(c) *Asymmetry of contraries* If one token has a contrary while another has none, they differ in meaning. '"To love", also, used in the frame of mind has "hate" as its contrary, while used of the physical activity (kissing) it has none: clearly, therefore, "to love" is an equivocal term' (*Top.*, 106b, 2).

(d) *Difference of intermediates (106b, 3)* If one token (and its contrary) has intermediates and another has none or if both have intermediates but not the same ones, the tokens differ in meaning. For instance, in one occurrence, 'conscious' may take an intermediate, 'semi-conscious' ('The prisoner was conscious'), and in another may not ('Human beings are by nature conscious').

An example of *different* intermediates: between 'white' and 'black', used to classify persons, there are different intermediates than there are between 'white' and 'black' classifying colors.

(e) *More intermediates* Similarly, if one token, in relation to its contrary, has *more* intermediates than another, the tokens differ in meaning: e.g. between 'white' and 'black' for colors there are many shades, whereas between 'white' and 'black' for people there are only a few: 'yellow', 'brown', etc. In the vocabulary of the model to be used later, despite the sameness of the color words, the words belong to different predicate (classificatory) schemes or lexical systems (as some would say). For example, 'black' may have the same 'sense' meaning when its *linguistic* meaning is different.

'Intermediate' is ambiguous and used equivocally in the above examples. In sense 1, there is an intermediate, K, between L and M, just in case anything to which one of the three predicates may apply is such that only one may apply to it. In sense 2, the applicability of the first predicate excludes one but not the other of the remaining two: 'alive', 'half alive' and 'dead'. In a scheme for primary colors 'orange', 'yellow', 'green' and 'blue' are intermediate between 'red' and 'violet', whereas in a color scheme for people, 'black' and 'white' are included, and there are intermediates like 'red', 'yellow',

41

'brown' and 'olive', but not 'orange' and 'purple'. Those words that belong to both schemes have different 'sense' meanings and different linguistic meanings. (See C. I. Lewis' seminal 'Linguistic Meaning and Sense Meaning', 1962.)

But what of 'black' and 'white' applied to cows? There are different intermediates from 'black' and 'white' applied to people. 'Black' applied to cows, as David Schrader pointed out, does not differ in 'sense' meaning (cf. Lewis 1962) from 'black' applied to automobiles, and yet 'purple' is an intermediate for cars and not for cows. That indicates that 'black' is equivocal, has different linguistic meanings in the two cases, although the kind of 'color experience' needed to apply the predicate is the same. That casts doubt upon Aristotle's test because we would not ordinarily say 'black' differs in meaning in those two cases.

The difficulty here is created by the fine line between commonplace falsehood and unacceptability of the sentence. In the context of classification by racial color, is 'Some people are purple' an unacceptable sentence or just obviously false? Is 'Some cows are purple' a commonplace falsehood, or is it unacceptable? I think we should interpret Aristotle's test as follows: when intermediates for the one occurrence are unacceptable in the environment of the other (see chapter 3 for a more precise statement of the condition), we have a difference of meaning; when the inapplicability of intermediates is due to commonplace falsehood but not unacceptability of the sentences, the test has not revealed a meaning difference; and where we are not sure whether there is unacceptability or commonplace falsehood, the test fails to yield a usable result.

(f) *Difference of contradictory opposites* Where the contradictory opposite of a token is a different word or a homonym of the contradictory opposite of another token, the word has different meanings. For instance, Aristotle indicated that the contradictory opposite of 'to see', namely, 'to fail to see', can mean 'to fail to possess the power of sight' and 'to fail to put that power into active use'. Thus, 'Bats do not see' may mean that they do not have the power of sight or that they do not exercise it.

'Having the power to F' and 'exercising the power to F' are different meanings of any predicate, F, which is capable of such differentiation. Needless to say, there are other meanings for 'to fail to see' such as 'to overlook'. So, if a pair of occurrences of 'to see' differs in what is the appropriate contradictory opposite, or if a common contradictory (e.g. 'to fail to see') is homonymous, then they differ in meaning.

(g) *Homonymous privatives* If the words that denote the *privation* (or *presence*) of a certain state bear more than one meaning, then a common word naming the state (or its privation) does also. Thus, if 'to lack sense' has more than one meaning, then 'to have sense' also does. So also, if 'to fail to read' has more than one sense, so does 'to read'. Similarly, if in two sentences 'makes sense' occurs (e.g. 'Crusoe made sense out of the signals' and 'That sentence makes sense') where the appropriate *privation* would in the one case be '*failed* to make sense of' ('found no meaning in') and in the other 'contained no meaning inherently', then 'make sense' is equivocal. Aristotle's example is that 'to be wanting in sense' as applied to soul and to body are different things, and therefore, 'to have sense' as applied to both is equivocal.

(h) *Different meanings in inflected forms* Here Aristotle shifted ground somewhat: if an inflected form of a word has more than one meaning, then the word has more than one meaning; his example is 'justly' and 'just'. For instance, 'justly' may mean 'appropriately' or it may mean 'fairly'; 'just' is similarly equivocal.

Aristotle said there is a meaning of the uninflected word corresponding to each distinct meaning of the inflected word. We have an English counterpart of that in 'to smoke'. Just as there is an 'active present' sense, in which we might say 'the fireplace *is smoking*', so there is, corresponding to the inflected form, a dispositional sense in which we might say 'Jones *smokes*' or 'Jones is a *smoker*' and there is also a proclivity sense in which we say a flawed fireplace *smokes* even when it is not actually smoking and even though we do not (though we might, according to the theory to be developed) say that it is a *smoker* (as a repairman might classify it).

(i) *Differences in predicates signified* As Aristotle stated it, if different occurrences of the same word differ in the predicates they signify, then they differ in meaning. He illustrated with 'good', which signifies 'productive of pleasure' in some applications to food and in others, merely, 'not harmful to health', and, in the case of medicine, 'productive of health'.

Frequently, just what is at issue is *whether* different occurrences of the same word signify the same predicates or not. In those situations, other considerations settle whether the significations differ, perhaps the other tests Aristotle provided.

As I classify the material in *Topics*, I, 15, there are two sub-tests under 9 (107a, 3–36) that can be applied in some of the disputed cases: 107a, 18–31 and 107a, 31–35. If the genus of the objects denoted by one occurrence is different from and not a subalternate to the genus of the objects denoted by another, the common word is equivocal. Thus, if 'a fish' and 'a thief' and 'a cold' are the respective 'catches' (designated by the cognate accusative of 'to catch') and they belong to a genera different from one another, genera not subalternate to one another, then 'catch' differs in meaning when applied to them.

Aristotle used a common name for different sorts of things – 'donkey' as a name for an animal and for an engine – and argued the equivocity of the name from the fact that the genus of engines was neither the same as nor subalternate to that of animals. His test can be generalized: where a transitive verb allows different sorts of thing-names to be substituted for its cognate accusative ('the catch'), if these diverse *sorts* are not species of one genus or species subordinated to one another or ordered as determinates to determinable, then the common verb also has different meanings. Thus, in 'He jumped the fence', 'He jumped the king', 'He jumped the trembling victim', and 'He jumped bail', there are different kinds of differences of meaning, and no pair of the occurrences of 'jumped' is univocal.

As *Topics*, 107a, 33–6 indicates, the same considerations, if applicable to the *contraries* of a pair of same words, will mark the equivocation of the latter as well.

(j) *Difference of contextual definition* Aristotle noted the value of contextual definitions: if the definition for a word in one combination of words, when compared with the definition appropriate to it in another combination, is found to differ, then the word differs in meaning in its two occurrences. Thus, 'clear body' and 'clear note', when contextually defined, with the notions of 'body' and 'note' later abstracted, do not yield the same definition: 'a . . . of such and such color' and 'a . . . easy to hear'; so, 'clear' differs in the two occurrences.

If 'clean record' and 'clean floor' are compared, we get something like: 'a record that does not indicate crimes or reprehensible behavior' and 'a floor without untoward indications of stains or dirt'. Then, dropping the terms 'record' and 'floor', we are left with *definition frames* that are clearly different, exhibiting a difference of meaning between the two occurrences of 'clean'.

Comparison of contextual definitional frames is a serviceable test, in fact one of the most easily applied and most illuminating of all the tests. It can be applied, as I usually do, simply by listing near synonyms, opposites, determinables, determinates, hyponyms, etc., for the one token and asking whether the same expressions are both co-applicable with and stand in the same semantic relation to the other.

(k) *Equivocation within contextual definitions* Aristotle recognized that in any of these definitional processes, the first stage may yield another term *common* to both occurrences; e.g. 'healthy' may yield 'what is related commensurably to health'. To use a contemporary example, in the cases of 'sound ship' and 'sound melon' and 'sound argument', analysis or contextual definition might yield '*x* that does not exhibit or contain a defect' (Mavrodes 1970: 747). But the mere presence of common words in a pair of definitions does not sufficiently indicate sameness of meaning because the common word itself may be equivocal. Aristotle said, 'Often in the actual definitions, as well, ambiguity creeps in unawares, and for this reason the definitions also should be examined' (107b, 7).

In general, the mere fact that a pair of predicates seem to be determinates of a common determinable (e.g. 'unfit for its purpose') does not show that the determinable is applicable *univocally* to both designates. Nor does it follow that because a given determinable has the same set of determinates in two contexts, that either it or the determinates apply univocally in both. (This has important applications to philosophical analysis, see chapter 8, section 2 (c), p. 189, below.)

In fact, one cannot, practically, *establish* univocity of a pair of words in differing sentence frames; one can at best (by getting negative results from tests like these) render equivocation improbable. For this reason, I suggest that *same words are univocal unless equivocation is indicated* (linguistic inertia).

(l) *Difference of comparatives* This can also be generalized. Aristotle suggested that a word differs in meaning if the one instance admits of a *comparative* and the other does not, or if, while both admit of comparison, they do not admit of (non-figurative) comparison to one another. This seems especially useful. A sharp flavor and a sharp note are not non-figuratively comparable in that the flavor might be sharper than the note. A fast car is not faster than a fast color. Long hair is not longer than a long book. Sometimes the affirmative comparison is acceptable when the negative or privative is not, and a meaning difference is also thereby indicated.

Having the same comparatives will not, however, assure univocity because the comparisons are sometimes possible just *because* of the differences of meaning. For instance, one man may be more intelligent than another and any man is more intelligent than any dog and some dog is more intelligent than some man; and the reason the three may be true is that 'intelligent' has three (at least) different meanings (that are revealed by some of the other tests). But Aristotle's test, as he stated it, is sufficient in the cases where comparisons are *blocked* either because one token does not take a comparative ('The patient was alive') while another does ('This class was alive, more alive than most'), or because, despite the possibility of comparatives, the one is not to be compared non-figuratively to the other ('dull day', 'dull knife').

(m) *Generic opposition of the realms of applicability* In one occurrence the word is the *differentia* of a genus that is different from and not subalternated to the genus of the denotata of the other. 'Sharp' differentiates note from note and, likewise, one pin from another, whereas 'pin' and 'note' do not denote things of the same or of subalternated genera. As a result, non-figurative comparison fails (even though both occurrences take comparatives); e.g. 'That note is sharper than a pin' is hyperbolic emphasis. The reverse is harder to provide an environment for, because the effect of hyperbole is more likely to be blunted: 'That pin is sharper than a note'.

(n) *Difference in the class-partitioning properties* Aristotle suggested that a word differs in meaning if the *differentia* under the word in the one case is not the same as that in the other. Thus, if the common word is 'color' and the ranges of application are bodies and tunes, then if the *differentia* of the ranges are different (shades for color and

46

modality in melodies), 'color' differs in meaning. 'Crooked' applied to paths and to moral behavior has different 'differentia'.

(o) *Difference in predicable status* Finally, if in one case the word is the species and in another the *differentia*, the tokens differ in meaning because 'the species is never the *differentia* of anything', (*Top.*, I, 15, 107b, 33). Thus, 'the rational' sometimes means 'that by which men are differentiated from beasts' and sometimes means 'what is reasonable to believe'. So too, 'rational' as the *differentia* of the genus 'animal' and 'rational' as a *species* of numbers differs in meaning.

Aristotle's interest in tests for equivocity arose not in discussions of analogy but in providing practical helps for scientific thinking in the *Topics*. Nevertheless, his tests help to disclose meaning differences in cases where competent speakers of the language are in doubt.

Aristotle's tests are, as I have emphasized, not the only ones we can employ. (Nor do we have to rely upon any one of them alone.) For instance, if modifiers appropriate to one occurrence are not appropriate to another, that often marks a difference in meaning. So also, when the same modifiers are applicable but differ in meaning: 'He jumped the fence *swiftly*' can mean that he moved *quickly* in doing so. But 'He *swiftly* jumped bail' does not require that he move at all but only that he jump bail soon; so 'jumped' differs in the two cases.

In a doubtful case, a congruence of two or more of the various tests that disclose asymmetry of contraries, antonyms, modifiers, qualifiers, inflections, comparison, genera of objects denoted, and of contextual definitions, will probably be sufficient to nudge intuition to recognize a difference of meaning. Furthermore, one can apply even the congruence of these tests cautiously, holding that in *general*, though perhaps not in every case, such a congruence reveals equivocation, but only when one's educated and adjusted verbal 'ear' is not offended by the result.

5   SEMANTIC CONTAGION

Semantic contagion consists of the *dominance* of one word (or group of words) over another (or group of others). It is observable as a process, relationship or event, depending upon how the examples are arranged. I prefer the relational description because it does not

47

involve the misleading suggestion of *changes* of meaning. That is, differentiation is a synchronic relation, although, of course, it is manifested diachronically, too, as evolving meaning.

Consider the sentence frame: 'He cancelled the (N.P.)', completed with 'check' and completed with 'appointment'. 'Cancelled' adjusts its meaning to the completion noun. So too, with 'He wrote for a (N.P.)', completed as: 'He wrote for a living' and 'He wrote for an appointment'. The reverse occurs as well: 'He (V.P.) for a living', (i) 'He wrote for a living'; (ii) 'He married for a living'. (That, of course, is ambiguous between 'as an occupation' and 'to avoid having to work'.) Adjustment, (in the sense of 'fit'), occurs in the single concatenation of words, the meaning of 'for a living' in (i) is not *altered* in (ii), or vice versa, but rather *what* 'for a living' means in (i) and (ii) is (within a range of possibilities) *settled* by what words it is combined with.

The 'completion' word (in a pair of sentence frames) sometimes adapts to the frame elements already present and sometimes the frame words (or one of them) adapt to the completion word, depending upon which dominates.

The distinction between completion words and frame words is entirely relative to what one supposes one is *given* to be completed. If one is given something wanting a word or two to make a sentence, it is a frame; if one perceives oneself as given words wanting a *structure* as well as words to make a sentence, one needs a sentence frame. Although it is a matter of *gestalt* which one sees oneself as having and, consequently, lacking, the dominance relations are not arbitrary, as my examples will illustrate.

I want to counter the impression that the completion words and the frame elements 'already have some context-neutral kernel of meaning' that adjusts or adapts when they are combined. Outside a context a word has no signification at all (nor any denotation) but has (in its other contexts of occurrence) partly delimited *possibilities* or *ranges* of signification that are adapted, fitted, to context. The various adaptation results are the species of differentiation (analogy, metaphor, denomination and mere equivocation). J. Lyons (1977: 567), made a similar observation: 'Furthermore polysemy – the product of metaphorical creativity – is essential to the functioning of languages as flexible and efficient semantic systems.' Lyons was wrong that polysemy is the product of metaphorical creativity alone, or even chiefly. Other kinds of differentiation (proportionality and denomination) are even more common in discourse, as the 'clusters' described in chapter 4 will illustrate.

Lyons did not fully appreciate how words interact through dominance to make room for new ideas. Potentially infinite polysemy is the feature upon which the indefinite expressive capacity of language rests and by which it can make room for endless new ideas. (See section c, following.)

I disavow Lyons' emphasis upon *metaphorical transfer* as the source of polysemy because it is myopic. He is right that the ability to make metaphors and understand them is 'an integral part of every speaker's linguistic competence and . . . in the child's acquisition of language' (1977: 556). And he is right that, 'The distinction between homonymy and polysemy is unrelatedness v. relatedness of meaning (cf. 1.5); and it is clear that this is the relevant and important consideration. . . . Indeed it is arguable that it is the only synchronically relevant consideration' (1977: 551). But metaphorical transfers are *only a species of a more general competence*, to 'compute' or 'assemble' sentence meanings as resultants of dominance and indifference relations among verbal components. Polysemy is only *in part* a 'product of metaphorical creativity' (1977: 567). There is a generic linguistic ability of which 'metaphorical transfers' form only one class of analogous manifestations.

That adaptation to context is *explanatory* is displayed by its operating *causally*. If the sentence frame were written out twice: (iii) 'He dropped his (N.P.)' and (iv) 'He dropped his (N.P.)', and if (iii) were completed with 'friend' and (iv) with 'book', 'dropped' in each would have a determinate and different meaning that could be altered simply by erasing the completion words in the two cases and interchanging them. The interchange of completion words *causes* 'dropped' in (iii) and (iv) to *change* meaning and displays that *semantic dominance* is explanatory. Such *changes* of meaning are not common outside poetry, e.g. Cummings, occasionally in novels, and in jokes and puns, and word plays.[2]

Why 'dropped' adjusts to 'friend' and 'book' rather than the reverse (as would be the case with 'He . . . the books' completed by 'wrote' and 'audited') is explained in chapter 3. For now, the fact that there is dominance, that it has a *causal* structure and that it is law-like in its regularity (that is, *would* have altered the meanings *if* we had interchanged the completion words) is what is to be acknowledged.

49

Finally, there can be more differentiated meanings than there are actual occurrences of the word, the others being implicit in contrasting modifiers which *successively* differentiate the word as if it were severed and repeated; 'John *likes* blondes and chocolate ice cream'. The same effect can be created with *pronouns*: John Fowles (1977: 17) 'Before you *have your way* and we . . . go our separate *ones*.' 'Ones' does the trick of putting 'way' into the plural and under the domination of 'go our separate' in contrast to the double entendre for 'have your way'. The figure of speech, zeugma, employs this structure (see chapter 6). Lyons (1977: 408, example 28) did not consider these cases against a large enough background and missed the law-like structure.

In Summary:

Def. II–2: Meaning differentiation: Meaning differentiation is a *relation*: the relation of *differing meaning* among same words caused by contrasting, *dominating* environments.

The *existence* of meaning adjustment is indubitable because it is observable. And so is the dominance of contrasting completions. 'He watched . . .'; 'He watched by the bier of his friend'; 'He watched his feet'; 'He watched his step'; 'He watched while they slept'. Furthermore, the explanatory role of dominance was demonstrated by its *causal* operation when I interchanged completion expressions. Now we have to find out how dominance is achieved and why one word dominates another and why the dominance patterns seem to vary so much.

One thing we can tell already is that dominance involves exclusion: meanings are 'selected' by the *exclusion* of others because the resulting sentences would be unacceptable in the environment. (To the extent that more than one resulting sentence is acceptable and probable, the expression is ambiguous.)

6 EVOLVING EXPRESSIVE CAPACITY

The synchronic differentiation structure causes diachronic evolution of expressive capacity. What *has* occurred in discourse is the foundation for new possibilities. If W^1 is metaphorical in relation to W^0 (same term), then there can be W^3 that is metaphorical with W^1 and not univocal with W^0, and this can be *contextually induced* through domination. Similarly, just as 'investigator' is a paronym

50

of 'investigate', so, as 'investigate' acquires new senses, even meta-phorical ones, 'investigator' will tag along, picking up new meanings denominatively (see discussion of paronymy in section 9 of chapter 5).

And, of course, once a word has acquired a meaning by a combination of simple metaphor and denomination (e.g. 'to cashier', extended from a simple metaphor for sending an employee to the paymaster to be 'paid off', dismissed), by abstractive analogy it can generalize into 'to dismiss or discharge from office or employment' ('The President cashiered General McArthur'), and by further personification and abstractive analogy, will apply to a critic's unfavorable review of a play, as *if* he were an owner–boss dismissing employees for bad work: 'The New York Post cashiered Porter's *Happy Way* last night.'

There are diachronic manifestations of the analogy structures. Yet ordinarily there would be little sense to tracing out the history of differentiations of a word; for one thing they are not adequately indicated in the recorded corpus. And why would a person want to trace 'force' (magnetic fields) back through actual differentiations to 'force' used experientially in observations like 'He ought not to force that stone into place'? A *constructed* series of step-wise adaptations from the one use to the other ought to be sufficient to display the continuity of meaning.

The real interest in the diachronic manifestations of analogy is that analogy of meaning (and, of course, thinking by analogy) is at the very heart of the expansion of the expressive capacity of natural language. But that is adequately explained by the dominance relations, as is the endless diachronic differentiation they necessitate.

New concept systems, only tangentially related to previous ones, cannot be incorporated into artificial languages without a new vocabulary. Whereas, in ordinary language all one needs is a suitable rearrangement of the affinities and oppositions of existing words. And that can be *induced* by new arrangements of their sentence frames. Thus, 'pressure', 'volume', 'rate', 'amplitude' and the like apply to liquids, to electricity, and to automobile traffic and commercial exchanges.

7   MULTIVALENT DOMINANCE

Sometimes dominance between words is mutual (but in different respects), e.g. in such phrases as 'physical attraction'. For instance, (a) 'The physical attraction of persons married to others is better sublimated than indulged' or (b) 'The physical attraction of the metals was determined by careful measurement'. The term 'attraction' is partially captured by 'physical' in (a), which is itself determinable and is captured by the rest of the sentence frame. 'Attraction' in (b) is dominated in a dimension left open in the first frame to 'physical' (e.g. in contrast to 'emotional' or 'intellectual'). There is a parallel indeterminacy in the second occurrence of 'physical attraction' (e.g. where 'physical' is ambiguous between 'electrical', 'gravitational', 'nuclear', etc.). Reciprocal dominance (e.g. of 'attraction' over 'physical' and 'physical' over 'attraction') is an instance of multivalent dominance. In this example a single word 'attraction', is dominated in distinct respects by *different* expressions in the environment, 'physical', 'married to others' and 'indulged'.

8   RELATED AND UNRELATED MEANINGS

Mere equivocals have no discernible 'relatedness', e.g. *sharp*/sign, *sharp*/edge or *charge*/criminal, *charge*/battery, *charge*/purchase. Analogous words are related in meaning: '*wise* law', '*wise* man', '*stop* a vehicle', '*stop* a check', 'an *intelligent* creature', 'an *intelligent* reply'; 'to *collect* animals', 'to *collect* taxes', to *collect* one's debts'; to *include* a person', 'to *include* a paragraph'. Although I adopt no strict rule about the predicates 'differ in meaning' and 'differ in sense', generally when one is applied the other applies too. Very roughly, homonymy corresponds to 'have different meanings' and polysemy to 'have different senses' (see Lyons 1977: 550–69).

Having now completed the preliminary material, I summarize what is explained in chapters 4 and 5.

Whenever a person employs a word in an utterance, he employs it univocally or equivocally with respect to *each* of its other tokens (without regard for temporal order) within the corpus of the language. If univocally with respect to a given occurrence, there is no predicate scheme difference (see chapter 3) or predicate mode difference (see chapter 5). If equivocally with respect to a given occurrence, there is a difference of one or the other kind. If of the latter *only*, he employs it denominatively analogously (see chapter 5). If of the *former* only, he employs it non-denominatively but with a difference of predicate scheme (chapters 3 and 4). Thus the *same* token of a word, compared to a *set* of other tokens of the word, can be univocal, merely equivocal, analogous, denominatively analogous and metaphorical to various members of the set simultaneously.

The difference of predicate scheme is either such that no near synonym of the one occurrence is a near synonym of the given occurrence, or some near synonyms of the one, but not all, are near synonyms of the other. If the former, the term is merely equivocal with the given one. If the latter, it is analogous by proportionality. If the predicate schemes stand in *asymmetrical* implication relations, the expression is employed metaphorically and if not, not. If the expression is employed metaphorically, it may be employed figuratively as well: that depends upon whether there is, additionally, a relation of analogy, paronymy, or certain referential differentiations, in the shortest step-wise adaptation to the given occurrence from the tokens being compared.

In brief, when a word recurs, it either differentiates or not with respect to every other same word in the corpus, taken pair-wise. If it does, it differentiates merely equivocally or analogously. If analogously, either metaphorically or non-metaphorically. If metaphorically, either figuratively or non-figuratively. And if in *any* way, either denominatively or non-denominatively. Thus the speaker does not have to *know* the laws of differentiation because, whether or not he knows them, his words obey them: as objects fall, so words go together to make what sense they can. Later chapters show how this happens.

3

Predicate schemes:
an explanatory model

Predicate schemes are the meaning-relevant portions of *paradigmatic sets*

1 PARADIGMATIC SETS: CO-APPLICABLE WORDS

Contrast and meaning To have meaning, an expression must be *in contrast of meaning*; it must have *differential* meaning – function contrastively to something else (Lyons 1966: 422; 1963: 59). Equivocal words stand in diverse contrast patterns with *other* words: for example, they may not have the same opposites (*sharp:dull; sharp:flat*). That provides the purchase for modelling the meaning relationships under inquiry.

As Lyons described combinatorial contrasts, there are two basic kinds: syntagmatic and paradigmatic (1966: 70ff, 117, 428f, 460; 1977 vol.1: 48, 55). An expression *paradigmatically* contrasts with all other expressions that could have been inserted in its place (the remainder of the sentence remaining substantially unchanged) to produce replacement sentences that are semantically *acceptable* within the given environment and preserve the consistency (or inconsistency) of the original. A native speaker must not find the substituted result so incongruous that his critical reply would be the equivalent of 'That's not English; one doesn't say that'.

The set of words in paradigmatic contrast with a given word may be imagined as a vertical list of words substitutable (under the conditions mentioned) for the same place, or role, in a given sentence frame, e.g. 'The youth/young man/boy/urchin/girl/matron/etc. asked for a job.' It is the list of *co-applicable* words (see definitions below).

Syntagmatic contrasts are the differing semantic and syntactic *limitations* expressions impose linearly upon what can be combined with them into an acceptable sentence. For instance, 'He kicked him with his *nose*' is usually excluded syntagmatically; even more, 'He kicked

him with his *skin*'. Apart from a presupposition-cancelling environment, 'kicked ... with' syntagmatically requires an instrument-
completion belonging to a semantic field that includes 'foot', 'shoe',
'heel' and the like and excludes 'nose' and 'skin' (cf. Lyons 1977:
250–69). Syntagmatic contrasts may be imagined as *difference* of
acceptable completions *linearly* in the sentence frame, depending
upon the syntactic and semantic presuppositions of elements
'already' given, direction being irrelevant.

Lyons, in his earlier book (1966), overemphasized that words in
paradigmatic contrast for a given token are related in meaning to
one another the way members of a lexical field are related. Redundancies in the environment sometimes do restrict substitutions to
words belonging to recognized lexical systems or semantic fields,
like kinship relations, cooking terms, and so forth. But it is not
always so, as will be illustrated.

Lyons (1966: 137ff) partly enlightened us about 'can also occur in
the same context', when he discussed 'acceptability'. I add other
observations. Certainly some combinations of words are grammatically impossible. But, contrary to the apparently widespread belief
among philosophers that some grammatically well-formed expressions are inherently nonsensical ('It's Tuesday everywhere I look'),
there is no grammatically well-formed string of words that is in all
environments semantically impossible or semantically unacceptable.

For instance, 'Green ideas sleep uneasily' is perfectly sensible in
talk about an inventor's impetuosity to enter production without
adequate reflection. Consider Patrick White's *Voss*, p. 60: 'Air
joining air experiences a voluptuousness no less intense because
imperceptible.' In context it is meaningful. And see in the same
work, p. 86, 'The darkness was becoming furious.' Something is
nonsense only relative to an environment.

Edward Erwin decided that 'to be meaningless' means 'to be *a
priori* false' (1970: 152). And undoubtedly some scientists and philosophers of science, calling statements meaningless, may mean that
they are *a priori* false, though I would have thought *a priori* falsity to
be incompatible with being meaningless, e.g. 'There is a largest
natural number'. Erwin's analysis does not even begin to take
account of the many related senses of 'That's meaningless' and of the
correlated senses of 'That's nonsense'.

Theodore Drange (1966: 11) gave an initial list of eight sentences

55

that includes 'Smells are loud' and 'I have eaten a loud clap', insisting that 'we must understand that sentences (1)–(8) are to be interpreted literally, without any of their terms being taken in an unusual way'. And to those who regard such sentences as 'odd' rather than meaningless, Drange observed (1966: 12): 'But it should be realized that what makes them odd is the fact that unlike ordinary sentences, sentences such as (1)–(8) need to be given some *special* interpretation in order to be understood.'

He, of course, equated 'literal' with 'usual' and 'non-literal' with 'unusual' 'special', etc.

As often happens, the way the question is put prejudices the answer (see Wittgenstein, *P.I.*, 114). For we can also say we are unfamiliar with the expressive possibilities of such sentences, not recognizing any *use* for them, but as soon as a function is found or described, they are intelligible. The problem is rather to describe what is missing when we create environments in which they *cannot* have senses that we can understand, to identify the semantic difference between an environment in which 'a thinkable proposition' is expressed and one where nothing is expressed. (See the explanation of linguistic nonsense at the end of section 7 (c) below.)

Some presupposition-cancelling, metaphorical or figurative environment is possible for any grammatical string of words. The notion of 'presupposition-cancelling feature' is not systematically investigated here. But some things can be said about it.

(1) Syntagmatic relations are, as Lyons (1968: 440) says, relations of presupposition: 'This notion of syntagmatic interdependence, or presupposition, is of considerable importance in the analysis of the vocabulary of any language (cf. 9.4.3). . . . There are presuppositions holding between particular classes of nouns and verbs . . . (e.g. *bird: fly, fish: swim*) . . . (*blond: hair, addled: egg*) . . . (*drive:car*) . . . (*bite:teeth, kick:feet*).'

(2) *Any* presupposition, whether 'weak' and merely associative (drive:car vs. drive:nails vs. drive:a well) or logically implied (bachelor:unmarried male, husband:male spouse) can be contextually (environmentally) negated (suppressed) by dominant words. 'Husband' can mean 'The formerly male-role bearer' and 'bachelor', 'a person resistant to marrying or mating'. Each semantic presupposition that an expression has in one context-environment is *defeasible* in some environment or another. It can be defeated by resistance to unacceptability. To the extent that environment suppresses what is a

56

typical and frequent presupposition of a word, it is said to be presupposition-cancelling environment. Though 'the theory of relativity' is usually taken to describe, even to name, a scientific theory, it differentiates to designate a perceptual, cultural or aesthetic theory. And it differentiates denominatively (see chapter 5) into a definite description (and even a name) for a book, stack of papers, particular file drawer and even a *place* (e.g. the place where the copies of the theory belong or where the file drawer for the copies of the theory belongs).

Though any presupposition can be cancelled (and that is the basis of differentiation, chapter 4), a word cannot *acquire* by contextual domination just any presupposition, only those of the other words to which it gains affinity and opposition of meaning as a logical consequence of *giving up* affinity or opposition to some *other* word.

Inconsistency cannot assure meaninglessness, as philosophers should be aware. Yet, every grammatically well-formed string has some constructible environment in which it is semantically *unacceptable*. Indicia of an expression's unacceptability in an environment are (a) its irrelevance to the truth or falsity of the rest of E, (b) its *incongruity* in E and (c) most importantly, its being uncomputable relative to E; e.g. 'the milkman left pines of mills for the sky', 'fresh rot milks cans', or 'intermittent carnoids secure incipient pachyderms'. How meaninglessness occurs is discussed later on.

Lyons (1966: 428) remarked:

For instance, *husband* and *wife* are not synonymous, but they are semantically-related in a way that *husband* and *cheese*, or *hydrogen* are not; *good* and *bad* are different in sense, but more similar than *good* and *red* or *sound*; *knock, bang, tap*, and *rap* are related in a way that *knock* and *eat* or *admire* are not. The relationships illustrated here are paradigmatic (all the members of the sets of semantically related terms can occur in the same context).

As I said, Lyons (1966: 429) associates the study of such relations with the study of lexical systems, observing, 'The meaning of each term is a function of the place it occupies in its own system. (Cf. 2.2.1, with reference to Russian and English kinship terms.)' It may happen that the context and environment restrict the applicable expressions to a single field, though no test of or criterion for 'sameness of lexical field' was provided by Lyons. But it may also happen that there is no such restriction in the discourse environment. For instance, 'He swallowed . . .' might be completed by *food* terms or by *metal* names ('nickel') or by *coin* names ('dimes') or *vapor* names ('smoke') or *abstraction* names ('words' or 'fear'), or even *day* names ('Tuesday'). So, I do not restrict 'paradigmatic set' to expressions belonging to the same semantic field.

Rather, given a complete context (and a disambiguating environment), the entire class of words that can be substituted in the same sentential role, the remainder of the frame remaining substantially unchanged, with the replacement sentences being acceptable within the given discourse environment (truth values being ignored but consistency or inconsistency being preserved without *new* differentiation) is the *paradigmatic* set for a given term occurrence (see Def. III–2 below).

I begin model-construction with the theoretically primitive sentence relation, 'is a sentence *acceptable* within the given discourse environment (E)'; this predicate has among its necessary conditions (which I do not pretend to specify but only to suggest from the pretheoretical comments above) that the replacement must be recognized by competent writer–speakers to *be* a sentence of the language and to be 'computable' in the environment. The condition of 'having approximately the same meaning' does *not* apply here; nor does 'preserving truth'. But 'preserving consistency or inconsistency of the original' does apply to replacements, as does 'not newly differentiating any word of the sentence frame'.

Employing numbered superscripts to distinguish term occurrences (T^1, T^2, ...) and similar superscripts to distinguish sentences (C^1, C^2, ...) and expressions of the form 'C^1 (in E)' to refer to a sentence in a given environment (e.g. chapter 1 of *A Tale of Two Cities*), I introduce some explications and definitions, to which others will be added as I go along.

Def. III–I: Individual term occurrences: 'T^1 in C^1 (in E)' For example: T^1 is 'best' in C^1, 'It was the *best* of times' in E, that portion of Charles Dickens' *A Tale of Two Cities* which contains mandatory or exclusive syntagmatic relations to any term in C^1. (See Def. III–3.)

Def. III–2: Paradigmatic set for T^1 in C^1 (in E): The distinct words each of which may be substituted for T^1 in C^1 to produce a replacement sentence $C\star$ (otherwise the same as C^1) which is acceptable in the environment (E), truth values being ignored. 'Otherwise the same as' permits syntagmatic adjustments that maintain grammar and consistency (or inconsistency) but not new differentiation of any word in the sentence frame.

58

Def. III–3: Extent of discourse environment for T^1 in C^1 (in E): the number of units, measured in meaningful words used, in any direction, beyond which no mandatory or exclusive syntagmatic relation occurs for any word in C^1.

Def. III–4: W is co-applicable with T^1 in C^1 (in E) iff: W, substituted for T^1 in C^1, with the remainder of the sentence remaining unchanged and *with no other word in C^1 being newly differentiated,* completes a replacement sentence C★ that is acceptable in E. Again 'remaining unchanged' allows syntagmatic adjustments to *maintain* grammar and consistency or inconsistency.

Whenever a word is subject, modifier, verb, or other predicate, there is objectively at least one other word that can be substituted to yield an acceptable sentence, and there is at least one other expression that, if substituted, will produce a sentence unacceptable in the environment. And there is always at least a second expression that a competent writer–speaker does, or would, find thus substitutable (assuming he understands the conditions).

If the writer–speaker would count *no* other expression as appropriately in contrast, nor even an opposite of the one employed, then the word employed would have no linguistic meaning subjectively, because it is not relevantly in contrast to anything. Thus, if a sailor were reporting the color of a ship he had seen, 'It was egg-shell white', and refused to consider acceptable (but opposed) 'It was pea-green', or any other color word, we would have to conclude that either he does not understand the substitution condition, or his expression, 'egg-shell white' has no linguistic color-term meaning for him.

The generalizations above are included within a more abstract regularity: *for an expression to have meaning in a given environment, it must have contrastive meaning with other expressions that are also acceptable in that environment and must be in meaning contrast to some expressions not acceptable in that environment.* The expressions acceptable in a given context-environment are the expressions *co-applicable* in it (Def. III–4 above).

When the condition that there be such contrasting expressions is not satisfied by 'primitive languages' imagined by philosophers who talk about 'language games', I doubt that such signal-systems are languages at all.

Verbal classifications roughly 'project', indicate, the distinctive contour of paradigmatic sets. So the properties of classifications may be of interest. Still, the inquiry of this section is subsidiary to the main arguments of the book and the reader can press on to section 3, p. 63 below, without loss of continuity.

Among the classifications that are objective in the language and among those that are craft-objective, some are *articulate*. A classification is articulate just when the members form a finite, disjoint, fixed and exhaustive set of determinates under a univocal determinable, and are co-applicable over a wide range of contexts: for instance, the animal names, plant names, fish names, color words, blood-relationship names, insect names.

By 'objective classification' I mean a disjunction applicable over a wide range of environments in approximately the same contrast relationships to one another. The classification is *linguistically* objective if competence in the language and familiarity with the words, without familiarity with any special skill or craft, is sufficient for confidence about whether sentences employing them are, for the most part, acceptable. And a *craft-objective* classification is one where familiarity with the skills of a certain kind of craft is needed for the interpersonally confident determination of acceptable sentences, say, legal skill or medical skill or cabinet-making skill.

'Disjoint', 'fixed' and 'exhaustive' need some definition, as well as 'determinate–determinable'. A classification is *disjoint* just in case nothing correctly designated by any given label is also correctly designated by any other label belonging to it. A classification is *fixed* in membership just in case what members it has is not a matter of an individual speaker's preference but is determinate over a large corpus, like animal names in various regions of the world. A classification is *exhaustive* just in case the labels include at least one for everything within the range of its common determinable word, e.g. 'animal'; if for every kind of plant, where the language is used, there is a distinguishing particular name, and for every blood-relationship or military rank there is a distinct name, then the classifications are exhaustive. A determinate, relative to a determinable, is a word, say, 'red', that names one of the disjoint, exhaustive and mutually exclusive classes of things more abstractly or generally named by the determinable (e.g. 'color'). W. E. Johnson (1921) developed the notion 'determinable' this way (Searle 1967:357–9).

The predicates for expressing times of day (as clock readings), geographic positions (in latitude and longitude), bodily units anatomically, constituent parts of sailing craft, biological constituents of trees, and the like, are all, in my opinion, linguistically objective and articulate in English (though some might think some of these schemes are merely craft-objective).

Other articulate classifications, probably craft-objective only, are for washing machine parts, automobile parts, elements in electrical and telephone systems, divisions within an economic system, positions in a university hierarchy, clothes and shoe sizes, types of cloth, military titles, kinds of surgery, garden tools, kinds of pipe threads, screw types, concrete types, office furniture, laboratory glass, tobacco, trees, natural stone, coal, glass, grass ('orchard grass', 'fescue'), pencils, hardware ('latches', 'hasps', etc.), wood mouldings, grammatical relations, wood joints, a police manual's classification of crimes, a connoisseur's classification of the wines, etc.

Although one might disagree that one or another classification is linguistically objective rather than craft-objective or is articulate rather than non-articulate, it should be obvious that there are many articulate classifications objective in the language and many others objective in various crafts.

Objective classifications may be, in various ways, *inarticulate*. (1) If 'having a gradeable degree of academic accomplishment' is the determinable, it may not be fixed, either in the language or in the particular teaching craft, whether 'poor', 'fair', 'good', 'excellent' are its determinates or 'bad', 'adequate', 'superior', 'outstanding', 'brilliant', 'incredible', or some other set of expressions. Membership in such a classification is not objectively fixed, even though the *existence* of (varying) classifications for academic performance is linguistically objective.

(2) An objective classification may be inarticulate because its members do not exhaust the common determinable, or do not do so mutually exclusively. For instance 'to kick', 'to punch', 'to slap' are exclusive and determinate forms of 'to strike' but they do not exhaust the kinds of striking. And a student's work can be *both* excellent and brilliant, and hence, the members of that classification are not mutually exclusive and the classification is not disjoint.

61

Similarly, 'second', 'minute', 'hour', 'day', 'week', 'month' and 'year' are not exclusive in one direction and are exclusive in the other. The determinable adverb 'in a certain manner' might take as determinates, 'happily', 'eagerly', 'unkindly', 'hastily', and so forth, which disjunctively do not exhaust the field of application and some of which do not exclude one another.[1]

And sometimes an objective classification may not have a name for a common determinable: 'to be', 'to become', 'to have'. What are they determinates of? 'A cow', 'a calf', 'a bull' – determinates of ...?

The objective classification, including 'to run', 'to walk', 'to crawl', 'to dawdle', 'to totter', is not articulate because the membership is not fixed in the language; the members are neither disjoint nor exclusive (one could both dawdle and totter) and are not exhaustive of the range of the determinable. Nevertheless, the set has craft-objective subsets which are articulate (e.g. choreographic schemes for walking).

The contrast-dependent pair 'determinable–determinate' has been applied analogously above, automatically differentiating in comparison to its application to articulate classifications. In the latter there must be a plurality of determinates for each determinable, the determinates must be finite, exclusive and exhaustive and must designate disjoint ranges.

In non-articulate classifications, the determinates are only *like* their counterparts in articulate schemes, but are not disjoint, exclusive, exhaustive of the realm, etc. But that's just typical of the inexorable differentiation of classifications brought about by the suppression of a presupposition to avoid unacceptability in new environments.

Def. III–5: The objective paradigmatic set for T^1 in C^1: is the set of distinct words W^1–W^1, projected by an objective classification, substitutable for the given term, T^1, in its particular environment (with all the contextual and environmental presuppositions taken into account) to produce acceptable replacement sentences, without introducing new differentiation of the other elements (and preserving grammar and consistency/inconsistency).

Objective paradigmatic sets are roughly, incompletely and idiosyncratically approximated by subjective paradigmatic sets – the distinct words a speaker does or would consider co-applicable. Although various crafts have articulate classifications of kinds of cloth, metals, wire, paper, gasoline, rope, tools, printing type, brick, chairs, and practically any other kinds of things we can name, without special expertise one has only crude approximations of the classification. A person who buys rope may say, 'Give me ten yards of the one-inch nylon stuff', when in his subjective classification 'nylon' and 'dacron' are *not* opposed, while in the objective paradigmatic set they are.

The tension between a speaker's subjective classification and the craft-or language-objective classification (approximated by the utterance) creates the discordance felt by more sophisticated speakers at hearing the 'loose' usage of the less well-trained. That tension also justifies certain claims that a speaker does not understand what he is saying, that what is said makes no sense and certain claims that what was in fact said was divergent from what the speaker *meant*.

Someone, feeling that he has not had his money's worth in a transaction, might call it 'a fraud'. That offends pious legal ears. Yet, if 'fraud', as applied by the speaker, has any linguistic meaning at all, it has meaning contrastively with other words (like 'honest deal' and 'wonderful bargain' and 'robbery') that *he* would consider to be relevantly in contrast. But what 'fraud' contrasts with in his subjective paradigmatic set is different enough from the contrasts within the legally objective classification (and, therefore, its objective paradigmatic set) to create significant felt tension for a craft-conscious hearer.

3 PREDICATE SCHEMES: MEANING-RELEVANT SUBSETS OF PARADIGMATIC SETS

The meaning relationships of same words cannot be modelled directly as relationships of paradigmatic sets. First, the sets may be the same when the tokens differ in meaning and, secondly, the sets may differ when the tokens are the same in meaning. So, not every word that is a member of a paradigmatic set for a token is *meaning-relevant* to that token. I am, therefore, concerned with the co-applicable expressions that are meaning-relevant to a given token. These are its predicate schemes.

Def. III–6: The predicate scheme for T^1 in C^1 (in E): is the set of distinct words $(W^1–W^n)$ *co-applicable* (cf. Def III–4) with T^1 in C^1 (in E) and *meaning-relevant* to T^1 in C^1 (in E).

When predicate schemes for distinct occurrences, T^1 in C^1 and T^2 in C^2, are under discussion, rather than repeat such long strings of abbreviations, they will be indexed as follows. 'PS^1' for 'the predicate scheme for T^1 in C^1 (in E^1)' and 'PS^2' for 'the predicate scheme for T^2 in C^2 (in E^2)'. Thus I can form expressions like 'if T^1 in C^1 differs in meaning from T^2 in C^2, it does not follow that PS^1 differs from PS^2' and so forth.

Predicate schemes (meaning-relevant distinct words) can model word meanings particularly enough for the distinctions I want to make in chapter 4. Furthermore, such a model presents meaning relationships as contrasting patterns of distinct words. That accords with my underlying hypothesis that linguistic meaning realizes *differential* expressive capacity and that difference of expressive capacity is exhibited by distinct patterns of co-applicable words. Same-word tokens can enter *any* combination of words in place of one another. So if they differ in meaning, it has to be something other than a difference of *their* combinatorial possibilities (the way we might map the difference of meaning for distinct words). And that difference is in the patterns of *other* words that can be substituted for the particular token in its given context. For if every word co-applicable with W^1 were also co-applicable with W^2 and would stand in the same relations of affinity and opposition of meaning to still other words, then W^1 and W^2 would be univocal; there would be no linguistic meaning difference between them. (I do not consider inherence modes for now. See chapter 5.)

Secondly, nine of the fifteen equivocation tests (chapter 2) that I extracted from Aristotle's *Topics* explicitly suppose that where separate occurrences of the same word differ in meaning, that difference is reflected by differences of other words co-applicable with the one (or its opposite) and not co-applicable with the other (or its opposite). For instance, if what is a contrary of T^1 is not of T^2, Test 1; if the contrary of T^1 is homonymous with a contrary of T^2, Test 2; if T^1 has a contrary while T^2 does not, Test 3; if T^1 has other terms that are intermediate between it and some opposite while T^2 has no intermediate between it and the same opposite, Test 4; or if between T^1 and some opposite the intermediates differ from those between T^2 and some same-term opposite, Test 5; if T^1 has a different term as its contradictory opposite from that which is the contradictory opposite of T^2 or if a same-term contradictory opposite for T^1 and T^2 is homonymous, Test 6; if the terms W^1 and W^2 (in C^1 and C^2)

that denote the privations of what T^1 signifies in C^1 and of what T^2 signifies in C^2 are equivocal, then T^1 and T^2 are equivocal in C^1 and C^2, Test 7; if T^1 signifies a class of predicates (the predicates of the appropriately identified entailed statements) which differs in membership from the class signified by T^2, then T^1 and T^2 are equivocal, Test 9; if T^1 takes a comparative while T^2 does not, or if they differ in the comparatives they take, then T^1 and T^2 differ in meaning, Test 12.

Thirdly, I need that kind of model to represent meaning differences for words prior to and independent of representing entailment differences, paraphrase differences and all other sentence-meaning differences. That is because difference of same words can be the explanation of difference in sentence meaning in a way that the latter cannot explain the former.

Although different meanings of the same word can be represented by different lists (or the internal semantic relations of lists) of co-applicable words, not every difference of co-applicable words corresponds to a meaning difference. In some contexts 'husband' and 'wife' are not co-applicable, but do not differ in meaning from contexts where they are co-applicable: 'Wives may have cosmetic surgery without permission of their *husbands*'. If 'wives' were substituted for 'husbands' the result would be unacceptable, *and* consistency with the original sentence would not be preserved. Where *redundancy* excludes a word syntagmatically, the predicate scheme is not on that account different.

I reject an idea-in-the-mind-attached-to-the-inscription theory or a concept-signified-by-the-word theory as to what constitutes the linguistic meaning of a word. Rather, meaning is inherent in well-formed sentences (as expressive capacity), and is a medium of thought. Thought is impossible without (but never identical with) a realization in a medium: words, images, memories, notation, gestures, postures, actions, dreams, feelings, etc. And differences among one's thoughts subsist in the oppositions (contrasts) among the elements of the thought medium. Consequently, there cannot be distinctions of thought in a medium that does not permit suitable contrasts. But in some media, e.g. feelings and, as we shall see, words as well, the same opposition (or distinction) within the medium can realize different contrasts of thought, just as the same opposition of colors can in paintings realize distinct representations or expressions.

Even so, there would be no way of representing differences of *linguistic* meaning, differences of those relationships among words and larger expressions of the language that determine the expressive capacity of grammatically well-formed strings of words, without correlating such differences with oppositions of other verbal expressions or other linguistic items, e.g. semantic features in an ideal dictionary, etc. (see Katz 1972; Fodor and Katz 1964.)

Differences of *linguistic* meaning are not differences of thoughts, ideas, images, referents, or any of the other things that have been mistakenly said to *be* the meanings of words. They are differences of combinatorial acceptability (relative to an unspecified range of environments), that realize differences of expressive capacity (i.e. differences in what the expression *can* be used as a whole or part to mean). Why cannot 'snow is white' *mean* wrens are expensive? *Why* can you not *say* the latter by *uttering* the former, without merely correlating them, as with a code? (See Wittgenstein, *P. I.*, 510.)

So, I turn to the meaning-relevant words that are predicate schemes. A difference of predicate schemes (other than mere inclusion or exclusion by redundancy) constitutes a difference of meaning. Yet there are differences of meaning (of predicate mode) that are compatible with sameness (or inclusion) of predicate schemes.

To simplify vocabulary problems, let me *stipulate:*

Def. III-7: T¹ (etc.) has the same predicative meaning as T²(etc.) if and only if PS¹ is the same as or entirely includes or is entirely included within PS².

Same 'predicative' meaning is sameness (or mere inclusion) of predicate schemes. This is to stand in contrast to difference of predicate *mode* (denominative differentiation) which is compatible with sameness of predicate schemes (see chapter 5).

At this point a major *intra-theoretical* choice has been made, to explicate 'being meaning-relevant' as 'being co-applicable in the given context and *not* being co-applicable (or being co-applicable but *not* in the same affinity or opposition of meaning) with the same word in *some* other context where the not being co-applicable (or not being in the same affinity or opposition of meaning) *marks* a meaning difference'. The details of this account might require substantial restatement if a more satisfactory analysis of meaning-relevance were devised.

Difference of paradigmatic set is not sufficient for difference of meaning because not every such difference is meaning-relevant: some words are syntagmatically excluded because of other words than the ones they are to be substituted for: C^1 'When Smith first married (entered into marriage), he married his first cousin'; C^2 'When Smith first married (performed a marriage), he married his first cousin.' 'His aunt's son' is substitutable in C^2, but not in C^1, for 'cousin'. But the two occurrences of 'cousin' do not differ in meaning, rather the two occurrences of 'married' do. Note that if one substituted 'aunt's son' in C^2 for 'cousin' it would dominate 'married', compelling it to mean 'performed' (though that of course could be defeated, e.g. by 'who was a successful transsexual').

On the other hand, not every difference of meaning for T^1 and T^2 results in a difference of co-applicable predicates (sortals or characterizing terms) either. Some differences are modal, as is the difference between a disposition, 'he cheated', and the exercise of the disposition 'he cheated'; and the difference between an apparent state (e.g. of shape, motion, color) and the real (dispositional) state: 'He was hunched over' can mean 'looked as if he was', 'really was', 'looked to be and really was'; 'the stars were blue' can mean '*looked* blue' or '*were* blue'.

The meaning-relevant words are the ones whose *not* being co-applicable somewhere else *marks* a difference of predicate meaning. For instance, if no word substitutable for one token were similarly substitutable for another token, we would not hesitate to say the two differ in meaning. In fact, if no near synonym[2] of one is substitutable non-homonymously for the other, then they are merely equivocal: 'bank/bank'. So, also if W^1 is an opposite (whether contrary or contradictory) of T^1 in C^1, but when substituted as W^2 for T^2 in C^2, does not stand as the opposite of T^2, then T^1 and T^2 differ in meaning: *wide* vs. *narrow*/shoe; *wide* vs. *narrow*/'how wide is it?'.

On the whole, the *near synonyms*, the *contraries*, the *determinables*, the *determinates*, and the *predicates of correct contexual definitions* are *meaning-relevant*.

Def. III–8. The class of expressions that are meaning-relevant to T^1 in C^1 is the subset $(W^1, \ldots, W^n)$ of the paradigmatic set for T^1 in C^1 which, if any of its members, e.g. W^2, were not substitutable for T^2 in C^2 or were not to stand, upon substitution, in the same semantic relation (contrast) to T^2 that W^1 stands in to T^1, would, on one or more serviceable tests of equivocation, yield that T^1 and T^2 differ in meaning.

Near synonyms, opposites of various kinds, determinables, and determinates do not exhaust the portion of the paradigmatic set that is meaning relevant. Professor Henry Hoenigswald (1965: 191–6), commenting upon Lyons' classification of *Antinomy, Hyponymy, Converse Terms* and *Consequent Terms*, indicated other ways words can be meaning-relevant. If two tokens differ in *Antonyms*, whether non-gradeable (*single: married*) or gradeable (*big:small*) or *Hyponyms* (e.g. *grass: fescue; composition: sonata*), or *Converse Terms (buy:sell)* or *Antecedent-Consequent Terms (become:be)*, then they differ in meaning. So too, if in one context, 'form' is *Contrast-Dependent* upon 'matter' ('Every physical thing is composed of matter and form' where 'form' means 'the actuality of matter' and 'matter' means 'the capacity for form') and in another is not ('Some art critics are exclusively concerned with compositional form'), then 'form' differs in meaning.

Although I cannot list comprehensively the semantic relations that make words meaning-relevant, it is highly likely that they are not confined to those already mentioned. No doubt there are other useful classifications of such affinities and oppositions of meaning that would be congenial to my theory, too.

I want to replace Def. III–8, with Def. III–9, below, to avoid the counterfactual form: that the meaning-relevant words are those that if any had *not* been co-applicable and in the same affinity or opposition of meaning, then the given word would have had a different meaning. Without counterfactual form, I prefer Def. III–9.

Def III–9: W^1 is meaning-relevant to T^1 in C^1 (in E) if and only if:
(1) W^1 is co-applicable with T^1 in C^1 in E (that is, belongs to the paradigmatic set for T^1);
(2) For some disambiguating context-environment C^n in E^n, W^n is not co-applicable with T^n, a same word with T^1, or does not bear the same affinity or opposition of meaning to T^n that W^1 bears to T^1;
(3) T^n differs in meaning from T^1;
(4) The non-co-applicability of W^n with T^n or W^n's not standing in the same semantic relation to T^n that W^1 bears to T^1, *marks*, on serviceable tests for equivocation, a meaning difference from T^1.

Suppose that, in general, a word, W, belongs to the predicate scheme for T^1 (in C^1 in E^1) if W stands to T^1 in semantic relations such as the following:

$$W^1 \text{ in } PS^1 \text{ is a} \left\{ \begin{array}{l} \text{determinate} \\ \text{determinable} \\ \text{contrary} \\ \quad \text{(close contrary, rough contrary)} \\ \text{contradictory opposite} \\ \text{comparative} \\ \text{antonym} \\ \text{hyponym} \\ \text{contrast-dependent} \\ \text{antecedent–consequent} \\ \text{consequent–antecedent} \\ \text{converse-term} \\ \text{near synonym} \end{array} \right\} \text{ for } T^1 \text{ in } C^1.$$

Considering the above list, we can distinguish three kinds of predicate scheme differences: (1) difference of co-applicable expressions; (2) difference, among co-applicable expressions, of words that are meaning-relevant; and (3) difference of semantic relationships among meaning-relevant words: a word that is an *antonym* of T^1 in PS^1 may be a *rough synonym* of T^2 in PS^2.

These kinds of differences might occur simultaneously. That is, some word in PS^1 is not in PS^2 and some word, W, that belongs to both PS^1 and PS^2 bears a different semantic relation to T^1 than it does to T^2; for instance, 'to scan' in PS^1 has a near synonym 'look over carefully' and in PS^2 'to scan' has an antonym, 'look over carefully'.

(1) 'He *twisted* the wire' and (2) 'He *twisted* the words' have many common co-applicable words some of which, like 'misapplied' and 'unraveled' are, themselves, differentiated when substituted. But certain words co-applicable in (2), like 'changed the purport of', are not co-applicable in (1) because the result is unacceptable in the supposed environment. That asymmetrical non-co-applicability clearly marks a meaning difference in the two occurrences of 'twisted'.

Similarly, (3) 'The orchestra corrected the *sharp* opening chord', (4) 'The car negotiated the *sharp* bend', and (5) 'The dealer negotiated the *sharp* reduction in price' employ 'sharp' equivocally, with differences of meaning-relevant expressions. 'Hairpin' is co-applicable in (4) but is unacceptable in (3) and (5); and 'below pitch' is acceptable in (3) but not in (4) or (5).

Can a difference in meaning-relevant expressions obtain among univocal occurrences? No. Univocal terms can differ in which words are co-applicable, but not in which co-applicable words are meaning-relevant. E.g. 'He married his cousin' does not permit 'aunt's son' but 'She married her cousin' does permit 'aunt's son' and yet both 'married' and 'cousin' are univocal. (Redundancy is the key; syntagmatically 'he' and 'married' exclude a male complement, unless 'married' is to differentiate.) Further, analogous terms can differ in meaning-relevant words but not in all of them. 'He expected a raise' and 'He expected a delay' permit 'anticipated'.

Lastly, to use one of Lyons' examples that Hoenigswald comments upon, (1965:193), if 'width' is opposed to 'narrowness' in C^1 'The *width* of the horizon was breathtaking' but is not similarly opposed in C^2 – 'He measured the *width* of the hall and found it too narrow for the furniture' then 'width' is differentiated; its predicate schemes differ.

If insuperable defects emerge in this analysis of meaning-relevance, one might, perhaps, reconstruct the concept, so that words that are non-co-applicable are meaning-relevant. But that is opposed to the present theory. The near synonyms, opposites, contraries, contradictories, determinables and determinates, antonyms, hyponyms, consequent terms, and converse terms for a word are meaning-relevant because there is an actual or constructable context in which they are not co-applicable (or only co-applicable if not bearing that semantic relation) and where, on that account the token is equivocal with the first.

4   THE MUSIC ANALOGY: INHERENT MEANING AND
    DIFFERENTIATION

In traditional diatonic musical notation, *which* note (musical character) is indicated by a certain mark on a page of music is dependent upon harmonic contrast relationships, just as *which* meaning the word 'bank' has depends upon which predicate scheme it belongs to.

Predicate schemes function semantically the way 'shadow' triads function harmonically.[3] They are 'there' identifying what occurs, even when not explicit, not scored.

A harmonic character achieves its identity through its contrast relationships, through the distinct triads to which it belongs. Beginning on any staff position (on, or adjacent to, the five-line-four-space staff), one can inscribe a diatonic array, w w ½ w w w ½

70

(whole tone, whole tone, semitone, whole tone, whole tone, whole tone, semitone).

w w ½ w w w ½

Each of those scale positions (marked with an X) belongs to three triads, each of which is a group of three 'notes' composed of and including two intervals, a major fifth between the outside 'notes' and an included major third either between the root and middle 'note' or between the middle and uppermost 'note'. (I use quotation marks around 'note' to warn the reader that such entities do not have to be written out or even marked with a dot or an X.)

The array of triads for the scale positions in D major is:

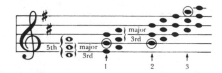

Whenever any note in the scale of D major occurs, it belongs to three and only three of the triads listed. (See circles in figure above.) And in order to satisfy the triad condition (for each triad to contain a perfect fifth and a major third), both the first space (F) and the third space (C) must carry sharp signs, provided the diatonic array begins on the space below the first line. It is the structural relationship within the array of *triads* (by which positions are sharp, flat or neutral *to create the pair of intervals that constitute the triads*) which determines the semantic key as against the merely nominal key (see Webster 1971a). Whether a given mark on the staff indicates the tonic, sub-dominant, median, leading tone, or the like, depends (a) upon which set of 3 triads it belongs to and (b) how the triad of which it is the root is related to the other six triads of the diatonic array, beginning at a certain staff position. Certain combinations of triads, I–IV–V or IV–V or V–I, if given in a score, *determine* where the diatonic array begins on the staff and thereby determine what

71

key the note belongs to. Thus, although the key signature might be 'C major', a composer might have shifted to the key of the dominant of C major, namely G major, without having used an F sharp. Although the key would appear nominally (syntactically) to be C major, it is really (semantically) G major. (see Webster, 1971a).

If

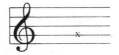

occurs, then X must belong to three triads and three only:

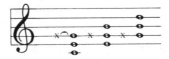

And if the 3 triads have no positions altered by flats or sharps, then we have G dominant; if the first triad has a C sharp, we have G subdominant; if E is flat, we have G submediant, and so forth. G can function in each of the 7 harmonic positions of the diatonic array and the key varies with and is determined by the triad relationship.

The demonstrable consequence is that the harmonic *identity* of a given note in a score is dependent upon which are its three triads.

Analogously, whenever a predicate occurs, it occurs as part of some predicate scheme (a set of co-applicable and meaning-relevant distinct words), just as a single note occurs only as belonging to three triads. When the same word (like the same note sign) belongs to different predicate schemes, it (like a note sign which in different occurrences belongs to distinct sets of shadow triads) has a different semantic identity.

All words, like all note signs in diatonic scores, are in principle equivocal because capable of occurrence within distinct predicate schemes, as are the notes within distinct sets of three triads.

Thus if 'good' is in relevant contrast to 'bad' and 'wrong' and in another context to 'weak' or 'rotten', where 'bad' and 'wrong'

72

would, when substituted, produce unacceptable sentences, then it is as if a certain note sign (the term 'good') belongs to two distinct sets of shadow triads; it has a different semantic identity in the two cases. The meaning-relevant words for a given word token are its shadow triads, its identity makers.

Since any given word, like any given note sign, can in distinct contexts belong to distinct predicate schemes (like sets of shadow triads), the meaning of any given word can, in a given context, be represented as a certain class of meaning-relevant words. Distinct predicate schemes for equivocal occurrences of the *same* word represent differences in their meanings, just as different triple triads for the same note sign represent different harmonic identities for that note.

A 'harmonic identity' is a *semantic* role, e.g. 'leading tone in key of . . .', the kind of thing governed by rules of harmony and counterpoint; linguistic meaning is also a *semantic* role, the kind of thing governed by rules of logic, rhetoric, composition and style.

5   CONTEXT VARIANT SCHEMES: MULTIPLE SCHEME MEMBERSHIP

Predicate schemes for the same word are covariant with certain differences in context. For instance, in C^1 – 'He caught a *cold*' – and C^2 – 'He tried to measure the *cold* by calculating the freezing time for water' – 'cold' occurs in distinct predicate schemes, loosely, the 'affliction' scheme and the 'weather' scheme. 'Heat' is co-applicable, antinomously, in C^2 but is not co-applicable in C^1. The determinables, 'infection' and 'ailment' for 'cold' in C^1, are unacceptable in C^2; and similarly, 'circumambient temperature', a determinable in C^2, is unacceptable in C^1.

What *explains* the fact that 'cold' in fact occurs in two different schemes, rather than in the same scheme in both sentences? The dominance-indifference relation to be described below (section 7).

C^3, 'The minister *married* his own son', and C^4, 'The man *married* his own cousin after his first wife died'. 'Became the spouse of' is co-applicable in C^4 but not in C^3. Because it is not co-applicable in C^3, is co-applicable in C^4 and is meaning-relevant in at least one, 'married' is differentiated. The schemes differ.

Among distinct schemes, the only difference that does *not* constitute a meaning difference is *inclusion* (redundancy):

C^5. 'Smith married someone who was already related to him, his *cousin*.'
C^6. 'John supported a blood relative, his *aunt*.'

In C^5, aunt, niece, sister-in-law, first cousin, etc. are co-applicable. But the group (a) father, brother, uncle, etc. is excluded because of the syntagmatic requirement of femininity communicated from the masculine pronouns, 'him' and 'his', and the gender asymmetrical 'married'. The group (b) mother, sister, etc. is syntagmatically excluded from the frame for C^5, ' . . . married his/her . . . ', where the pronoun is *reflexive*. But these are not differentiating; they are contextual redundancies.

In C^6, because no sexual asymmetry is required, groups (a) and (b) are co-applicable but the *in-law* relationships are syntagmatically excluded by the frame expression 'already related to him by blood'. The inconsistency of the excluded substitutions is not the basis for their unacceptability. Many inconsistent sentences are acceptable. Rather, it is the failure of the substitution to *preserve* the consistency (or inconsistency) of the original.

In C^7, 'Smith was married to someone who was already related to him, his *cousin*' and C^8, 'Jones supported someone already related to him by blood, his *cousin*', the objective *paradigmatic sets* would have to differ, with C^7 excluding both (a) and (b), and C^8 permitting (a) and (b) and excluding the in-law relationships.

With respect to *cousin* in C^7, there is some context C^n in which the fact that 'aunt', 'niece', 'father' and the like are *not* co-applicable accounts for (marks) the fact that 'cousin' (C^7) is equivocal with 'cousin' (C^n). For instance, C^n, 'Alligators are first cousins to cobras'. In most environments for C^n, although various kinship words yield acceptable sentences ('Alligators are brothers, sisters to cobras'), 'father', 'mother', 'child of', and such, would usually (but not always, of course) be excluded: the resulting sentences are unacceptable in their environments. Yet the non-co-applicability of 'father', 'mother', etc. in C^n will not mark a meaning difference with 'cousin' in C^7, because 'father', 'mother', etc., are also not co-applicable in C^7. This difference is simply not a difference of co-applicable words. Pretheoretically we know that 'first cousin' in C^n is metaphorical in relation to 'cousin' in C^7, as is 'cousin' in C^9, 'Scarcity is the *first cousin* of greed'.

If a plumbing supply salesman, excusing his inability to identify a part from my inept description, said C^{10}, 'All these elbows are *cousins* of one another', 'mother', 'father', 'grandfather' and the like would not be co-applicable. The non-co-applicability marks a meaning difference with respect to C^8.

We have a *difference of predicate schemes for T^1 in C^1 and T^2 in C^2* if: some W, co-applicable in either C^1 or C^2, is not co-applicable in the other and its not being co-applicable, relatively to the other (C^1 or C^2), is differentiating. *W's not being co-applicable in C^1 and C^2 is differentiating if and only if* the fact that it is not co-applicable in both but is co-applicable in one (on the tests of difference of meaning) *marks* the equivocation of T^1 and T^2.

Because the predicate scheme is as extensive as the environment permits, and because the presuppositions of environment may syntagmatically *block* expressions from the *scheme* (because the sentences with such substituted words would be unacceptable), while the same words are not blocked from the scheme for another occurrence in a different environment, the schemes for the same word can be objectively different. ('Blocking' avoids resultant unacceptability of a sentence involving the 'blocked' word.)

Because of that, apart from a complete context, such a word is *scheme indifferent*. Scheme difference is *multiple scheme membership*. *Scheme indifference*, for a word apart from a dominating (scheme determining) environment, is logically the result. When I talk of a word as 'scheme indifferent' I do not mean, of course, that it has to be indifferent to noticeably different schemes once its context has been completed. Rather it is indeterminate because, in various contexts, it belongs to different schemes and there must be something other than *it* that determines, in a given context, which scheme it belongs to.

One must not confuse the syntagmatic blocking, which represents and creates scheme difference, from syntagmatic restraints that have nothing to do with a difference of meaning-relevant words. Such redundancies can obtain when the words in question are univocal. C^{11}, 'After years of the parole officer's effort, he turned out to be a ...', 'an impostor', 'a saint', 'a pillar of honesty'. Another context might exclude honorific words: C^{12}, 'He was not only dishonest, he was a ...'. That might allow 'a crook', 'a fraud', and the like, but by the intensive 'not only' block 'a saint', and the like. In C^{11} 'crook' is co-applicable but antinomous with 'saint', while in C^{12} 'saint' is not (apart from figurative contexts). Thus we have a difference of co-applicable expressions. Is there a difference of predicate schemes? That depends upon whether there is also a difference of meaning-relevant words. Certainly, the fact that 'saint', 'pillar of honesty' and the like, are *not* substitutable for 'crook' is, in *some* contexts, differentiating (e.g. 'The shepherd reached out with his crook') but not here. Why not? Because redundancy in the environment excludes *all* antonyms for 'crook' (that is, all honorific contraries). Redundancy blocks words by making them fail to preserve consistency – inconsistency with the original. Hence, there is not revealed a difference of antonyms between C^{11} and C^{12}, because redundancy in C^{12} excludes antonyms, independently of what 'crook' means.

'To catch' may in C^{13} belong to a scheme where 'pitching', 'catching' and 'playing first base' are contrasting determinates of 'positions'. In C^{14}, 'catching' and 'missing' may be *antonyms* of one another and not determinates of 'positions'. In another scheme, C^{15}, there is no place for 'missing', it is not an antonym, as in 'catching fish'; but there is a place for 'losing', as 'Oh, I lost it'. Thus, 'catching' in C^{15} has a distinct antonym from C^{14}, and each *has* antonyms while C^{13} is better described as having contrasting determinates. Although both 'catching' and 'missing' may belong to a scheme that applies to catching a thief, 'missing' does not have the same meaning as it does in the case of missing a person who is absent. Though 'missing' sometimes belongs to the same scheme as 'catching', it also belongs to some schemes that do not include 'catching'; for instance, missing an appointment or 'shooting at and missing'. In another scheme, 'hitting it' and 'catching it' are not opposed (antonyms) but are near synonyms. For instance, one could catch a fly by hitting it with the fly swatter.

Every word in the language can appear in contexts diverse enough to exclude, syntagmatically, scheme members co-applicable in some other. Thus, every word is a member of context-variant schemes and is, apart from a determinate context, *scheme* indifferent over the range, at least of its actual schemes of occurrence.

Def. III–10: A context-environment E^2–C^2 *excludes* a scheme member of PS^1 just in case E^2 renders $C^{2\star}$, created by substituting W^1 from PS^1 for T^2 in C^2, unacceptable in E^2.

Those expressions in context or environment that 'select' the scheme from within the range of schemes to which the given term is indifferent are the *dominating* expressions (see no. 7 below). Exclusion, blocking, and scheme resistance (Def III–12) come to the same thing: that what is excluded and resisted is what would yield an unacceptable sentence.

A given token need not belong to one definite scheme *only*. The utterance may be ambiguous, or the word can occur in *more* than one meaning at the same time. *Double-entendre* is not the same as ambiguity: zeugma is an example: 'He *collected* men and support'. Ambiguity requires *indeterminacy* of scheme (over a range of probable and coherent ones), the absence of syntagmatic relations that reduce scheme indeterminacy below the level where evidently differing schemes are equally acceptable in the environment. *Double-entendre* (a pun), on the other hand, requires the very opposite: that the dominating expressions (in the environment) *require* that a term belong to more than one distinct scheme – 'You have your way and I'll go mine' (Fowles 1977: 17).

6   SCHEME BOUNDARIES

Objective schemes have a lower boundary, co-applicability. No word belongs to the scheme for a given token if it is (non-redundantly) blocked.

The environment, relatively to a given word, extends as far from its given sentential place in any direction as there are mandatory or excluding syntagmatic controls upon what is co-applicable in that sentential place. The upper boundary to objective predicate schemes is meaning-relevance: non-co-applicability, in some other context, of a word co-applicable in the given one, that marks a meaning difference.

Disputes about membership in predicate schemes are pretty much tangential to this theory. For one thing, *estimates* of objective predicate schemes by appeal to objective classifications are typically sufficient. And we can usually settle whatever is at issue by asking whether the near synonyms, antonyms, hyponyms, contraries, contradictories, and so forth, are co-applicable.

Note that there can be three kinds of environment relative to a given sentence: a *hospitable environment*, where dominance relations are definite enough to settle a determinate (or determinate range of) *linguistic* meaning for the sentence; an *alien environment* that leaves the linguistic meaning quite indeterminate (an evacuating environment, for instance – see chapter 7); or an *inhospitable environment* that dominates conflictingly or plays off dominance and entrenchment so as to create linguistic nonsense by *preventing* the words from coming to an *overall* meaning; for example, if, after the first sentence of the Gettysburg address, one writes 'Equal deficits harmonize shoes' and proceeds with the rest.

7 DOMINANCE AND INDIFFERENCE

These are the constituents of meaning adaptation. Contrasting adaptation causes differentiation. All the phenomena to be explained – mere equivocation, analogy of proportionality, metaphor, and denominative analogy – are kinds of differentiation.

(a) *Indifference*

Apart from a given complete environment, a word is *indifferent* to every scheme in which it actually occurs within the corpus.

There is no word that is not, apart from context, scheme indifferent, because there is no word that has the same meaning, the same predicative meaning, in every constructible occurrence. For the same reason, there is no word that is not ambiguous in some context that we can construct. Hence, every word is *dominated* at least some of the time; for instance, when it is not ambiguous. To be equivocal is to be dominated. And to be dominated is to have a scheme *selected* in context from among a number of schemes to which a word is, otherwise, indifferent.

When a word, indifferent over a range of schemes, is grammatically combined with expressions that are not indifferent to all such schemes, the *resistant* expressions *capture* and *dominate* the (apart from context) scheme indifferent word, causing it to have presuppositions that *fit* the context (non-indifferent – see Defs. III–11 and III–12, below). This is the principle of semantic dominance: a scheme-indifferent word is determined by (relatively) *intransigent* words with which it is combined in a given environment. The captured word can occur (where such schemes are syntagmatically possible) *only* in schemes syntagmatically compatible with the scheme(s) for the dominant and resistant expression(s). That is 'linguistic force'. For instance, 'late' can have 'former' or 'tardy' as its near-synonym, but not both (skipping zeugma for now). Which one it has is determined by dominance.

78

The dominance principle, that a scheme-indifferent word is captured and dominated by a relatively scheme-intransigent word, needs a number of refinements, though as a *generality*, it effectively conveys the central idea.

Entrenchment One indispensible refinement is that a word which, considered apart from context, is indifferent to schemes S^1 through S^n is usually *not equally indifferent* to each of them but has *typical* occurrences. A word is more deeply entrenched in some schemes than in others.[4] (By the way, there is no entrenchment in musical notation.) For instance, 'bachelor' is more deeply entrenched in a scheme where a meaning-relevant antonym is 'married male' than in a scheme where a meaning-relevant contrary is 'master' or 'undergraduate'. So, in recurring, 'bachelor' will need a more explicit dominator to select the latter scheme than it does to select the former. (Entrenchment of a word in a scheme is what I am concerned with; it would also be useful to study the entrenchment of schemes within bodies of discourse.)

Entrenchment is socially, geographically, professionally, habitually and idiosyncratically variable. Within philosophy, for instance, 'Bachelors are unmarried' is so entrenched, when used as an example, that it takes a detailed environment (e.g. a reference to or citation to a medieval university's rules for holding the position of bachelor) to force 'bachelor' into a scheme where 'unmarried' is not meaning-relevant (see Def. III–4) but is related as predicable accident rather than as genus (see Aristotle's Test 15 for equivocation, chapter 2, p. 47, above).

Contradictions A genuine semantic (non-syntactical) contradiction is created when dominance forces an expression to belong to a scheme that logically conflicts with the scheme demanded by some syntagmatic relation to a second word. Thus, 'some bachelors are married' becomes a hard-core contradiction when its environment *mandates* the 'male, not legally married' reading of 'bachelor' and the 'legally married, not figuratively married' reading of 'married'.

Entrenchment for philosophers sometimes causes the words to occur in those senses, when, for other persons, they would be equally indifferent to other schemes (and, so, ambiguous). Similarly, among brokers, 'closed-end funds must redeem their shares', because the words are well-entrenched in their contrast patterns, is a straight contradiction.

Wherever both environment and context permit an acceptable concatenation for the whole utterance, a sentence or utterance has that meaning instead of being unacceptable. That is the 'linguistic force' – 'resistance to unacceptability' – that causes 'fit' of meaning to context. So, if context (and that includes grammar) and environment (and that includes commonplace truths incorporated into word meanings) *permit* 'Saturday followed Mary' to mean either that a dog (a cat, etc.) named 'Saturday' physically followed a person named 'Mary' *or* that a certain day's events, designated figuratively with the day's name, metaphorically followed, namely 'haunted', some person, Mary, rather than that a certain day (*nonphysical* unit) *physically* followed a person, then the expression will have one of the former senses or be ambiguous and will not have the latter. (See the illustration of 'tearing' the expression apart in the Introduction, above.) And if the expression is entrenched in one set of schemes (e.g. because of its exemplar occurrence in poetry, a novel or a play, or its employment in a craft for a specific purpose, e.g. to illustrate contradictions), then it recurs in those schemes in the absence of reinforced dominance. The *intentions* of the speaker are irrelevant; an expression can be consistent even if he intends it not to be and an expression can be inconsistent even if he intends otherwise. A sentence or utterance (barring special contexts where extended meanings are conventionally excluded, e.g. logic exercises, accounting practices, tax forms) is objectively inconsistent only if consistent and coherent readings are excluded by the environment or if the expressions are entrenched in the inconsistent schemes.

(b) *Ambiguity*

Ambiguity is reduced to the extent that schemes (of scheme indeterminate terms) are selected through syntagmatic relations with expressions not similarly indifferent: for instance, 'wide' might be co-applicable with 'narrow' but not in 'narrow escape'. Thus, 'He . . . ed a *date*' contains 'date' indeterminately, permitting at least the schemes where 'date' means 'appointment', 'day of the year', 'romantic meeting', 'a palm fruit', 'a person with whom one goes to a dance or the like', etc. Now the sentence frame can be variously completed, for instance: C^{16} 'He *picked* a date', C^{17} 'He *appointed* a date', C^{18} 'He *fixed* a date', C^{19} 'He *wanted* a date', C^{20} 'He *borrowed* a date'. The resulting sentences are still ambiguous. Although 'date' in any one of its schemes excludes some of the schemes for 'picked', 'wanted', 'appointed', 'fixed', 'made', and 'borrowed', it does not exclude all but one for each. (One can check these exclusions by formulating the unacceptable replacement sentences, e.g. 'He appointed a palm fruit.') And, although each completion word, 'wanted', 'appointed', 'fixed', 'borrowed', excludes some of the schemes for 'date', it does not exclude all but one (or a few very similar ones). Hence, ambiguity persists and would have to be reduced (if we wanted to reduce it) by the addition of other modifying features; e.g. C^{21} 'He picked a date for the meeting by assigning a whole morning for it', C^{22} 'He picked a date for the dance by asking the cheerleader to go with him'. A residual ambiguity can be eliminated by indications that the time of the dance was not fixed by the choice of the cheerleader as a companion. But, no doubt, other ambiguities remain.

(c) *Dominance*

Where there is a scheme difference for the same word, the contrast between the two completion expressions (other expressions, expressed or implied, in the environment) selects the scheme, e.g. 'wanted': 'The beggar wanted money'; 'The bearing wanted oil'. The selection process is *exclusion* through the resistance (intransigence) of the completion expression to concatenating with any scheme for 'wanted', that contains any word that, substituted for 'wanted', would yield an unacceptable utterance.

Unacceptability is variously based and variously resisted (see Introduction). For example, C^{23} 'He *wanted* to be a plumber' ('desired'), and C^{24} 'His account *wanted* forty dollars to total a million' ('lacked'). In C^{24}, 'wanting' implies 'lacking'; 'wanting' in C^{23} does not (e.g. 'He was a plumber and wanted to be a plumber'). Secondly, various mental state words ('hoped for', 'enjoyed') are co-determinates of 'wanted' in C^{23} but none of those are co-determinates of 'wanted' in C^{24}. In C^{24}, 'account' is the dominant expression and, in the meaning appropriate to the environment, it does not concatenate acceptably with 'hoped for', and the like. That is, expressions of the form 'The account *enjoyed* forty dollars to total a million' are *unacceptable* in the supposed environment of C^{24}. Hence, 'account' is intransigent to the 'enjoyed/desired' scheme for 'wanted'. (See Defs. III–11 and III–12, below.)

Thus a sufficient condition for 'being linguistically nonsensical' relatively to a given environment, E, is: there is no pattern of predicate schemes for all of the sentence's constituent words where each and every substitution of scheme members constitutes a replacement sentence acceptable in E.

Def. III–11: F dominates T^1 in C^1 (in E): (a) if a given term, *t*, is indifferent, apart from context, to a number of schemes, and (b) if a given frame expression, F (for the sentence C^1 in E that contains *t*) is semantically (syntagmatically) resistant to (Def. III–12) *some* members of some of the schemes for *t*, then F dominates the scheme-indifferent *t* by restricting *t*'s range of schemes for the given context to schemes all of whose members are co-applicable (Def. III–9) with F (if there are any).[5]

Def. III–12: A sentence frame, F, (in E) is semantically resistant to some members, W, of some of the schemes for a completion expression *t*, just in case substituting W for *t* produces a replacement that is unacceptable in E.

Thus, F, 'The account . . . forty dollars to total a million' is resistant to the 'enjoyed' which is a member of some scheme for the completion expression, *t*, 'wanted'; substituting 'enjoyed' into the blank results in a sentence unacceptable in E.

Inconsistency is neither meaningless nor semantically anomalous and is not of itself unacceptable. Hence, while every member of the predicate scheme for T^1 in C^1 must be co-applicable in C^1, the resulting expressions do not have to be logically consistent, though they do have to preserve consistency/inconsistency with the originals.

It is a general law that a sentence frame that does not concatenate in acceptable replacement sentences with all of the members of all of the schemes to which a predicate T is indifferent, dominates and differentiates T to that (or those) scheme(s), if any, all of whose members, when substituted for T in F, create replacement sentences acceptable in the environment (E). Some of the purported counterexamples to this law assume that contradictions or otherwise inconsistent expressions are unacceptable. But that is the very opposite of the truth.

Deep entrenchment of a predicate in a scheme and a social or communicative value in preserving an inconsistency will offset the rather weak tendency of words to resist concatenation inconsistently. Sometimes, to get an inconsistency, you have to arrange a stand-off (an unresolved conflict) of dominance: 'Some bachelors are females' – where neither 'females' dominates 'bachelors' nor 'bachelors' 'females', and both are environmentally dominated or equally entrenched.

Conflict of dominance, resulting from opposed expressions, can result in (a) *double entendre*, (b) overriding of one expression (defeat of its dominance by a more dominant expression) or (c) a stand-off, 'some bachelors are female', with outright inconsistency or (d) 'the tearing apart' of the expression that prevents an overall meaning and manifests the very resistance to unacceptability that, in such a case, is the cause of unacceptability (see Introduction).

8 SUBJECTIVE SCHEMES

I explain differentiation (and its various kinds) by objective predicate schemes. But there are also subjective schemes, for the membership of which the individual speaker is the authority.

Def. III–13: Subjective scheme for S: A term, x, belongs to the subjective scheme of a person, S, who employs another given word y, just in case x belongs to the discourse vocabulary of S and S does or would regard x as meaning-relevant to y in context.

The class of expressions from which a given word is contrastively 'selected' provides important nuances of its subjective meaning. Thus, the fact that 'a fraud' as understood by a non-lawyer lacks the legally all-important element of 'reliance upon a knowingly or irresponsibly false assurance as to a materially relevant contemporaneous matter of fact', and stands only in gross opposition to expressions like 'armed robbery', 'good deal', and 'fair bargain', contributes importantly to the meaning it has in a particular pragmatic context (for instance, to what is *not* implied by the speaker).

9 NEAR SYNONYMS

Central meaning relationships are summarily described in terms of the substitutability or non-substitutability of the meaning-relevant near synonyms of one same word for another. A *near synonym* for T in C is a meaning-relevant expression that is *substitutable to produce a replacement sentence having approximately the same meaning as the original*. For instance, in 'He admired the mayor's integrity', 'honesty', 'moral soundness', 'probity', 'uprightness' or 'incorruptibility' might be substitutable in the environment to yield replacement sentences approximately the same in meaning as the original. Certainly, acceptability of the replacement sentence to *paraphrase* the original remark is necessary. But more is required: the replacement must be to the minds of competent informants 'nearly the same in meaning' as the original.

Def. III–14: W is a meaning-relevant near-synonym for T in C (in E) if and only if:
(1) W is co-applicable with T in C (in E) – Def. III–4;
(2) W is meaning-relevant to T in C (in E) – Def. III–9;
(3) The replacement context, C*, containing W, has approximately the same meaning as C.

There is nothing to be gained from trying to amplify 'sentence approximately the same in meaning'. What is satisfactory will, perforce, vary with speakers and communities. The basic idea is clearer than any analysis will make it: satisfactory as a way of saying nearly the same thing.

The terms that a *speaker* would regard as 'close in meaning' or as 'near synonyms' often provide a large enough sample of a subjective predicate scheme for my explanations. Thus in (a) 'That act *violates* my dignity', and (b) 'That act *violates* the law', if 'assaults' is close in meaning to 'violates' in (a), but is not to 'violates' in (b) or is, only when understood metaphorically, then the near synonyms differ and the predicate schemes for 'violation' in the two occurrences differ in membership.

If there is no meaning-relevant near synonym of either token of 'violation' that can be substituted for both tokens (but not merely equivocally or metaphorically) and in each substitution yield a replacement sentence having approximately the same meaning as the corresponding original, 'violation' is merely equivocal. If such substitution is possible, but there are still differences of predicate scheme, then the pair of same words is analogous in meaning, except in the case where the schemes differ only in that one is a subset of the other. (Where one scheme is a subset of another, the difference is accounted for by contextual redundancies that would otherwise cause consistency/inconsistency not to be preserved.)

10   LOGICAL CONSTRUCTS

Are predicate schemes logical constructions or real things? There really are paradigmatic sets of terms, approximated objectively by classifications in the language and within various crafts and subjectively within the vocabularies of individual speakers. Whether, within the paradigmatic sets there are *always* subsets of meaning-relevant words is more controversial but, it appears to me, well confirmed. At least some of the near synonyms, determinables, determinates, antonyms, contrast-dependent words, hyponyms, antecedent – consequent words, contraries and the like are such that in *some* context where they are not co-applicable (a) the same word is equivocal and (b) the non-applicability of the other expressions *marks* the presence of the meaning difference.

Nonetheless, my basic claims about the existence and law-like nature of differentiation and semantic dominance and about analogy, metaphor, denomination and paronymy, do not logically depend upon the real existence of predicate schemes. Those meaning relationships, though approximately mapped by means of predicate scheme relationships, may be logically antecedent to them and can be recognized and distinguished even by a person who denies the existence of predicate schemes or their utility to explain or model those meaning relationships. Still, I submit that the phenomena under inquiry are sufficiently well reflected in predicate schemes to be rendered more easily intelligible, more easily distinguishable from one another, and more easily described systematically than any other extant device allows.

4

Equivocation,
analogy and metaphor

1 INTRODUCTION

Earlier chapters show how mere equivocation, analogy of proportionality and metaphor all result from the domination of susceptible
words by contrasting, scheme-intransigent expressions.

'Pen' is indifferent to *instrument* schemes (that include 'pencil',
'quill', 'stylus', etc.) and to *enclosure* schemes (that include 'stall',
'paddock', 'run', etc.). The verb 'wrote' is indifferent to *means
expressing* schemes (that include 'telephoned', 'telegraphed', 'sema-
phored with', 'drew with', 'inscribed with', 'signed with', etc.). Yet,
concatenated into 'He wrote with a pen', 'wrote' is *not* indifferent to
the *enclosure* scheme for 'pen'; rather, it is *resistant* because it belongs
to a *means demanding* scheme which, concatenated with that enclosure scheme, would in the supposed environment yield an unacceptable sentence, e.g. 'He wrote with a barnyard enclosure'.
'Wrote' dominates 'pen'. And 'pen', thus determined, reciro-
cally dominates 'wrote' to exclude the *means expressing* scheme
('telegraphed', etc.) because that result would be similarly unacceptable.

Of course, in a story about stock exchange trading, 'He telegraphed with his pen' could mean that he sent a message by a
motion of his pen, and the context would be read so as to make 'telegraphed' means-demanding ('with his pen'). And 'ink' doesn't
always dominate 'pen'. In a story about counterfeiters hiding their
ink somewhere on a farm, 'They put the ink into the pen' might not
have 'ink' dominating 'pen'. Still, 'He put the pen into the ink'
would usually have 'ink' dominating because of the tight syntactical
link to 'pen' and the commonplace improbability of the other
reading.

That is pretty much what has been explained so far. Now I turn to
distinguishing mere equivocation from analogy.

86

Same words are equivocal if there is *any* difference of linguistic meaning among them at all. *Mere* equivocation, what linguists call homonymy, requires unrelatedness of meaning. (Lyons 1977: 551, distinguishes homonymy from polysemy in the same way but does not provide a practicable measure of unrelatedness.) Equivocal words are not, as Aristotle and Aquinas said, without partial sameness of meaning.[1] Even the most disparate meanings for the same word ('run' in baseball, 'run' as in 'hole in a stocking') have *some* semantic overlap; there are at least a *few* general words that are subsitutable univocally, or at least not *merely* equivocally, in both frames. By any plausible criterion of similarity of meaning that I can think of, e.g. common elements of intension (Lewis 1946), common entailments, univocal more general terms, and the like, mere equivocals can be similar in meaning. The mark of mere equivocation is not lack of similarity but unrelatedness. (And that is what I think Aristotle and Aquinas really meant, too.)

The lists of meaning-relevant *near*-synonyms (see Def. III–14) are disparate for a pair of mere equivocals (as is also true for other meaning-relevant words). There are *no* common, non-homonymous words of suitable specificity to produce replacement sentences for both corresponding originals.

Further, among mere equivocals, the complete equivocation *repeats itself* at the predicate scheme level: (1) 'He *charged* the account for the purchase'; (2) 'He *charged* the line of opposing players'; and, (3) 'He *charged* the defendant with assault'. All employ 'charged' merely equivocally with respect to one another. Iterated application of the tests for equivocation discloses that common near synonyms, if there are any, are merely equivocal (or metaphorical) and that *their* near synonyms fail to yield replacement sentences approximating the meanings of the originals.

Thus, if 'charged' in (1) and (3) has a near synonym, 'made x liable for' (with a syntactic change to make (3) coherent), 'made x liable for . . .' when substituted, differentiates merely equivocally. The sense in which an account is made liable is quite different from the sense in which an accused is made liable; the accused is 'liable' in the sense of 'is subject to being found guilty of', whereas the account is 'liable' in the sense of 'is reduced by the amount of . . .'. Even if the mere equivocation of 'made x liable for' had not disclosed itself immediately, it would under further substituting of near synonyms for common words. The predicate schemes for mere equivocals are demonstrably lacking in significant overlap.

These features distinguish merely equivocal (synchronically unrelated) same words from analogous (synchronically related) same words.

Def. IV–1: Mere equivocation: Term A is merely equivocal in complete sentential contexts (1) and (2) just in case:
(1) A occurs equivocally in (1) and (2).
(2) The predicate schemes for A^1 and A^2 differ.
(3) There are other contrasting terms or expressions (expressed or implied), x and y, in the environments which have distinct predicate schemes and which cause A to differentiate.
(4) The predicate schemes for A^1 and A^2 are disparate and common members of comparable specificity are *merely equivocal* (recursively satisfying all five conditions).
(5) And, either (a) or (b) or both:
    (a) No near synonym, s, for A^1 or A^2, when substituted for A^1 and A^2 in both (1) and (2) will yield a pair of sentences each of which has approximately the same meaning as its corresponding original, unless s is merely equivocal.
    (b) Every near synonym of A^1 or A^2, substituted for the other expression (e.g. a near-synonym of A^1 being substituted for A^2 in (2)) either (i) produces an unacceptable 'replacement' sentence, (ii) occurs metaphorically, or (iii) causes new differentiation in other terms in the context frame.

There is, logically, an overlap in conditions (4), (5a), and (5b); it might be possible to derive (5b) from (5a) and (5a) from (4) through careful definitions, and (4) entails (2). But the object of stating conditions here is not economy as much as utility and perspicacity.

Mere equivocation, like equivocation in general, is symmetrical: if A^1 is merely equivocal with respect to A^2, the latter is merely equivocal with respect to the former. But mere equivocation is not transitive. If A^1 is merely equivocal with A^2 and A^2 is merely equivocal with A^3, it does not follow that A^1 is merely equivocal with A^3, because A^1 and A^3 could be univocal or analogous.

The first three conditions are, of course, common to all (predicatively) differentiated same words, while conditions (4)–(5) (5a, 5b) distinguish merely equivocal terms from analogous terms.

Consider:
(1) Benjamin Franklin *was delegated* to Paris by the fledgling American government.

(2) Deciding whether or not to prosecute antitrust suits *was delegated* by the President to the Attorney General.

In (1) 'was deputized', 'was sent as representative', and the like, are near synonyms; in (2) 'was trusted to the care of', 'was committed to', 'the authority for y was transmitted by x to z', 'the exercise of x's discretion for y was transmitted by x to z', are near synonyms.

If the near-synonyms of 'was delegated' in (2) are substituted in (1), either unacceptability, metaphor ('was committed to'), or a new differentiation of other expressions in (1) results and there is not a replacement sentence approximately the same in meaning as the original (1). This is as condition (5b) provides.

If 'was trusted to the care of', or 'x transmitted to y the authority for' were substituted in (1), not only would the result be grammatically and semantically unacceptable in the environment, such substitutions would not yield a sentence having approximately the meaning of the first. And the same is true of substitutions of the near synonyms of the first into the place for 'was delegated' in the second. This is as condition (5a) provides.

The above conditions for mere equivocation are jointly sufficient (though they are not independently necessary, because redundant), and concern those characteristics of merely equivocal terms that are relevant to distinguishing mere equivocation from analogy. The three distinctive conditions (4, 5a, and 5b) for mere equivocation, labelled informally, are (i) 'disparity of predicate schemes' (ii) 'non-substitutability of near synonyms' and (iii) 'induced differentiation in other expressions'. Some examples will, I hope, further clarify these conditions. Nevertheless, the details of the following subsections A, B and C are merely amplifications. The reader can profitably move directly on to section 3, *Analogy of Meaning*.

(a) *Disparity of predicate schemes*

(1) 'The judge *charged* the jury' and (2) 'The army *charged* the enemy' employ 'charged' merely equivocally. The predicate schemes for the two occurrences are disparate. I do not mean that no common words apply in both cases – for instance, 'did something to'; for in nearly every case *some* common more general expression is substitutable, and often such expressions apply univocally. But the expressions that are meaning-relevant to the one are, typically, not even co-applicable with the other. Antonyms, hyponyms, contrast-dependent terms, and the like, are *disparate*.

89

The judge might have 'instructed', 'given directions to', 'ordered', 'explained law and facts to'; the army might have 'attacked', 'run towards', 'threatened'. But none of those words belongs to the predicate scheme for the other. So too with the opposites (e.g. 'evade', 'avoided', 'fled from', and the like) in (2) which have no corresponding contraries in (1).

Expressions like 'badgered', 'belabored', 'hammered', 'stormed at', may apply in the two cases but in neither are they meaning-relevant (see Def. III–9); both occurrences are metaphorical, and the resulting sentences are not 'approximately the same in meaning as the corresponding originals'.

Consider another example. 'The guard *checked* the passenger's luggage' and 'The new law *checked* the flow of cash.' In the first, a focal idea is 'inspected', with associated terms like 'looked carefully at', 'officially investigated'; in the second, a focal idea is 'interfered with', with associated ideas like 'brought to a halt', 'stopped', 'hindered'. (A focal idea can be determined from the near synonyms which give us an apt paraphrase of the sentence in its environment, that is, not only approximately the same in meaning, but *nearly* or 'almost exactly' the same.) The opposite of 'checked' in the first case focuses upon 'ignored', 'failed to investigate' and the like; in the second, the opposite is 'increased', 'exacerbated', and 'failed to stop'. There is no significant overlap of near synonyms or opposites for the two occurrences; certainly not of *meaning-relevant* words.

(b) *Non-substitutability of near synonyms*

As more formally stated, the condition is:

No near synonym of either A^1 or A^2, when substituted for A^1 and A^2 in both (1) and (2), will yield a pair of sentences each of which has approximately the same meaning as the corresponding original, unless the substituted term is in its two occurrences merely equivocal.

No near synonym of the one expression can occur *univocally* as a near synonym of the other. For a given word, having the same meaning in both occurrences, to be a near synonym of a pair of expressions that are *unrelated* in meaning would be inconsistent: the very fact that a pair of expressions have a univocal near synonym *constitutes* relatedness of meaning.

If a common expression is substitutable as a near synonym, but not univocally, it must be differentiated, too. Of differentiated words, there are only the analogous and merely equivocal; and among the analogous, there are only the symmetrically analogous (by proportionality and denomination) and the asymmetrically analogous (metaphors). There is no difficulty created by the hypothesis that a substituted word is itself merely equivocal (and possibly, metaphorical) for that *would* allow the creation of a pair of sentences approximately the same in meaning as their corresponding originals. But what of analogous terms?

The difficulty is that a *near* synonym need not be an *exact* synonym. It can, and usually will, differ somewhat in meaning from the expression for which it substitutes. Hence, a single word, substituted as a near synonym for a pair of merely equivocal tokens, can differ somewhat in meaning from each of them. Why then can it not be symmetrically analogous? (Remember, the asymmetry of metaphors is *superimposed* upon the symmetrical differentiation that creates analogy.)

The two replacement sentences (as I call the sentences created by substituting a near synonym for a pair of equivocal tokens) would have to have approximately the same meaning as the originals to which they correspond. Now, the terms replaced are *unrelated* in meaning, by hypothesis, but the replacing terms are *related* in meaning, because any analogous pair is related in meaning. Because *symmetrical relatedness* (not 'near synonymy') is *transitive*, symmetrically analogous terms cannot be substituted as near synonyms for mere equivocals (which are unrelated). So a same word can't be substituted as a near synonym for a merely equivocal pair unless it is merely equivocal.

Consider this example: (a) 'The judge *charged* the jury'; (b) 'The garage-man *charged* the battery'. In (a), 'charged' means 'instructed', and in (b), 'restored the electrical storage power of'. The schemes have no discernible community of members; 'instructed', 'directed', 'explained the law and their duties', and the like, are close to the first but not to the second. Suppose 'juiced up' is suggested as a common near synonym. It is metaphorical in both cases but, comparatively, merely equivocal: the determinates, antonyms, hyponyms, antecedent-consequent terms, and the like, co-applicable with the one 'juiced up' are not co-applicable with the other. E.g. an antonym for (b) is 'drained'; substituted in (a), the resulting sentence is unacceptable in the environment.

Mere equivocation discloses itself, eventually, in the absence of near synonyms that can be substituted without repeating failure of

91

the replacements to approximate the originals, whereas among analogous terms, the overlap of predicate schemes repeats.

(c) *Near synonym substitution creates unacceptability, metaphor, or induces differentiation of other expressions within the sentence frame*

(a) 'She *dropped* a friend who was insulting' and (b) 'She *dropped* a stitch.' 'Dropped' in (a) has near synonyms like 'discontinued associations with', 'no longer confided in', etc. (depending upon the wider environment, of course); and 'dropped' in (b) means 'She missed, skipped or incorrectly formed', etc. Now if you put 'ignored' into the two contexts, one would become metaphorical (and also fail to approximate the meaning of its original); if you put 'passed by', the same would happen. In fact, substitution of near synonyms for mere equivocals, by creating unacceptability, metaphor or new differentiation, effectively blocks the creation of replacement sentences having approximately the same meaning as the originals.

The key element in the distinction of analogous from merely equivocal same words and the feature that accounts for condition 6 and for the principle of double homonymy (below) is: *if a pair, or more, of same words are merely equivocal (in their complete sentential contexts), then no near synonym of either, when substituted for the equivocal pair in both the original sentences, will yield a pair of replacement sentences having approximately the same meanings as the originals (unless the common near synonym itself is merely equivocal).* Exactly the opposite obtains in the case of analogous terms.

Double (iterated) homonymy: words substitutable non-metaphorically as near synonyms for a pair of merely equivocal words, are themselves merely equivocal.

Qualifications and cautions are necessary. First, a word may be merely equivocal, given a certain pair of environments, while in the same sentential contexts in contrasting environments it is *not* merely equivocal. Secondly, because the criterion for mere equivocation offered here is articulate and explicit, it will not accord exactly with unreflective intuition and in a few cases may demand revision of intuition. Some words, which one would have regarded as merely equivocal, on this criterion will appear as analogous (synchronically related) in meaning. Still reflection supports the test I have chosen. For if a pair of tokens that at first appear unrelated in meaning, upon examination, have a meaning-relevant near

92

synonym substitutable for *each* of the pair, yielding replacement sentences approximately the same in meaning as the corresponding originals, then if the substituted pair is not itself merely equivocal the original pair *must* be related in meaning. That follows from the symmetry of 'having approximately the same meaning' and the fact that 'having approximately the *same* meaning' entails 'being related in meaning'.

There is no vicious circle in the iteration of the test. The substituted near synonym, replacing a pair of merely equivocal words, is itself tested for the presence of a near synonym (or contextual definition) that can be substituted for *it*, to produce a pair of sentences having approximately the same meaning as the original pair of sentences.

If 'indicted' *were* merely equivocal in 'The grand jury indicted Smith for the crime' and 'Smith's father indicted him for lying', then there would *not* be a near synonym like 'accused . . . . of', that is substitutable in both contexts to yield sentences approximately the same in meaning as the originals, unless 'accused' were itself merely equivocal or metaphorical. But this is a case of analogy.

Revision of intuition will, I conjecture, almost exclusively reclassify as analogous what might have appeared to be merely equivocal, e.g. *drive*/car, *drive*/nail. Still, if on occasion (I can think of no example), a pair that we would have regarded as related in meaning is found to satisfy the 'merely homonymous near synonyms' test, then our prior opinion should be revised.

Many merely equivocal pairs so clearly satisfy the conditions stated above that one's imagination staggers to find even a candidate for a non-homonymous near synonym of both: e.g. 'The ships sailed up the *sound*', 'The amplifier increased the *sound*', 'The mate began *to sound*', 'The bells began *to sound*'. The competent speaker would often say that the occurrences are of two different *words*. I do not do so, under the constraints adopted here (see chapter 2). But the idea is the same: there is *nothing* (of any significance) in common in their meanings; that exhibits itself in the disparity of their predicate schemes.

3 ANALOGY OF MEANING

As I said, the basic difference between merely equivocal and analogous terms is that the mere equivocals have disparate predicate schemes. Consequently, mere equivocals have no non-homonymous near synonyms and no significant overlap of common contraries, contradictories, modifiers, expressions in appropriate contrast, similar paraphrases, and the like. Some of these features are matters of degree. But the absence of non-homonymous near synonyms, substitutable for the mere equivocals to yield replacement sentences having approximately the same meaning as the corresponding originals, is absolute.

There are always *some* substitutable near synonyms for a pair (or *n*-tuple) of analogous terms. For example, 'clean record' and 'clean floor' have in common, 'spotless', 'unblemished', 'stainless' and other near synonyms of 'clean' in a given context and have similar opposed expressions, 'dirty', 'unclean', 'stained', 'blotted', 'blemished', and may have similar comparatives, 'dirtier', 'dirtiest', etc., and related paraphrases, denials and the like.

But are *all substitutable meaning-relevant near synonyms* for a pair of analogous words also analogous? Yes. By 'substitutable', I mean 'capable of replacing the other of a differentiated pair so as to yield a replacement sentence, otherwise identical in constituent words with the original, and having approximately the same meaning, in the given environment, as the original'. I do not, of course, deny that some co-applicable expressions may be univocal[2] and, frequently, metaphorical, but they will not be near synonyms. There can be no *univocal* meaning-relevant near synonyms because a *meaning-relevant* expression will be dominated by the same factor that differentiates the analogous term. *Analogy, too, is iterative.*

As far as I can tell, the classical writers also thought an analogous pair could not be satisfactorily replaced by a univocal term.[3] This was made central to their discussion of religious discourse where, it was argued, there are no univocal terms to designate the positive attributes of God and the attributes of creatures. The two theories, the classical one and this one, employ different notions of 'satisfactory substitute', but with consonant results.

Under my condition for substitution (above), the resulting pair need not exhibit the *same* meaning contrasts as the originals. The classical analogy theory regarded as an adequate substitute only such words as would yield a pair of replacement sentences approximating the meanings of the originals *and preserving the distinctive contrasts of meaning of the terms replaced.* Under those conditions the replacement terms could not be univocal. Of course, a non-

94

analogous same-term pair cannot constitute an 'exact' synonym for an analogous pair or preserve the same contrast relationship that is presented by an analogous pair. This accords with the classical theory. Further, a replacement word is dominated and differentiated just as was the original analogous word and cannot be univocal.

Meaning-relevant near synonyms for an analogous pair cannot be merely equivocal, either, because 'being related in meaning' is transitive. That is established as follows:

(1) If W^1 and W^2 in C^{1*} and C^{2*} are merely equivocal, they are not meaning-related.
(2) If W^1 is a meaning-relevant near synonym for T^1 in C^1, W^1 is meaning-related to T^1.
(3) If W^2 is a meaning-relevant near synonym for T^2 in C^2, W^2 is meaning-related to T^2.
(4) 'Being meaning related' is a transitive, symmetrical relation.
(5) If T^1 is analogous with T^2, then T^1 is meaning related to T^2 (definition of analogy).
(6) Therefore, W^1 is meaning related to T^2 and, thus, to W^2. Hence, assuming that a same-term meaning-relevant near synonym substituted for both of an analogous pair is merely equivocal leads, within the conceptual framework developed here, to an explicit contradiction.

Thus we find that a meaning-relevant near synonym for an analogous pair can be neither merely equivocal nor univocal.

The classical division of analogy of meaning into two broad classes, denominative analogy (relational analogy) and analogy of proportionality (analogy based upon the relations of relations) accords well enough with the linguistic phenomena and can be mapped with predicate schemes. The classical subdivision of analogy of proportionality into 'proper' and 'metaphorical proportionality' is not intuitively so obvious. Yet, if you consider the *Miller's Analogies* cases (see chapter 1) where proportionalities depend upon the *metaphorical* application of a word, the point of that classical subdivision emerges, too. Nevertheless, I do not base the distinction between analogy and metaphor upon the contrast between 'proper' and 'improper' proportionality, but upon an asymmetry to be described in section (4), below.

Def. IV–2: Analogy of Meaning (of Proportionality):
Term A is analogous in meaning, in complete sentential contexts (1) and (2) if and only if:

95

(1) *A* occurs equivocally in (1) and (2).

(2) The predicate schemes for A^1 and A^2 differ.

(3) Other terms or expressions, *x* and *y*, in the environment, are in predicate scheme contrast and syntagmatically *dominate* and differentiate A^1 from A^2.

(4) There is a discernible overlap of scheme members, including near synonyms, for A^1 and A^2 and the semantic contrasts *among* scheme members for A^1 and A^2 are discernibly related (e.g. same-word antonyms, same-word determinables, etc.) along with differences of scheme members or of intrascheme contrasts or of both.

(5) The difference of meaning between A^1 and A^2, mapped into the contrasting predicate schemes, directly reflects syntagmatic contrasts (and syntagmatic overlaps) between the schemes for *x* and *y*.

(6) Some meaning-relevant near synonyms of A^1 are substitutable for A^2, or vice versa, yielding replacement sentences approximately the same in meaning as the corresponding originals.

(7) Some meaning-relevant near synonyms for A^1 or A^2, when substituted in both (1) and (2), satisfy condition #6 and are differentiated but not merely equivocal, and do not newly differentiate expressions belonging to the original sentential context.

(8) There are no substitutable near synonyms that are merely equivocal.

Analogy of meaning is symmetrical: if A^1 is analogous to A^2, then A^2 is analogous in meaning to A^1. But analogy of meaning is nontransitive: if A^1 is analogous to A^2 and A^2 is analogous to A^3, then A^1 may or may not be analogous to A^3, depending upon whether conditions (6) and (7) are satisfied by the latter pair as well as by the former pairs. Another way to put it is this: in an *n*-tuple of analogous terms, although every term is analogous to *some* other same word, not every occurrence is analogous to every other; there may be mere equivocals. The series may form a chain without forming a circle (an important consequence; see later).

The fact (condition 5) that the difference in schemes for A^1 and A^2 reflects contrasts between the dominating expressions *x* and *y* is not peculiar to analogous terms; it is characteristic of merely equivocal terms as well. In 'He charged the account' and 'He charged the fort', if 'fort' designates a physical place and 'account', a construct within a financial institution, they partly determine the schemes 'charged' belongs to. In the first, 'charged' is in contrast to 'credited' and fairly close to 'debited', 'posted' and 'disbursed from'. In the second, 'charged' is in contrast to 'surrendered to' and is fairly close to 'attacked', 'stormed', 'besieged', and the like. With mere equivocals the effect of the contrasting and dominating contexts is not the *reorganization* of the schemes in relationship to one another (as happens in the case of analogy) but the *substitution* of one scheme for the other, the selection of a disparate scheme. Still, the differing schemes for the common term reflect contrasts between the dominating completion expressions.

The pages immediately following explore some of the consequences of these analogy conditions, particularly concerning the relatedness of analogous words and clustered meanings. The reader concerned with the overall line of thought can proceed directly to section 4, *Simple metaphor*.

The relatedness of the analogous Consider:
   (i) 'He *allowed* the farmers to pass over his cartway', and
   (ii) 'He *allowed* each of the sailors a proportion of the profits.'
The first involves permission or non-hindrance, the second, either promise, provision or disbursal. These are merely equivocal, even though 'permitted' can be applied in both situations. 'Suffered' and 'tolerated' are unacceptable for the second, though they roughly approximate the first. Now if (ii) had read, instead, 'He *allowed* each of the sailors *to take* a proportion of the profits', we would have had *analogy*.

The schemes for 'allowed' in (i) and (ii) differ greatly. For instance, the *passivity* feature in suffering and tolerating is excluded by the *activity* feature in the promising, providing or distributing of due shares; and the *control* element, involved in allotting shares for the crew, is negated by the *external proposal* element in 'consented to'.

Is the accord/bestow/allot/assign scheme for 'allow' so different from the tolerate/suffer/permit scheme that 'allow' is merely equivocal? That depends. When 'permit', 'sanction' 'accord with', 'consent to' can be substituted non-metaphorically and not merely equivocally as near synonyms in both contexts, 'allow' is analogous. And where 'permit', 'sanction' and 'accord with' are *not* co-applicable with 'allow' (as in ii), their non-applicability effectively *marks* the equivocation: 'I did not *allow* enough time for driving to the train.' 'Sanction' and 'accord with' are unacceptable; 'permit' *might* be acceptable; but in 'I did not *allow for* the uneven window-sill', 'permit', 'sanction', 'accord with' and so forth are not acceptable. Of course 'allow' is also merely equivocal, in the 'assign–allot' vs. 'recognize–admit' senses and in the 'take into account' vs. 'concluded' senses. Differentiated uses can extend so that every one is analogous to *some* other, but merely equivocal with respect to others. (So, mere equivocation is a consequence of analogy.)

The expression 'carry out' differentiates according to whether the context is of *accomplishment* (completion) or of *undertaking* ('to carry into practice').

(iii) He *carried out* the assignment.
(iv) He *carried out* his contention.
 (v) He *carried out* his threats.
(vi) He *carried out* his beliefs.

Thus, 'put into action', 'set in motion' and the like apply in (v) and (vi) but only equivocally in (iii) and (iv). Yet these four occurrences of 'carried out' are analogous to one another, whereas 'He *carried out* his wife' employs the same word merely equivocally to (iii) through (vi).

A term is used analogously in any pair of contexts that, because of presuppositions of environment, exclude (as unacceptable) the meaning-relevant near synonyms, antonyms, modifiers, and the like, from being the same for both and yet permit an overlap of meaning-relevant near synonyms, opposites, and of contrasts with other words.

Frequently one can recognize and even put a name to the similarity that obtains throughout a cluster of meanings (senses). For instance 'carry' in the 'physical-transport' senses differentiates from 'carry' in the more abstract senses in which one can carry or convey news to another. And those two kinds of meanings of 'carry' belong to a *cluster* of meanings (focused upon modes of transmission by bearer) that is quite different from the clustered 'to bear the weight of' senses, that also may be either particular or abstract. These in turn form a different cluster, with overlapping foci, from the 'continuation' and 'extension' senses of 'carry' that may *also* be particular or abstract: 'The plan carries the window line almost to the roof'; 'The police carried the investigation to every passenger who entered the terminal'. Neither physical-transport schemes nor the bearing-the-weight-of schemes are acceptable, given the presuppositions of 'window line', 'plans' and 'police investigation' in the contexts given.

That is not to deny the possibility of a context in which 'The plans *carried* the alliance with the other nations' would be acceptable in a 'support' scheme, even a *physical*-support scheme, for instance, where 'plans' functions *denominatively* as a name for the paper or book embodying the plans and 'alliance' functions similarly.

Clusters created diachronically Clustered meanings are diachronically necessitated by the various 'resistances' to variously based unacceptability. The senses of a word will string out from one another (we don't need to know word histories) as mutations of presupposition (of affinities and oppositions to other words) and mere equivocation between links in diverse chains for the same word is inevitable. So besides its other sources (direct borrowing from other languages, stipulation and misuse), mere equivocation is the diachronic 'fallout' of differentiation.

How a single expression, 'carry', came to have diverse, clustered meanings, especially so diverse as the foci, 'to transport from one place to another' and 'to support the weight of' and 'to continue or extend in space or time', is probably no longer recoverable. But the account of differentiation I offer not only predicts such phenomena, it allows us, by hypothetical sequences of successive differentiations of the same word in distinct contexts, to *simulate* the process.

Differentiation of words into diverse clusters is the rule rather than the exception. See, *Webster's Third New International Dictionary*, unabridged. 'It becomes clear from more than seventy-five years of work upon the great historical dictionaries, that multiple meaning for words is normal, not "queer".' (Fries 1961:41.)

There is enormous *thought efficiency* in natural languages, whose multivalent discriminations do not have to be consciously devised by speakers because the mere concatenation of the words will make distinctions more subtly than the speakers could (practicably) even conceive beforehand. Earlier examples, for instance, senses of 'allowed' in various contexts, illustrate that. They show how effectively and unobtrusively a word is differentiated, with its sense being quite *obvious* to the experienced reader who has, only a few paragraphs before, been reading the same word in quite different senses, and usually, with no *experience* of change.

Philosophical inquiry into the ways to describe the distinctions we *actually* make in ordinary discourse (for instance, in the senses of 'voluntarily' and 'freely'), shows how complex and difficult it is to describe the ordinary language distinctions of meaning among co-occurrent expressions (cf. Austin 1962). If, to make such distinctions, we had first and separately to think them out, a speaker would have to have the skills of the best linguistic analysts to make the kinds of statements that are second nature to him now. The language would cease to do part of our thinking for us. Now we can think *in* the distinctions of word meaning without having, continuously, to think *of* the distinctions of word meaning.

Analogy and clustering Consider these examples:

(1) He *charged* the gun before firing it. (loaded)
(2) He *charged* the jury, explaining law and facts. (instructed)
(3) He *charged* his assistants to watch the financial markets. (instructed with authority and actually burdened, etc.)
(4) He *charged* her with information as to her opponents. (mentally burden, to load)
(5) He *charged* her with murder. (accused – as in manner of informer)
(6) He *charged* her with murder. (accused – as in manner of judicial officer requiring plea)
(7) He *charged* him with carelessness. (to impute or ascribe)
(8) He *charged* him with responsibility. (to impute, ascribe, lay to one's charge)
(9) He *charged* the others maliciously. (attack verbally)
(10) He *charged* their account with the debts. (to make a pecuniary charge, to make liable for)
(11) He *charged* more than the law allowed. (to fix a price, to set a price)
(12) He *charged* the little boy too much. (to collect a price)
(13) He *charged* the estate for his services. (to place a debit upon)
(14) He *charged* the battery. (to restore electric potential)
(15) He *charged* three roses. (heraldic: to assume a heraldic bearing)
(16) He *charged* the guns. (military: leveled, to place on target)
(17) The bishop *charged* his clergy. (authoritative instruction in responsibility, *almost* same as (2))
(18) The dog *charged*. (to *squat* with its head on its forepaws – said of dogs)

Some of these occurrences of 'charged' (and we must imagine full, disambiguating, discourse environments) are merely equivocal with one another: e.g. (1) and (2), (1) and (3), (1) and (4), (1) and (5), (1) and (6), (1) and (7), (1) and (9)–(15), and (1) and (17)–(18). The occurrences in (1) and (2) are unrelated, even though the common terms 'loaded', 'burdened', or others might apply merely equivocally or metaphorically in both sentences.

But the occurrences in (2) and (3) present a different case: here too 'charged' is not univocal, but common near synonyms are co-applicable in both sentences: e.g. 'instructed', 'authoritatively direc-

100

ted', 'informed' and, sometimes, 'ordered'. And (3) and (4), while related in meaning, also differ: 'directed' and 'ordered' both apply in (3) but not in (4), where 'instructed' and 'informed' both apply, as they do in (3). In (2) and (3) 'charged' occurs analogously; so also in (3) and (4) and in (2) and (4). The predicate schemes of analogous words overlap (because there are at least some common meaning-relevant near synonyms) but are rearranged and reorganized, relatively to one another. For instance, (3) allows (contrast this sense with 'allows' above) 'instructed', 'informed', 'ordered', 'commanded' and 'directed'; but (4) does not allow 'ordered', 'commanded', or 'directed', yet does allow 'instructed', 'informed', and the like. The latter includes a portion of the scheme of the former and the contrast *among* 'charged', 'informed' and 'instructed' is similar to that within the scheme for 'charged' in (3).

There is no relatedness of meaning between 'charged' in (1), (2) or (3) and in (5), (6), and (7), despite the generic legal environment of the latter three. 'Accused x of', 'laid to x's account', 'formally recorded the accusation of', and the like, are near synonyms for 'charged' in (5), (6) and (7) and are not acceptable (i.e. will not yield an acceptable replacement sentence) in (1), (2) or (3). (Notice the automatic differentiation of 'acceptable' now applied to words, instead of sentences.) None of the near synonyms of 'charged' in (1), (2) or (3) is acceptable in (5), (6) or (7). Here is discernible *un*relatedness of meaning – mere equivocation.

On the other hand, (5), (6) and (7) *are* related in meaning: 'accused' 'laid to x's charge', 'ascribed to' and the like can be substituted, though each differentiates. There is a performative element in a grand jury charge or an arresting officer's charge that is absent in a private citizen's charge against another; the former charge, accusation or ascription is conceptually incomplete without an answer. Thus 'charge'/'answer' are antecedent–consequent terms in some schemes and not in others.

The clustered meanings of 'charged' have overlapping foci: (a) the fixing of prices, (b) the collecting of money and (c) the allocation of financial responsibility. They are internally related but are merely equivocal with each of the non-overlapping foci: (d) the military or gun-loading-and-leveling senses of 'charged', (e) the legal accusation senses, (f) the authoritative–instruction–command senses, and, lastly, (g) the physical-mental-attack senses.

There are, thus, *clusters* (e.g. (a), (b) and (c), above) of related but differentiated uses of 'charged' where *within* the cluster there is discernible analogy of meaning and *among* the clusters there is mere equivocation. Are (e) and (g) a single cluster because they can both be considered attacks? No, metaphorical near synonyms are not enough. As Aristotle and Cajetan described it, the designata of mere equivocals have nothing in common but the name.[4] Battery charging, the heraldic charging, and dog charging represent three meaning clusters whose members are merely equivocal in relationship to one another and to all the other clusters that have been mentioned. Clustered, differentiated words are analogous to one another. *There is an analogous use of any given word, corresponding to each of its distinct near synonyms in a given context-environment.*

Consider: 'He acted deliberately, after considering all his options.' In one disambiguating environment, it means he acted leisurely, unhurriedly or imperturbably; in another, it means he acted with forethought, intentionally, premeditatedly. Though there is a correlation between imperturbable, unhurried actions and premeditated, intentional actions, the two are different meanings of 'deliberately'. In fact, when we compare the lists of near synonyms, and also the antonyms, we find no significant overlap in the predicate schemes. The term, in those two senses, is merely equivocal, e.g. 'The piston moved deliberately through the forward stroke.' Mere equivocation is sometimes a waste product of dead metaphor, though in my opinion, it is more often the fallout of analogy.

Nevertheless, the speed–of–motion ('The judge moved deliberately to the bench'; 'The clock hands moved forward deliberately') and mental-state clusters for 'deliberately' *internally* exhibit meaning *foci*, not a single definite meaning shared by all. There is a difference between acting intentionally and acting with premeditation; and one can act with premeditation without acting upon mature consideration. In some environments, 'deliberately', 'intentionally', 'premeditatedly', and 'upon mature consideration' are near synonyms; in others, 'deliberately' is differentiated so that only one or another of those terms is a near synonym. The cluster, exhibiting overlapping meaning foci (like intersecting spotlights on a stage floor), are analogous with one another. Dictionary entries are for statistically *typical* meanings from *within* a given cluster. So one ought not to assume that between the entries for the same word, each entry being characteristic of a distinct cluster, there is mere equivocation; quite often that is not true.

Clustering is the *result* of analogy of meaning, the result of having predicate scheme overlaps, and not its explanation. That is why 'focal meaning' talk is unsatisfying; it offers no prospect of a real explanation, even if we grant that as far as it goes, it is descriptively true.

(a) He *established* that there are philosophical errors in ancient thought. (proved, demonstrated)
(b) He *established* his business in 1920. (started successfully)
(c) He *established* himself within the community. (created a good reputation)
(d) The king *established* judges for civil matters. (appointed permanently in law)
(e) The president *established* control over Congress early in his term. (acquired by design)

Each of the above meanings further differentiates, within the general focus indicated by the example and the explanatory parenthesis. None of the above meanings belongs to the cluster that surrounds one of the others, though some terms, like 'proved himself' can occur (merely equivocally) in the scheme for 'established himself' as well. That none belongs to the cluster indicated by any of the others is evident because the near synonyms acceptable for one diverge so much from those acceptable for the others. Nevertheless, there are differentiated senses of 'established' which cluster around *each* of the examples listed above.

A dictionary of synonyms provides the following lists of words that, on occasion, serve as near synonyms for 'establish'. (I do not mean that more than one item listed is a near synonym in every case where one of them is, but only that in some context or another, each of the expressions listed is a near synonym and that in some contexts, more than one of the listed terms may be equally applicable.) Establish: confirm, institute, found, build up, verify, endow, fulfil, prove, ratify, set up, authorize, demonstrate, substantiate, fix, plant, carry out, settle, constitute, organize, determine.

The five specimen contexts, (a) through (e), do not exhaust the senses of 'establish'. For instance, (f) 'He established a college at Cambridge in 1640' is *close* in meaning to (b) 'He established his business in 1920' but not the same. 'Endowed' can be substituted for the first but not for the second. The sense of 'established' in (f) clusters with (b) and is also merely equivocal with all of the others.

103

Clearly, the { proved/confirmed/verified/demonstrated/substantiated/determined } cluster for 'established' is meaning-related, and the { founded/built up/ratified/authorized/organized/set up/planted/carried out } cluster for 'established' is also internally related. The first cluster occurrences of 'established' are *all* merely equivocal with the second cluster occurrences. And occurrences of 'established', synonymous with distinct members of the first pattern, are analogous to one another.

Even though every word in the first pattern, above, is a near synonym for 'established' in (a) and is not co-applicable in each of the others, (b)–(c), still there can be occurrences of 'established' that discriminate even more finely, not being co-applicable with all *those* words. Because the near synonyms are not *exact* synonyms of one another, there can be occurrences of 'established' where it is synonymous with *one* of the synonyms in contrast to (in distinction from) the others, e.g. where, in effect, 'proved' is distinguished from 'verified'. *Thus, the class of meaning-relevant near synonyms for an occurrence defines a cluster of analogous meanings for that word.* For example, when 'established' means 'demonstrated' and *not* 'verified', 'confirmed' or 'determined', as in 'Anselm established the existence of God'.

Thus, the first pattern identifies a cluster of related meanings for 'established' in (a) just because (i) each member is a meaning-relevant near synonym for 'established' in (a); (ii) there is a range of *differentiated occurrences* of 'established' for which the members of the first pattern are severally meaning-relevant while not *all* are co-applicable; and (iii) differences of *sense* for 'established' within that range are represented by the meaning *contrasts* among the near synonyms, particularly by the non-co-applicability of one or more of the near synonyms in a given context. (In other words, sometimes 'established' means 'found out' in *contrast* to 'verified', etc.)

When one distributes the synonyms from a dictionary of synonyms over the five specimen contexts, (a)–(e), one finds very few that can be substituted in more than one and, where substitution is possible, the substitution is metaphorical or merely equivocal. Further, some of the substitutions are strained. 'The king fixed judges for civil matters' is infelicitous and misleading. And others, 'He founded himself within the community', may be intelligible, but are metaphorical. *Within* the clusterings, we find analogy of meaning; *among* them, mere equivocation.

Consider another set:

(a) The wreck *collected* barnacles and seaweed on the sand.
(b) The ornithologist *collected* specimens of birds.
(c) The sanitation engineers *collected* garbage in the city.
(d) The meterman *collected* shillings from the gas meters.
(e) Everywhere he goes, he *collects* friends.
(f) The student *collected* his books before going home.
(g) The detective *collected* that the butler was out. (gathered, inferred)

These expressions, except (g), permit 'avoided' as an *antonym* (in appropriate environments), though in (a) and (e) 'avoided' is the *very opposite* of 'collected' and is, nevertheless, merely equivocal, while 'avoided' in the others is merely *an* opposite; and 'dispersed' is the very opposite in (f) and possibly in (c), while 'dispense' would be the very opposite in (d). Nevertheless, with the exception of (g), these uses, (a)–(f), can be said to form a single cluster of related meanings: such expressions as 'gathered', 'picked up', 'accumulated', 'amassed', 'aggregated' apply *roughly* in all cases. But the distinctions *among* such terms and among the antinomous expressions, and also among the meanings of modifiers (such as 'slowly' and 'quickly') which would apply in most of the cases, are *different* (the intrascheme contrasts differ). That is, occurrences (a) through (f) are senses of 'collected' with overlapping foci (as indicated above) and are analogous to one another.

A wreck collects barnacles by no *active* process, as against the activity features of the other cases. The ornithologist collects 'selectively' or 'discriminately' in a way that sanitation workers do not select and discriminate in collecting garbage, though they too (under a different sense of 'select' and 'discriminate') may select and discriminate in collecting garbage. The meterman collects shillings indiscriminately, not selectively or discriminately in the way that either the ornithologist or even the garbageman may be said to select or discriminate, despite the fact that the meterman may not 'accept' bad shillings, etc. Of course, the sense of 'collect' in these cases is different from the sense in which the canvasser for a charity collects money, where he does not usually select or discriminate but gathers, assembles, amasses, aggregates, and the like, *receptively*, as against the ornithologist, meterman, and student, who act *acquisitively*.

The student may collect his books discriminately or selectively without being a collector in the way of the ornithologist or in the

105

way of the garbageman or meterman, or even a train conductor. And of course, to collect friends in (e) can either be like the receptive gathering of the ship in (a), or like the discriminating acquisitiveness of the ornithologist, or the receptive, non-acquisitive but possibly selective acts of the charity solicitor or it can involve an active *seeking*, like the ornithologists and ticket collectors, and unlike the garbageman (who, in another sense, actively seeks). Thus 'collect' in (e) can be even more finely differentiated in a hospitable environment.

Within the same general scheme one idea and its opposites, 'selectivity', 'acquisitiveness', 'receptivity', and so forth, may control the other kinds of intrascheme contrast. In different contexts, the control may change, so that the contrasts, the oppositions of terms, are partially rearranged. A pair of equally close synonyms in one context may be forced out of tandem into opposition by the presence of another contrasting factor in another context (cf. wide/narrow and much/little as in 'how wide?', 'how little?'). Those contrast-making and contrast-rearranging factors are contributed by the expressions (express or implied) in contexts or environments which are the *dominating* and scheme-determining expressions.

We can roughly segment same-word meanings in two ways: into clusters, analogous senses that have overlapping foci (e.g. physical-transport senses of 'carry') and, *among* the clusters, the merely equivocal meanings: for instance, the physical-*transport* cluster and the physical-*support* clusters for 'carry'. Some words may substitute in both senses – for instance 'bears' for 'carry' – but they too are merely equivocal or metaphorical across clusters.

There need be no *focal sense* of a word, no 'primary sense' among analogous senses. (Though, perhaps, Aristotle may have been right that in *some* cases there are, especially relatively to some theory or some explanatory objective.) Yet there are overlapping foci within clustered senses. Thus 'to carry' in its physical-transport senses overlaps the focus of 'to carry' in the abstract-transport sense. Yet most of the fifteen, or so, dictionary senses of 'bear' belong to distinct clusters; for instance, 'to bear' in the sense of 'to support the weight of' and 'to endure' do not exhibit enough community of near synonyms and of opposition to other words to converge upon a common focus.

As the classical theory supposed, there really is similarity of meaning when words are analogous; but not the sort that one might naively have expected, that one word token would appear directly similar in meaning to another, or that there is one 'prior' meaning to which the 'derived' meanings are similar. Rather, the physical transport and the verbal report of a message are similar, when regarded as *similarly in contrast* to other expressions that are meaning-relevant to each, like 'losing' and 'failing to deliver', and are *similarly in contrast* to the physical-holding and figurative-support senses of 'to carry'. That is exhibited by their similar differences in predicate scheme from occurrences of the latter kind. Analogy of meaning is based not upon direct resemblance but upon similarity (with difference) of semantic relations, particularly similarity of contrast relations. (That is pretty close in spirit to Aquinas' emphasis upon 'proportionality', similarity of *relations*.)

Similarity of meaning matrices Every word in a sentence stands in a meaning matrix, a pattern of affinities and oppositions of meaning to its predicate scheme members, and to other words.

Meaning affinities and oppositions may be variously classified, of course, and distinguished from one another without limit. But assuming any useful classification of such affinities and oppositions (such as are mentioned in this book and in Lyons' books, (1963, 1966, 1977), like synonymy, hyponymy, contrariety, and so forth), every word stands in a pattern of such relationships. In fact, the linguistic meaning can be represented as the pattern of such relationships.

Any analogous pair has discernably similar meaning matrices. Thus the proportionality, A:B::C:D, that Aristotle and Aquinas noticed and that I illustrated with Millers Analogies examples in chapter 1, has a correspondent in the present theory, $T^1:OW^1::T^2:OW^2$. That is, T^1 is to other meaning-relevant words as T^2 is to its meaning-relevant words, not exactly the same, but similarly. And the similarity is in the *patterns* of meaning opposition and affinity.

I think that has been satisfactorily illustrated in the preceding discussion of clusters. The theoretical importance of this matter is, as far as I now see, limited to explaining how one kind of discourse can be *embedded* cognitively by analogy of proportionality, similarity and continuity of meaning relationships, in another (see chapter 7).

Abstraction Words in one predicate scheme often belong to more abstract schemes within the same cluster. Thus, in 'The arch *carries* the weight of the roof', we could substitute 'bears', 'holds', 'sustains', or 'supports'. So too, in 'The first premise *carries* the weight of his argument'. The mentioned near synonyms for the first occurrence are also near synonyms for the second, though each is differentiated from the first and the contrast *among* 'holds', 'bears', 'sustains' and 'supports' is not a contrast in modes of *physical* activity but, rather, a contrast of 'holds', 'bears', 'sustains', 'supports', etc. *as a group, with their opposed ideas, without the supposition of contrasting physical activity.* That is, the intrascheme contrast of {holds/bears/sustains/supports} is not a contrast in modes by which one physical object is said to impede the gravitational pull on another but is so adjusted as not to presuppose *physical* activity at all, with the contrasts *among* the words remaining otherwise unaltered.

That is what *abstraction* is, linguistically: a comparative relation among same words where one is *more abstract than* the other just in case the tokens are not merely equivocal and the scheme members and intrascheme contrasts (affinities and opposition of meaning among scheme members) of both are the same, or markedly similar, and one token is dominated so as to presuppose the applicability of *determinable* words that are *excluded* from the context of the other. ('Physically' is acceptable in one and not co-applicable in the other.)

What distinguishes abstraction from metaphor? A metaphorical occurrence (as metaphor is explained in the next section) is often *more abstract than* a correlated literal occurrence. But there can be literal occurrences which are more abstract than a given metaphorical occurrence (metaphorical relatively to some third occurrence). Analogy that is not metaphor can be abstractive. Nevertheless, all metaphor is abstractive, relatively to some class of not merely equivocal tokens.

Abstractive analogy is not always metaphorical. The pair may not 'line up', and frequently do not, as the conditions for simple metaphor require. 'Wires *carry* messages' and 'Couriers *carry* messages'. The first implies transportation *without* movement, the second, transportation *with* movement. The contrast among the substitutable 'deliver', 'bear', 'block', 'impede' and 'lose' in the first case is among modes of transmission *without movement* and its contraries, whereas the contrast in the second case is of transmission, and its opposites, *with* movement. The former may be more abstract than the latter but it is not metaphorical with it.

'Metaphor' sometimes designates figures of speech of all kinds, any 'non-literal' occurrence of a word or expression. That, however, is not the way I use the word here. A simple metaphor, as understood here, is a particular kind of analogy, 'analogy of impro-per proportionality', as Cajetan called it[5] (though I cannot adopt his presumption that metaphors are literally false); and frequently meta-phor corresponds to the substitution of one member of a propor-tionality for another that Aristotle described in *Poetics* 1457b, 16–30.

In chapter 6, a wider thesis about *figurative* discourse is defended: that figurative discourse is characterized by words that are differen-tiated, by a shortest step-wise sequence that contains both simple metaphor and analogy or paronymy, from typical non-figurative occurrences. But simple metaphor is not by itself figurative discourse.

'Simple metaphor' denotes some of the linguistic phenomena we correctly call metaphors. Others, as correctly called metaphors, do not satisfy the conditions for simple metaphors. Nothing of import-ance follows from that because 'is metaphorical' is used both meta-phorically (as in the title of Susan Sontag's book, *Illness As Metaphor*) and analogously. Even the metalanguage predicate, 'is metaphorical' applied to *sentences* is denominatively analogous and means '*contains* a predicate used metaphorically', while 'is metapho-rical' applied to a *predicate* means 'is *used* metaphorically'. And in 'Poetry is metaphorical', 'is metaphorical' means 'is characterized by metaphors'.

The linguistic phenomena we, pretheoretically and without further distinctions, call metaphors do satisfy the conditions to be offered. Nevertheless, I emphasize, *the phenomena* are not all of exactly the same sort; they *are analogous* and the words in the analy-sis itself differentiate when applied to them. In fact, I classify metap-hors under paradigms and simulations based upon variations within two dimensions of the paradigms, not because that captures the 'essence' of the phenomena but because it organizes disparate things according to salient similarities.

Simple metaphor is asymmetrical meaning-related equivocation. The metaphorical instance (e.g. a *volley* of insults) has the meaning it has because the same word, occurring elsewhere, has another meaning which implies or has associated the predicate scheme contrast the

109

word has here, but the 'implying' meaning (or presupposition) is excluded from the present sentence because of the unacceptability, platitudinousness, impropriety or commonplace falsity that would result, whereas the present meaning is mandated by dominant expressions. As Mary Hesse suggested, on my account the metaphorical scheme is 'poorer' than a correlatively literal one.

Thus the predicate 'is a simple metaphor' *has* to be analogous (a) because there are distinct 'exclusion' conditions (unacceptability, triteness and commonplace falsity), of which only the first applies in all communities using the language, the others being indigenous to, and relative to, various discoursing groups; and (b) because 'implies' and 'has associated' are equivocal, sometimes meaning 'strictly implies' and sometimes only 'calls to mind' or the like.

I recapitulate the account of metaphor offered by Nelson Goodman (1968: 'Transfer', 74–80 and 'Modes of metaphor' 81–5). It is insightful, simple in form, compares usefully with the account to be offered and facilitates distinctions, especially between analogy and metaphor, that Goodman did not develop.

For Goodman, a metaphor is created when a word belonging to a label scheme or classificatory scheme (he uses 'schema') that has a certain prior realm of application (say, to persons or animals or parts of the body), is subsequently applied to something not belonging to that realm and, by implication, segments the realm into ranges of referents corresponding more or less well with the contrasts among the original label scheme. For instance, words for classifying parts of the body apply to a new realm, spatial relationships on the earth, so that we talk of the foot of a mountain, the head of a bluff, the neck of a point, the shoulder of a hill, the arms of a range, and the like.

Lexical field theorists could describe metaphor as the novel application of a member of a lexical field (and, by implied contrast, the application of the *remainder* of the lexical field as well) to a realm of objects no one of which belongs to the realm of objects formerly and literally classified under that lexical field and where the realm of new application is partitioned by means of the contrasting members of the lexical field. This approximates Goodman's idea. And like Goodman's idea, it neither explains what the contrasts within the label scheme consist in nor how those contrasts are preserved in the application to a new realm.

110

Goodman speaks of metaphor as the emigration of a predicate scheme to a new land (p. 73), to new habitats (p. 77), to new homes, 'an immigrant scheme' (p. 80), 'territory for invasion' (p. 74), and as a 'revitalizing' but 'bigamous second marriage' (p. 73).

His description is revealing but not satisfying. ('The home of a scheme is the country of naturalization rather than birth', p. 74). For instance, the 'literal' sense apparently corresponds to the prior habitat, ('antecedent practice channels the application of labels', p.74), but we find no criterion of 'literal' meaning or means for identifying 'prior' habitats. Of course, Goodman might count as, relatively, 'literal' any class of 'prior' applications to a disjoint realm. But that would not distinguish metaphor from mere equivocation, unless Goodman also thinks it necessary and sufficient for mere equivocation that the label schemes be disparate. (His semantics is one-dimensional, a mapping of labels onto parts of the world.) Still that would not satisfy me as to what constitutes the difference between the literal and the metaphorical, because 'metaphorical' is not symmetrical, though 'is equivocal' is, and because no distinction between analogy and metaphor is proposed.

I explain simple metaphor, under the traceable inspiration of Goodman's account, differently, making literal/non-literal strictly a synchronic distinction that applies pairwise to n-tuples of same words but without dependence upon the notion of 'prior' applications or senses. One term may be literal, and univocal, with respect to another and metaphorical with respect to a third, and so forth, without any assumed temporal priority among the occurrences or any postulated 'prior' application to a disjoint realm of objects. 'Another practice' supplants Goodman's 'antecedent practice', (1968:74).

One feature that most noticeably distinguishes the meaning relations to be called 'simple metaphor' is a asymmetrical meaning-relatedness: an implied presupposition of the literal occurrence is also mandated in the metaphorical occurrence, while an implying presupposition of the literal occurrence is excluded in the metaphorical occurrence. Thus far, the explanation accords with Goodman's. The difference is in the way the 'implying' presupposition is 'excluded' from the metaphorical occurrence and in the fact that these relations are simply subcases of adaptation and resistance to unacceptability.

My account is also compatible with the 'interaction' view of Max

111

Black. It employs broad senses of 'imply', as Black himself does in 'Presupposition and Implication' (1962: 48–64), and accords with his insistence that the very words we use have implications (1962:62) and with Black's recognition that 'metaphor', even restricted to linguistic relations, is not a single phenomenon but a series of related phenomena.

In simple metaphors the same word is equivocal (a symmetrical relationship of difference of meaning) and is related in meaning (also symmetrical). The one token is 'literal' in comparison to the other, while the other is 'metaphorical' in comparison to the former. The asymmetry is created by the mandating of a *double* presupposition, an 'implying' and an 'implied' presupposition in the 'literal' token, and by the mandating of the (relatively) 'implied' presupposition in the metaphorical token and the *exclusion* of the 'implying' contrast; here 'mandating' is, of course, accomplished by *dominant* expressions in the environment.

In (1) 'The clouds *swept* the moon', (2) 'His gaze *swept* the crowd', (3) 'The workman *swept* the halls', and (4) 'The police *swept* the suspects into the station', we have several *different* simple metaphors, relatively to (3). If we suppose that 'swept' in (3) is in contrast to 'washed', 'polished', 'mopped', 'scrubbed', 'dusted', and the like (a lexical field of cleaning terms), there is also associated with that predicate scheme (a) a contrast of characteristic *motions* involved in such actions, (b) a contrast of characteristic *apparent* movements involved in producing such effects, and (c) a contrast of perceivable or apparently perceivable *effects produced*, and, no doubt, many other associated and subsidiary contrasts (such as contrasts of attitudes of an agent or observer and the like), some of which have not even been noticed or articulated as yet.

If the environment *excludes*, as yielding unacceptable sentences, a contrast among the physical actions of a *person* (a presupposition that is characteristic of the field of *cleaning terms*), but presupposes actual or apparent motions, then by selecting a word from that lexical field to complete the context, I create a simple metaphor, relatively to occurrences that involve (imply) the physical cleaning actions of persons (see Black 1962:45).

Suppose the contrast is among *observable effects*, e.g. 'the clouds washed and then polished the sky'; and suppose that contrast is implied by a contrast among *physical acts* (e.g. 'Jones *washed* and *polished* the floor'). Some environments permit both the implying and

112

the implied presuppositions; others permit only the implied presupposition, e.g. the clouds and sky, above. In that case, the latter is metaphorical with respect to the former. Both can of course be metaphorical in relationship to some third.

Metaphor is a non-transitive, not an intransitive, relation. Nevertheless, it is not symmetrical. Thus when two occurrences are each metaphorical in relation to a third, they are not *both* metaphorical in relationship to one another, though one may be metaphorical in relation to the other. That implies that a given t^1 (*crept*/ship), can be metaphorical with respect to t^2 (*crept*/baby), which is, therefore, literal in relationship to t^1, while t^1 is also metaphorical in relation to t^3 (*crept*/disease), when t^3 is also metaphorical in relation to t^2.

'Implying contrasts' and their presuppositions. Implication, involved in metaphors, includes both logical entailment and weak linguistic association. A person cannot polish, rather than wash, a floor without also engaging in contrasting characteristic physical motions; a person cannot drive a nail, twist a nut, or turn a screw, without also engaging in contrasting physical motions (driving, twisting, turning) and (usually) displaying different mental states. So associated contrasts of various kinds are strongly (even when not analytically) implied in the physical contrast of driving, twisting and turning. There are, also, loose implications, based upon associated personality traits. Such associated contrasts are also 'implied'. In fact, 'implies' includes every relationship of 'attachment' by which a condition functions as a presupposition for a predicate and has presuppositions (conditions) attached to *it*. Thus if T^1 presupposes C^1 and C^1 presupposes D^1, then if there is a context that mandates a sense of T^n that presupposes D^n but *excludes* its presupposing C^n, then T^n is metaphorical to T^1(see Black 1962: 43–4).

Thus the basic idea of 'a simple metaphor' that analogously characterizes the diverse cases is: a meaning-related, equivocal occurrence of a word in an environment that excludes a certain intrascheme contrast (or its presupposition) that (in some given or canonical context) implies a contrast relationship (or presupposition) that the metaphorical context mandates. Metaphors don't have to be made, they can just happen as words fit their contexts.

'Exclusion' relations As I remarked earlier, there are various conditions for 'cancelling out' presuppositions. The condition men-

113

tioned already is 'unacceptability' of what would be the resulting sentence. Unacceptability is sufficient to exclude a presupposition whenever an acceptable result is possible. Thus where a sentence 'read' in a relatively literal sense would be linguistic nonsense – for instance, 'My brother writes electricity' – metaphor is compelled by the environment if that result is acceptable.

But other conditions also exclude the presuppositions of 'implying' intrascheme contrasts. For instance, metaphorical reading is sometimes compelled by the commonplace falsity ('John's a bird'), or by the mere platitudinousness ('He's a thing') of a literal reading. There may be still other 'exclusion' conditions that vary with the kind of discourse (e.g. sports talk, legal discourse) or with the social and educational status of the participants. (We already know that what is understood metaphorically by some speakers is taken literally by others.)

'Hard-core' simple metaphors are the *paradigm*; the implication relation is 'logical' or 'analytic' and the 'exclusion' is on account of the unacceptability of the sentence 'read' literally (in the predicate scheme of a relatively literal occurrence).

There are many *linguistic simulations* of the paradigm, with differing exclusion conditions that compel an 'implied or associated' reading (by excluding the 'implying' reading). Because these are linguistic simulations, with new ones, further new ones become practicable as simulations of both the paradigm and the extant simulations (see Thinking metaphorically, below).

Need metaphors be literally false? Metaphors are not necessarily false. Frequently a metaphorical sentence can be read 'literally' and, as so read, is false. But if you insist that combinations that make linguistic nonsense (as defined in chapter 7) when read literally (in the predicate scheme of a relatively literal occurrence), like 'night sings posts', cannot have a truth value when so read because they do not express statements, then it follows that hard-core simple metaphors are *never* literally false.

Furthermore, when the basis for the 'exclusion' is triteness or platitudinousness, the metaphor, read literally, *must* be true. So, Cajetan overstated things in saying that 'to be predicated metaphorically means that what the name signifies is found in that of which it is predicated according to a likeness *only*' (Cajetan, *Comm. in S. T.* I, 13, 3, (I)). 'Taken literally a metaphor is always false' is false.

114

And contrary to my earlier opinion (Ross 1958), I do not think Aquinas was actually committed to the view that all metaphors are literally false, even though Cajetan reads him that way. When he says (*Ia*, 16, 6c), '*ratio propria non invenitur nisi in uno*', Aquinas is actually talking about a broader class than metaphor and is not saying all such utterances are literally false. R. McInerny (1964, 1968) reads him in the same way, I think.

Complex metaphors Metaphors can, of course, be far more complicated than the simple metaphors described. 'Plunge', a verb in contrast to 'lunge', 'slip', 'waddle', etc. becomes *denominatively* analogous by adaptation in 'the plunge' (of the diver), and *abstractly analogous* by contrasting adaptation in 'the plunge' of the financier (where physical action is not required and is in fact excluded); it becomes *metaphorically* and antinomously differentiated into honorific and pejorative senses (the hero's plunge into the river; the foolhardy plunge into ruin); further, it differentiates *denominatively* into a name not for the action but the effect (the plunge of the plane), and further, *metaphorically*, into the plunge (steep drop) of the Dow Jones Average.

Thus the last occurrence is related to the first by a hypothetical sequence of contrasting adaptations: denomination – abstractive analogy – metaphor – denomination – metaphor. Similarly, figurative discourse can be analysed as hypothetical construction (by hypothetical sequences of adaptation) from non-figurative occurrences of the same words. (Further details in chapter 6.)

Another kind of complex metaphor is the metaphorical and denominative differentiation Aristotle mentioned, where one word from a verbal proportionality substitutes for another: 'Bring your stuff into my zoo' (referring to one's library), where the relevant proportionality is 'Books are to a library as animals are to a zoo'. These are the kinds of 'transfer based upon analogy' that Aristotle had in mind (*Poet.*, 1457b, 16–30). A more complex example, a sports headline, 'Beans beat Beef' may be based upon denominative substitution of 'Beans' for 'Boston' and 'Beef' for 'Chicago' where the place names are already functioning denominatively for baseball teams located in the cities.

Cajetan remarked upon a relationship between metaphor and analogy of attribution (a subcase of denominative analogy in this theory) but described it poorly:

... an analogon, taken metaphorically, predicates nothing else than that this thing bears a likeness to that thing, and this likeness cannot be understood without (knowledge of) the other extreme. For this reason analogous terms of this type are predicated by priority of those things in which they are properly realized, and by posteriority of those things in which they are found metaphorically. As is clear, in this respect they resemble terms that are analogous by analogy of attribution. (*De Nom. Anal.*, N.76.)

Not every metaphor involves denomination, of course; but many do. Still, 'he's a pig' means he *exemplified* piggery not merely 'he is *like* a pig'. Metaphors do not reduce to likeness (as Cajetan and Aquinas seem to have thought). Rather, likeness may rest upon, and simile reduce to metaphor, as Black (1962:37) and Goodman (1968:77) proposed.

Thinking metaphorically There are two features by which metaphor acquires modes. The first is variation upon the 'implying' relationships, variations from 'logical implication' all the way to loose forms of 'verbal association' (see Black 1962:43, 'specially constructed systems of implications'). The second is variation upon the feature that *excludes* the 'implying' scheme's presupposition(s) from the metaphorical context. Ringing changes on those two elements makes the modes of metaphor.

One naturally wonders whether there is some common kind of thinking that these linguistic phenomena reflect, say 'thinking metaphorically' or 'metaphorical structuring of experience.' I think there is. (A science fiction writer called that sort of thinking, when it classifies entirely new experience under the categories of old experience, 'metaphorical deformation of reality').

And Aristotle remarked, (*Poet.*, ch.22, 1459a, 5–9):

'But the greatest thing by far is to be a master of metaphor. It is *the one thing* that cannot be learnt from others; and it is also a sign of genius, since a good metaphor implies an intuitive perception of the similarity in dissimilars.' (Italics added)

It is sometimes startlingly instructive to classify things with words whose presuppositions are inconsistent with predicates the things are known (or believed) to bear. A 'different practice' provides friction to make a metaphor (Goodman 1968:76–77); e.g. to classify people with animal names, colors with sound predicates, inanimate motions with human action words.

116

It can be striking to contrast persons as animals either on the basis of appearance, personality traits, forms of life, gait, relative intelligence, longevity, or any other quality mapped into another pattern of word contrasts. A double-image, and rearrangement of the predicate boundaries to get a fit, really are part of metaphorical thinking. Goodman was right to think metaphors 'bigamous' and 'to be an affair between a predicate with a past and an object that yields while protesting' (1968:69); but he attributes to words, in this case, the characteristics of metaphorical thinking. Things are regrouped by force, by force of the conditions of contrast among the predicates in the classification.

The object metaphorically classified does not bear any predicate of the classification for the same reason that anything relevantly the same as any rigidly designated exemplar, or thing satisfying the stereo-types, does. Instead, it bears the one predicate, rather than another from the classification, either because its differences from other things are distinguishably projected from that point in the label scheme, or because contrasts among the objects classified seem more faithfully, more vividly or more informatively (or anything else one likes) delineated by distributing the classification names that way rather than another.

In *paradigmatic* metaphorical thinking, where none of the metaphorically characterized things bears its predicate (from the label system) for the same reasons as any of the literally classified things (that satisfy the presuppositions), metaphorical classifying is contrastive and coercive because it *regroups* (relative to other applicable classifications from which it differs by having a double reading on one of which it is not so, is trivially so, or does not make sense).

Linguistically objective metaphors Relationships among *dictionary types* (the types of which words are meaning-related and non-metaphorical tokens) fit the analogy theory. They can be merely equivocal, metaphorical or analogous. That amounts to an analogous differentiation of the predicates of the analogy theory itself because they now apply to occurrence *types*.

A further analogous differentiation occurs when we talk of a word token's being univocal (etc.) *with* a dictionary type, below. And notice how naturally, inexorably and irresistibly the adaptation occurred, as I predicted.

117

If the type 'bank' (place to keep money) is merely equivocal with the type 'bank' (raised shore of river or stream), then every word univocal with the first (or analogous by proportionality but not metaphorical with the first) is merely equivocal with every word that is univocal with (or analogous by proportionality and non-metaphorical with respect to) the second.

The relationships among the dictionary *types* can therefore be defined in terms of the already explicated relationships among particular tokens, and the very process of doing so illustrates the way words are dominated and differentiated in use, in this case, the predicates of the analogy theory. No contradiction comes from saying two dictionary entries are analogous or merely equivocal; rather the composition of the expression causes adaptation of 'analogous' and 'merely equivocal' so that 'is an occurrence *token*' or 'is in a complete sentential context', is not implied. Truth conditions for the predicates adapt by suppression. That is, by the resistance of these words, 'Word types are univocal, equivocal, analogous, and so forth' to concatenating in a way *evidently* unacceptable in the environment. The combination of linguistic inertia and universal linguistic force(s), sketched in the Introduction, accounts for the differentiation of the predicates of this theory as it is extended to word types, to relations of tokens to types, and, in chapter 5, to paronyms.

At the risk of being exasperating, let me repeat that the adaptations are automatic, irresistible, non-intentional, law-like and clearly intrinsic to the linguistic expressions in which they occur. I prove this by simply altering the context in the next paragraph so the truth conditions for 'is analogous with', 'is metaphorical with', etc. will alter right before your eyes.

Metaphor was first explained here, just as analogy and mere equivocation have been, as a kind of differentiation holding pairwise among same words. But the prevalence of statements of the form 'That's a metaphor', 'The term . . . is used metaphorically in that sentence', and the like, suggests that there are relationships between word tokens and dictionary *types* paralleling those already defined. So 'metaphor' analogously differentiates for the second time, as do the other metalanguage predicates of this theory, to apply to relations between a word *occurrence* and a *dictionary type*.

Thus, if the first dictionary entry for 'to bank' is 'to place valuables in secure keeping', and a given sentential occurrence of 'to bank' means 'to rely upon' (He banked upon my coming), the latter may be considered objectively metaphorical because the latter is metaphorical in relation to *every* occurrence that is either univocal with the dictionary paradigm or differentiated from it but neither merely equivocal nor metaphorical with it.

5 ANALOGY AND CATEGORIAL DIFFERENCES

Two distinct families of analogous occurrences are distinguished: (a) the *denominative* (attributive and ascriptive) differentiations, treated in chapter 5, and (b) the predicatively analogous words that typically correspond to a coherent (even if trivial) *proportionality*: e.g. 'seeing for oneself is to vision as holding in one's hand is to touching', namely '*grasping*'.

Words used analogously (e.g. the two implied occurrences of 'grasping') have sometimes been thought to reflect a categorial contrast among the things referred to, e.g. understanding and touching. Words typically differentiate with completions that contrast as 'the sensible' to 'the non-sensible', 'the living' to 'the non-living', 'the material' to 'the immaterial', 'the inorganic' to 'the organic', and 'the finite' to 'the infinite'. That suggested to me that categorial contrasts are the cause of analogy of common predicates (Ross 1970b), a mistake, unfortunately.

Analogy of meaning is not 'differentiation of same words in categorially contrasting contexts', neat as that might have been. There are cases of analogy (perhaps most cases) where there is no reason to postulate a categorial contrast at all. Categorially contrasting completions differentiate common (object-language) predicates; but differentiation has other causes as well.

Then, why is the 'Aristotelian' hypothesis, that a categorial contrast, say, in subjects, differentiates all common (object-language, positive) predicates (and at least some in a meaning-related way) true?

On this theory it is true by definition. *Two distinct expressions, forming a pair of object-language sentence frames, are in categorial contrast just in case they differentiate all common positive, object-language completions, and differentiate some of them in a meaning-related way.* Otherwise, how could a predicate be ultimate in classification if its *designata* were included in a common univocal sortal? And yet there are no distinct predicates that cannot occur in a pair of frames with common completion words (e.g. 'is something', 'a thing', 'some-

119

thing or another', and so forth). And there are no distinct expressions that make all common object-language, positive, completions for them merely equivocal. Thus, I suspect, the most extreme meaning distance that is actual in our language is the categorial difference defined above.

Categorially contrasting expressions *cannot* therefore concatenate with univocal, positive, object-language predicates. But they certainly do concatenate with analogous common predicates. Aristotle (*Meta.*, 1070b, 18), was particularly insistent upon that relationship among things of different categories. And it is a serviceable way to *define* categorial contrast of meaning because the results accord with other widely held ideas about categories: they are ultimate in classification; that they are not determinates of any common determinable or species of any genus, and so forth. Those attributes follow from the absence of any univocal common object-language predicates.

Furthermore, the predicate schemes for categorially contrasting words are not determinates (like the color names) of some common scheme of determinables (like 'color, taste, sound, smell, touch') which are themselves the determinates of some further common determinable (like 'sensation') that applies univocally to the *designata* of both. For there is no univocal (positive) common, object-language predicate and, therefore *no univocal more general sortal.* Thus we can say that categorially diverse expressions do not belong to a common tree of classification from which some more general word applies univocally to their *designata.* They are, therefore, classificationally ultimate.

No pair of distinct words is *always* in categorial contrast, not even in all their object-language occurrences, as was, no doubt, unreflectively believed about 'substance' and 'quantity' by some Aristotelians. Equivocation can negate opposition even among the category names themselves.

Categorial contrasts are possible between same words but, logically, they are derivative from categorial contrasts among distinct expressions, just as meaning differences among same words are, logically, derivative from meaning differences among distinct words. That is because same words, unless *dominated*, do not differ in meaning, whereas distinct words do not have to be dominated to differ from one another in meaning.

120

5

Denominative analogy and paronymy

There is another kind of analogy, *denominative analogy*, that results from contrasts of predicate mode. It consists of differentiated denominations (relational naming: to plow/a plow; to smoke/smokes), of which there are several kinds.

Denominative analogy is particularly important in accounting (a) for the relatedness among paronyms, (b) for figurative discourse (metonymy, synecdoche, antonomasia), (c) for the transfer of thing-names and event-names into verbs, and vice versa, and (d) for the relatedness of the same words used contrastively to impute activity, proclivity, tendency, disposition, and the like. For example, 'He cheated' (*once*) as against 'He cheated' (characteristically); 'He is a *responsible* young man'; 'His was a *responsible* action under conditions of great uncertainty'.

Denominative analogy sometimes involves *abstractive* analogy of proportionality (cf. chapter 4) along with contrasting predicate modes: 'Most of the employees at Newtown are *healthy*; Newtown, as the travel agents all say, is a *healthy* place.' The second 'healthy' is both denominatively and abstractively differentiated from the first. And there can be metaphorically denominative pairs, too, that is the basis of personification (see chapter 6).

What Cajetan (1498: ch.2, sec.10–15) called 'analogy of attribution' and Aquinas (*De Veritate*, 21, 4 ad 4 and *Principles of Nature*, ch.6, no.38) 'analogy because of diverse attributions', is a species of denominative analogy. For example, the analogy of meaning between 'healthy', applied to the intrinsic state of a dog, and 'healthy', applied to the appearance of its coat. Its distinguishing characteristic is that one of the words can be defined as signifying a causal, manifestive or representative (etc.) relation to *what is signified by* (the *significatum* of) the same word in another occurrence. But there are other kinds of modally differentiated, interdefinable same words as well.

After explaining denominative analogy and certain of its species (analogy of attribution, ascriptive analogy and representational analogy), I extend the classification to paronyms, both to expand the theory's descriptive scope and to reinforce the reader's perception of its truth, as the predicates of the analogy theory itself obey the regularities they describe, and differentiate (by proportionality) when applied to paronyms.

1   ORIGIN OF THE NAME 'DENOMINATIVE ANALOGY' AND
     WHAT IS ENCOMPASSED BY IT

Denominative meaning, relational naming, is referred to at the beginning of Aristotle's *Categories (Ia,* 13); the passage is rendered in various English translations with the word 'derivative' taken from the Greek for 'paronymous'.[1] St Anselm in his *Dialogus De Grammatico* speaks of 'grammatico' as one of the terms '*quae ... denominative dicuntur*' and proceeds to inquire 'Whether an account of their meaning shall at the same time involve an account of their reference.'[2]

But no systematic discussion that I know of (except for Anselm's which was directed at different objectives) occurred until St Thomas Aquinas distinguished some kinds of denomination (*De Ver.*, 21, 4, ad 2.)[3] In the sixteenth century Suarez (trans. Ross 1964) and John of Saint Thomas (trans. Simon et al. 1955) employed 'denomination' in the broad sense of 'naming' or characterizing something on account of its relations to something else, for instance 'father' or 'sister'. John Locke, (*Essay*, III, II, 17; VI, 9, and II, ch.25, sections 2–7), uses 'denomination' to mean 'relational naming' and explicitly distinguishes 'extrinsic denominations' (section 2), contrasts denomination with 'absolute' naming in section 3 and relates denomination to his general account of relations (section 5): 'The *nature* therefore of *relation* consists in the referring or comparing two things one to another, from which comparison one or both comes to be denominated.'

In section 7 Locke gives examples of things named denominatively that are the same as those discussed throughout the middle ages and in this chapter; e.g. son, father, friend, enemy, subject, islander, general, judge, patron, client, professor, servant, superior, older, digger, 'to almost an infinite number'; 'he being capable of as many relations as there can be occasions of comparing him to other things in any manner of agreement, disagreement, or respect whatsoever'.[4]

Denomination is relational naming (as contrasted with naming on account of an inherent, absolute quality). And denominative *analogy* is *differentiated* application of a common relational word, e.g. 'John is *awkward*', 'John's speech is *awkward*'.

Strictly, there are two cases for a pair of relationally differentiated same words: one of the pair is applied non-relationally (non-denominatively) and the other is applied relationally (denominatively), or both are applied relationally, but in contrasting relations.

A person is denominated 'judge' because of his political/legal role and, similarly, a person is denominated a doctor, drunkard, bungler, runner, racer, driver, vacationer, flier, sailor, patient, client and student by relationships to other things. So, too, God is metaphorically denominated 'Father', 'Bridegroom', 'Counsellor', 'Lord', 'King', and 'Lion'. In fact, whenever anything is classified contrastively, whether metaphorically or not, on account of (non-constitutive) relations in which it stands to things *other* than itself, it is classified denominatively.

Now, denominative classification is not, by itself, analogy. Rather, *differentiated same-word denominations* are analogous. And, as the rest of this half of the chapter will show, there are many different kinds of differentiated denominations.

To call Smith a runner and his teammate Jones a runner is not to differentiate 'runner'. But, to call something 'human' because it is constitutively human, i.e. a person, and to call clothes 'human' because they are human dress is denominatively to differentiate 'human', making each analogous (denominatively) to the other.

We denominate an historical period Victorian because of the reign of Victoria. We denominate things characteristic of that period as Victorian (of the Victorian period). And we characterize present day things that resemble things typical of the earlier period, as Victorian: customs, manners or morals. The three occurrences of 'Victorian' are denominations, differentiated from one another, and are analogous to one another.

To classify an agent with a common name that also classifies its characteristic function, activity, disposition, purpose, or effect, is also analogous. For instance, 'judge', to classify the activity that is the characteristic function of a certain kind of official, differentiates into an extrinsic denomination (common name) of the individual exercising the function: a 'judge'.

The same is true of instrument denominations. The word for the activity of a certain instrument (the activity *for* which it is made, e.g. 'drill') differentiates to name the instrument itself: a drill, a telephone, a plow, a hammer.

I put 'non-constitutive relation' in parentheses when describing denomination in general because I do not distinguish between what various medieval writers (and Locke) called 'extrinsic' and 'intrinsic' denomination. (Certainly, a parallel distinction could be elaborated, if needed, between predicates differentiated in virtue of constitutive and non-constitutive aliorelative relations.) Instead, I emphasize that denominations are *aliorelative*, a point Aquinas also made:

> All things that are ordered to one, even in different ways, can be denominated from it; thus from health which is in an animal, not only is the animal said to be healthy through being the subject of health; but medicine also is said to be healthy through producing health, diet through preserving it and urine through being a sign of health (*IIIa*, 60, 1c).

Aquinas distinguished two kinds of denomination, the one, where an expression applies to a thing because it stands in a causal relation 'which is the very meaning of the denomination': '*X* is *F*' *means* '*X causes* . . . to be *F*'. ('The food is healthy' *means* 'The food produces health in the ill'.)

In the second case, the causal reaction is not the very meaning of the word but, rather, the reason for (or ground) of the denomination. The causal relation between an author and his work is the ground (basis) for the differentiation in 'The author is brilliant', 'The work is brilliant'.

St Thomas observed:

> There are two ways of denominating something with respect to something else. One way makes the very relationship the *meaning* of the denomination. Thus urine is called healthy in relationship to the health of the animal. The very meaning of 'healthy' as it is predicated of urine is 'to-be-a-sign-of-health-in-the-animal'. In such predication that which is denominated with respect to something else is not so denominated because of any form inhering in it but because of something outside to which it is referred.
>
> The other way of denominating something in relationship to something else does not make the relationship the very meaning of the denomination but rather its cause. Thus when the atmosphere is called bright because of

the sun, this does not mean that the very relationship of the atmosphere to the sun is its brightness, but rather that the location of the atmosphere directly opposite the sun is the cause of its brightness (*De Ver.*, 21,4 ad 2.)[5]

Another translation may be clearer:

In another way, something is denominated in relation to another when *not* the relation but its *cause* is the reason of the denomination. For example, air is said to be lucid from the sun not because the reference itself of the air to the sun is the lucidity of the air, but because the direct opposition of the air to the sun is the cause of its lucidity. [italics added].

The second, involving a relational and a non-relational word, can be summarized first. To say the air is bright and to say the sun is bright is, on Aquinas' view, to apply the predicate 'bright' equivocally. The sun is *inherently* bright on account of what it is, while the air is bright derivatively – not on account of what it is but *because* it is lit up by the sun. It is like the present day relationship between *bright*/light; *bright*/room. Similarly, with 'brilliant' as a predicate for the author and 'brilliant' as a predicate of the book. For the brilliance of the book is causally derivative from the brilliance of the author. Yet 'bright' (air) does not *mean* 'caused by the brightness of the sun' and 'brilliant' (book) does not *mean* 'caused by a brilliant author'. The *basis* of those meaning differences is the causal relation between productive properties (bright sun, bright bulb and brilliant author) and resultant properties (bright air, bright room and brilliant book).

The first kind of denomination is just the opposite. The entire *meaning* of one denominating expression consists of the relation 'is the cause of...', 'is the sign of...' where the blanks are to be filled with *what is signified by* the same word in some other occurrence.[6]

Aquinas and Aristotle observed that we can apply a predicate, say, 'healthy', that belongs to some things because of their internal states (e.g. of biotic well-being), to the things and states of affairs that are signs, effects, symptoms, and causes of such internal states (e.g. of health in an organism). And we can define the one sense by means of the other. Thus we speak of a 'healthy complexion', 'a healthy diet' (better in English to speak of a 'healthful diet'), 'healthy kind of exercise' ('healthful' is better), 'a healthy (again, 'healthful' is better) environment', and (by abstractive analogy) 'a healthy society' and 'a healthy institution.' (I mean by 'healthy en-

125

vironment' not the analogue to 'having the biotic state of well being', which is analogy of proportionality, but the equivalent of 'healthful', which corresponds to the second mode of denomination described above and found in Aquinas, *De Ver.*, 21, 4 ad 4.) Similarly, we speak of an 'unhealthy' place, that is, a place where a certain disease is much more common than in other places, and more abstractly, of 'healthy' and 'unhealthy' places where bodily or spiritual well-being is causally affected to a noticeable degree, e.g. Arizona has supposedly a 'healthy' climate in a way New York has not.

That insight (derived from Aristotle and Plato, of course) is supported by the fact that a dispositional sense of 'red' can be defined in terms of the sense-quality meaning of 'red': e.g. 'to be dispositionally red is to have that physical condition which, under normal conditions of light and sensation, *ceteris paribus*, *causes* the experience of the sensible quality "red" (the "red-sensing" events) through light stimulation of the eye'.[7]

Someone might reverse the order of definition. But that would not affect the underlying idea that sometimes a word in one of its meanings can be defined entirely as *meaning* (signifying) a causal (or other) relation to the *significatum* of the same word in one of its other meanings. That is Aquinas' and Cajetan's notion of *Analogy of Attribution:* Whenever a word differentiates so that it signifies a relation (any of the Aristotelian four kinds of causing and also in any of the 'sign of' relations) to the *significatum* of another same word, there is analogy of attribution as Cajetan described it, and a denomination of the first kind that Aquinas distinguished: *able* performance/*able* performer; *agile* leap/*agile* dancer; *moral* man/*moral* act; *intelligent* man/*intelligent* statement.[8] The list of such differentiations in English is immense.

There can be other definitional relationships of the same general kind: 'is an *effect* of F', is a *sign* that F obtains' and 'is a *symptom that X is F'*. Any *significative* (manifestive, indicative, etc.) or *real change-effecting* relationship gives rise to attributional differentiations. In each case *F, within* the definition, is the *significatum* of *F* in another occurrence (or typical occurrence) outside the definition. So we can talk about a *priority of occurrences:* T^1 is prior to T^2 just in case T^2 signifies 'is the cause, effect, sign, symptom, etc. of' the *significatum* of T^1 as T^1 occurs in some particular or typical context.

When instrument names (hammer) are the same as the active

126

verbs for their functions, the activity word can be regarded as prior. For the names can be defined as 'the instrument, end, output, purpose, effect, means, sign, or symptom ... of *F*'. And where the output (or end) is named for the instrument (e.g. the *sound* of the trumpets is called 'trumpets', etc.) or the activity for the instrument, 'to combine' wheat (named for the instrument which *combines* the cutting and threshing operation), there is also analogy of attribution. Metonymy and synecdoche involve denomination (in fact, analogy of attribution) comparatively to typical other same-word occurrences.

2   DENOMINATIVE ANALOGY: WHAT CONSTITUTES IT?

Denominative analogy (the genus) involves differentiation (to sail/ a sail) by difference of relations of one thing to other things. Analogy of attribution (traditional) is a sub-class that involves a differentiated word with one token meaning a causal or significative relation to what-is-signified-by the other. And there are other differentiated denominations (he *cheated*/once; he *cheated*/characteristically) that are interdefinable but not cases of analogy of attribution.

Aquinas' explanation of a second kind of denomination and other passages, like the following, suggest that he realized that there are related denominations that are not analogous by attribution. But there is no reason to suppose that either Aquinas or Cajetan recognized a genus of denominations that *includes* analogy of attribution as a species. In *IIa IIae*, 57, 1, ad 3, Aquinas says:

> It is usual for words to be distorted from their original signification so as to mean something else: thus the word medicine was first employed to signify a remedy used for curing a sick person, and then it was drawn to signify the art by which it is done. In like manner, the word *jus* (right) was first of all used to denote the just thing itself, but afterwards it was transferred to designate the art whereby it is known what is just, and further to denote the place where justice is administered; thus a man is said to appear *in jure*; and yet further, we say even that a man, who has the office of exercising justice, administers the *jus* even if his sentence be unjust [italics added].

Cajetan's first condition for attribution is, 'only the primary analogate realizes the perfection formally, whereas the others have it only by extrinsic denomination' (1498: 16, no.10). And Aquinas says (*Ia*, 16, 6c.): '*Quando aliquid dicitur analogice de multis, illud inve-*

nitur secundum propriam rationem in uno eorum tantum, a quo alia deno-minantur.' That does not hold of differentiated denominations in general.

And Cajetan's second condition, (1498: 18, no.12) 'the one thing which is the term of the diverse relationships in analogous names of this type is *one* not merely in concept but numerically', is not satis-fied even by the clear cases of attribution. The fact that the health is Fido's and the condition of the coat is Hugo's does not affect the denominative differentiation or the inter-definition in (1) 'Fido is *healthy*' and (2) 'Hugo's coat is *healthy*'.

The problem here is to break loose from the narrow conditions for analogy of attribution that Cajetan formulated, to ask about dif-ferentiated denominations in general. What characterizes that kind of analogy?

Expressions, otherwise the same in scheme, can differ relation-ally. For instance, 'is truthful' in 'His statements are truthful', may mean 'are all truthful', 'are characteristically truthful', or 'are generally truthful'. The opposition of 'is truthful' to 'true', 'false', 'believed true', 'not believed to be true', and to other meaning-relevant words remains the same; yet the occurrences I mentioned differ relationally in meaning.

'He waters the plants' can mean 'He is in the habit of doing so', 'He is responsible for doing so', or 'He usually does so'. 'Waters the plants' is still within the same predicate scheme: it is still in the same contrast to 'prunes', 'cultivates', 'fertilizes', etc.

Because 'waters' is ambiguous if no explicit modifier or environ-mental factor dominates to indicate whether habitual, role-responsible or merely usual action is involved, it follows that the word *can* be differentiated to each of those meanings. For, of course, *the range of an expression's ambiguity is at least the range of its present potential for differentiation.* (Entrenchment in predicate modes can re-strict ambiguity but can be dislodged to permit further differentia-tion.)

And yet, I would not, on the model of chapter 3, call such dif-ferences of meaning (sense) differences of predicate scheme. There need not be a difference of meaning-relevant words where there is a difference of predicate mode. 'Waters' is in relevant contrast to 'fert-ilizes', 'prunes', 'cleans' and the like in each case. And those words, too, differentiate when substituted for 'waters', to acquire the same relational features that 'waters' possesses in the given environment.

In sum, *all the predicate scheme members, when substituted for a pair of modally differentiated terms, contract the same modal contrast.*

I distinguish predicate schemes from predicate modes. Words can differ in either to a considerable extent independently of the other. *All the (linguistic) meaning differences among same words that do not amount to a difference of meaning-relevant words (predicate scheme) are differences of predicate mode.* And contrasts of mode are contracted by substituted common-scheme members.

There are, in principle, indefinitely many contrast-dependent predicate modes distinguishable through dominance.

Consider an initial list of contrast-dependent predicate modes, commonly contracted from dominant words:

Type 1	Type 2
(1) cause	effect
(2) sign	sympton
(3) disease	syndrome
(4) character	characteristic
(5) characteristic	manifestation
(6) manifestation	indication
(7) activity	capacity
(8) activity	proclivity
(9) proclivity	tendency
(10) tendency	habit
(11) habit	disposition
(12) disposition	function

The list consists of contrast-dependent relatum denominations. If a given term '*t*' denominates something *as* a relatum of Type 1^n (for instance 'piano playing' as a *habit*, Type 2^{10}, as in 'His piano playing was malicious') then, *t* can also denominate something, in some context or another, *as* a relatum of Type 2^n (for instance, piano playing as a *tendency*. Type 1^{10}, in 'His piano playing is not inhibited by his bereavement'.) Another example, if 'dangerous' can denominate a characteristic, it can denominate something manifestive of the characteristic (dangerous look). Some words are remarkably facile, appearing in many (vertically) of these relata-opposed sets; for example, 'brave' man/'brave' deed, 4, 5, 10, 11.

I do not say that *if* there is an *a* that is a relatum type 1^n, then there is a *b* that is a relatum type 2^n, or vice versa. I make no such commitment to *things*. This is a meaning relationship, a contrast of denominations, not a relationship among things denominated or otherwise referred to.

129

The general idea can be stated simply. *There are contrast-dependent predicate modes such that if a given word is dominated to one rather than another, then the same word in some actual or constructable context, is dominated to the other.* And the difference of predicate mode can be formulated with a contrast-dependent pair of distinct words.

Contrast-dependent words are distinct words whose patterns of meaning difference are logically dependent upon and negative counterparts (reciprocals) of one another. They are, like matter–anti-matter, symbiotically in contrast. For instance, in one meaning of 'act', 'act' is contrast-dependent upon 'proclivity', 'ability', and 'tendency', etc. In another meaning it is contrast-dependent upon its meaning difference with 'potency', 'matter', 'form', etc. What 'act' means, in the first case, is opposed to what 'potency' means, and 'act' is co-applicable with 'form' in opposition to 'matter'. The list of modes, earlier, is of this sort.

Where distinct words are contrast-dependent (like 'matter/form'), (a) nothing can satisfy the one predicate without actually being different from and opposed to anything bearing the contrast-dependent predicate, and (b) you cannot *learn* that meaning of the one word without learning it as opposed to *what is meant* by the contrast-dependent word (even though the second word does not have to be mentioned or noticed in the learning process). In effect, you have to learn the two meanings at the same time and in opposition to one another in order to know either.

Verbs exhibit especially clearly the sorts of contrast, both vertically and horizontally, that I listed, above. 'He *shakes*' may indicate *effect* rather than *cause, symptom* rather than *sign, disease* rather than *syndrome, indication* rather than *manifestation, proclivity* rather than *activity*, or vice versa.

Every predicate is *determinable* with respect to predicate modes (inherence modes) though not every predicate is susceptible to the same modes as every other. For example, two different words may be determinable as to whether activity or disposition, or both, is meant, but perhaps only one may be determinable to 'causes F' *rather than* 'manifests F', the other having nothing to do with such a relationship at all.

Very many predicates, including most verbs, adjectives and adverbs, are indifferent in at least two dimensions: (a) as to whether a momentary appearance only ('looks F', 'seems F' or 'seems F'ly') or an abiding dispositional quality is attributed ('That paint not only looks red, it is red') and (b) as to whether 'looks F' or 'really is F' or both 'looks F and really is F' is meant. Thus, 'apparent/real' and 'momentary/dispositional' are contrast-*dependent* predicate dimensions within which practically all modifiers are indifferent.

The contrast-dependent feature of the modes is the 'a rather than b' opposition: any word that, being dominated, exhibits the one feature *rather than* the other (for any pair of features listed or generated to satisfy the opposition conditions mentioned), can also be dominated to exhibit the *other* rather than the former. Lastly, any word that *can* be dominated to one rather than another of a contrast-dependent n-tuple of inherence modes must (unless already entrenched) in order to be unambiguous, be dominated to one.

Def V–1: Denominative analogy: T^1 and T^2 are denominatively analogous (given the usual complete environments, etc.) just in case (i) T^1 and T^2 are differentiated, (ii) related in meaning, and (iii) T^1 and T^2 are both denominations or one is.

3   PREDICATE MODES AND INHERENCE RELATIONS

I speculate briefly that predicate modes are contrasts of inherence. Suppose there are two kinds of inherence relations (predicables): (a) *intrinsic* (being identical with, being the same thing as, being the essence of, being essential to, being constitutive of, compositive of, being part of, etc.) and (b) *extrinsic* (being a sign of, symptom of, incident of, disposition of, appearance of, manifestation of, cause of, etc.) *All inherence contrasts that can be expressed with distinct words in our natural language, whether of intrinsic or extrinsic modes, can be expressed through differentiation of same words.* And all sortals can have more than one predicate mode, can express inherence contrasts, while having the same predicate scheme.

Although *some* inherence relation is necessary for any predication at all, mode and scheme are logically independent in this respect: (a) words with the same schemes may be in different modes and (b) words with unrelated schemes, even different words, may be in the same predicate mode. However, I have not determined whether schemes restrict modes, though I suspect so, or whether contrast of mode can induce a contrast of scheme, though I doubt it.

Univocity requires not only sameness (or inclusion) of predicate schemes but also sameness of predicate mode (sameness of the inherence relations(s) of what is attributed). Any difference, either of scheme or mode, makes a difference of meaning. If 'He trembles' means 'He does it all the time' as distinct from 'He has a tendency to', then 'trembles' is differentiated even though *not* with respect to its contrasts with {shake, quiver, shudder, shiver, quake}. One can reassure oneself on the point by considering the invalidity of arguments in which the mode of inherence of a pivotal term is allowed to vary: 'People with Parkinson's shake; Jones has Parkinson's; therefore, Jones is shaking.'

Some inherence modes are entrenched; for instance 'is' recurs as 'exists', 'is identical with' or 'is characterized by' rather than 'represents' ('That's a hat'). That is simply a modification of inertia; instead of tending to recur in the same meaning as any one picked out for reference elsewhere in the corpus, words tend to recur in certain *typical* meanings (modes), unless dominated.

4   DOES THIS THEORY INVERT THE TRADITIONAL CLASSIFICATION OF ANALOGY?

Some students of the classical theory may think that what I have called *denominative analogy* (with the exception of the attributional analogies where one term is definable as signifying a causal, etc., relation to the significatum of the same term in another occurrence) is really classical analogy of proportionality because it involves sameness of *res significata* and difference of *modus significandi*, the key features of terms analogous by proper proportionality (Ross 1958: ch4; McInerny 1964, in Ross 1971:75–96). For, what I have called denominative analogy, in many cases but not all, involves sameness of predicate schemes and difference of predicate modes.

On the other hand, what I called *analogy of proportionality* in chapter 4 is said to violate the classical condition for sameness of *res significata* and difference of *modus significandi*, because my theory requires difference of predicate scheme membership (at least a difference of intrascheme contrast), whereas the predicate modes of two analogous occurrences may be the same. And so, it may be argued, this theory, while keeping the same names, actually inverts the traditional classification.

The comparison of same predicate scheme to same *res significata*, although inviting, is misleading. So is the comparison of difference of predicate mode with difference of *modus significandi*. The *modus significandi* differences contemplated in the classical theory, (for example the difference in the mode of knowing for a man and a cow) are great enough to create a difference of *predicate scheme*: for the meaning-relevant words for 'knows' in 'Plato knows the relationships among the great forms' and 'Bossie knows there are flies on her back' are not the same. Therefore, a difference of *modus significandi*, as understood by Aquinas, is sufficient to create a difference of predicate schemes. It follows that difference of predicate schemes is not the same as difference of *res significata*.

The two theories, the classical and the present one, do not divide the key meaning elements in the same way. Sameness of *res significata* is not congruent with sameness of predicate schemes; and sameness of *modus significandi* is not congruent with sameness of predicate mode.

5   ATTRIBUTIONAL ANALOGY WITHIN THE NEW THEORY

Although not every attributional analogy satisfies the first conditions I sketch (because some additionally involve metaphor or proportionality as well), they can be the more easily recognized against a background of simple exemplars.

I employ *analogous by attribution*, more broadly than Cajetan employed the cognate expression, to mean: *interdefinable, differentiated same words, one of which has a predicate mode that is contrast-dependent upon the predicate mode of the other*. For instance, 'That writer is brilliant' and 'That book is brilliant'. The differentiated pair 'brilliant' may stand in *disposition-manifestation* contrast, or an *inherent quality– ability-to-produce-that-quality* contrast, although the predicate schemes remain the same.

Thus analogy of attribution has two analyses: the traditional notion, developed by Aristotle, Aquinas and Cajetan, described in section 1, above, and the much broader 'interdefinable same words whose predicate modes are reciprocals of one another'.

Perhaps the latter should be called 'reciprocal denominative analogy', or 'analogy of reciprocal modes', or the like, to keep it unconfused with the traditional analogy based upon relations of causation and signification. Still, the traditional attribution cases are included within the broader group and that, in turn, within the generic 'denominative analogy' (differentiated denominations).

I have subdivided the broad class of denominative analogy into

(a) attribution, (b) ascription, (c) ascriptive attribution, and (d) representational denomination. Depending upon one's purposes, one might want to distinguish other kinds of denominative analogy: (1) *analogy of natural attribution*, the use of the same words for things naturally related: able performance/able performer; agile leap/agile person; (2) *analogy by restriction*: use of 'omnipotence' for a restricted sphere of absolute power – 'The energy czar is omnipotent'; (3) *analogy by generalization*: use of a word for anything with qualities *like* its other conditions of application: necrosis (death of part of the body, as of a bone) – the gradual and revolting decay of anything, e.g. the environment, the society; (4) *analogy by extended negation*: 'fresh' applied where it satisfies only the newness conditions – 'fresh paint', 'fresh start', 'fresh news'. But these phenomena seem to be by-products of the more general kinds of denominative analogy, the rest of which are described briefly in what follows.

6 ASCRIPTIVE ANALOGY

Some expressions, to be unambiguous, have to be applied from a definite point of view, either explicit or implied. 'Insensibly' for instance: 'He spoke insensibly' – from *his* point of view, from the author's, or some neutral point of view? Similarly for 'He spoke nonsensically'.

Differing points of reference, supplied by the context (sometimes merely by the word order), can induce meaning differences. So, words that are determinable in these respects, to be unambiguous, require a semantic vantage from dominating expressions: 'Unhappily, he graduated'; 'He graduated unhappily'. 'He suffered from a heavy burden but did not feel it', has a different sense on the supposition that the evaluation (via 'suffered', 'heavy' and 'burden') is from some reportorial point of view (as may be found in Dickens) rather than from the point of view of the subject, 'He'.

Shifts in supposition during an argument can create fallacious changes of meaning. 'Jesus was God, Jesus died on the cross; whatever dies on a cross, has died; therefore, God has died.'[9] Contextual contrast can account for whether a word occurs in personal, material or simple supposition (modes of reference); and those differences are meaning differences for the word. Whether 'man' is used to refer to John, to the word 'man' or to the species 'man' makes a meaning difference that can affect the validity of an argument and the truth of what is said. (Actually, it is meaning-difference that makes supposition difference, not vice versa.) Supposition differences are brought about by verbal dominance. So, we know the dominance phenomenon has something important to do with reference as well as the meaning.

It has too long gone unchallenged that what words 'man' concatenates with acceptably (e.g. 'is a species', 'is endangered', 'has three letters', 'is not an individual') *depends* upon what it stands for (supposits for, or refers to). Is it not obvious that what 'man' stands for is affected (perhaps, determined) by what words it concatenates with (in a given environment)? It is time to disentangle 'reference' and 'standing for' from some kind of labeling and consider it as another mode of linguistic meaning.

7 ASCRIPTIVE ATTRIBUTION

The two kinds of denomination already described interact to produce such pairs as 'thoughtful person/thoughtful gesture', 'deliberate act/deliberate decision', 'weary gesture/weary man', 'weary person/weary glance', 'careless step/careless person', and so forth. They involve the *ascription* of mental or internal states from some vantage or another along with analogy of attribution, applying the same word in reciprocal predicate modes.

8 REPRESENTATIONAL DENOMINATION

Another kind of denominative analogy is peculiar in that the differentiating relationship is 'x *represents* y', or similar relations (like, 'x *is an example of* y', 'x is a *picture* of y').

Plato, of course, recognized that the images of the forms would bear the same names as the forms, but in a different sense of the terms, and that parallel differentiation would be repeated with images of images.[10] And Aristotle and Aquinas observed that 'man' for a picture is equivocal with 'man' for Socrates.[11] Further, Boethius not only stated that the real and the pictured man do not fall under one genus, and therefore bear the name 'man' equivocally, but generalized: 'everything that is *in a subject* is predicated *about its subject* equivocally' ('*omne quod est in subjecto aequivoce de subjecto dicitur*');[12] to say *about* Smith 'he's human' is to equivocate relatively to what Smith *is,* a human.

135

Consider a simple case, where a teacher explaining a painting says, 'Look at the man's hat', in contrast to a social cynic criticizing a neighbor, 'Look at the man's hat'. The occurrences of 'hat' are different in meaning. To be a hat in the first case, the marks in the picture need only *represent* a hat (not even look like one) and certainly are not worn on anyone's head. Usually, (but not always) in the other sort of case, the referent must *be* a hat.[13]

The contrast-dependent relations – representation/represented, picture/pictured, image/imaged – exhibit characteristic *entrenchment*. The names for things represented, imaged or pictured, can occur denominatively as the name of the representation, image or picture. But such words are not 'ambiguous unless explicitly dominated', as with many of the other predicate modes.

In the terminology of Platonism, which survived through Aristotle's works and into Aquinas', anything that can be said to *participate* in another, can be characterized by some of the same words (analogously differentiated) that apply to the other. Thus Aquinas says the sensitive powers of man can be called 'rational' not 'by essence' but 'by participation', as Aristotle had observed in *Ethics*, 1, 13 (Aquinas, *Ia IIae*, 50, 4c).

Nowadays we customarily call a judge 'the court' and designate a place at a conference table and the occupant thereof as 'The United States', 'IBM', and the like. Similarly, the arguments of the appellant's lawyer are called the appellant's arguments. So the characteristics of the representative are imputed, in same words, to the represented, and vice versa. That happens, too, when the *statements* of the occupant at the conference table are said to be the statements of The United States, the philosophy department, and so forth. Antonomasia has denomination as its chief mechanism.

9 PARONYMY

Paronymy: is it analogy or like analogy? In Latin, *medicina sana* and *corpus sanum* are permissible, with no more than the gender change required for agreement with the noun, while in English, 'healthful', the sense in *medicina sana*, should not be used to render '*sanum*' in '*sanum corpus*' but rather, 'healthy'. And '*sanus*' and '*sana*' are paronyms in Latin while 'healthy' boy and 'healthy' girl in English are not. *Paronymy in one language ('healthy', 'healthful') is analogy ('sana medicina', 'sana complexio') in another.*

Paronyms are morphologically variant (and, for the most part meaning related, but not univocal) n-tuples derived (synchronically) from a common root. In Latin, the conjugation of a verb or the declension of a noun produces such meaning-related n-tuples derived (synchronically) from a common root. (So most of Aquinas' examples of analogy were actually paronyms.) In English, plurals, tense endings, ('tensing', 'tensed') and predicate mode endings (-able, -tion, -ness, etc.) produce paronyms from the root.

Def. V-2: paronymy is morphological variation upon a common root, in law-like correlation with meaning differences; for example 'explain', 'explanation', 'explicable' and 'explicability', and, in Latin, explaneo and explanatio.

As D. P. Henry (1967:62) indicated, *denominative* is the Latin adverb in 'things named paronymously'. He quotes Boethius' *Commentary on the Categories of Aristotle.*

Hence all those names are called 'paronyms' which differ from their root-name only by case-determination, i.e. by alteration only. Thus let the root-name be *'justice'*; from this the altered name *'just'* is contrived. Hence, things are paronymously named whenever they are called by a name which derives from a root-name, and differ from the root-name merely by case determination (*solo casu*), that is, by a name-alteration alone.

Boethius used the words *'justitia'* and *'justus'* which, of course, differ not merely in *case* endings. (Boethius recognized the broader phenomenon but did not choose the right word for it.) So one can easily see how the discussion of denominative analogy turns toward questions about paronyms. For one thing, the Latin word *'denominativa'* is rendered in Henry's English translations by 'paronyms', a word, he points out, used by French grammarians to refer to 'near homonyms having some fairly close resemblance in sound or spelling'.

My characterization of paronymy, as morphological variation upon a common root in law-like correlation with (denominative) meaning differences, is broader, more accurate and includes the classical cases as well. And it allows me to extend the descriptive scope of the analogy hypotheses.

Evidently, there is a relationship between paronymy and analogy. Analogous words in one language often correspond to paronyms in another. So, it is inevitable that we should ask whether the meaning relationships among paronyms are the same as or paral-

137

lel to the the relationships among same words. In some respects they are not the same; there are no univocal paronyms; and the meaning difference among meaning-related paronyms, at least in part, corresponds to *denominative* differences for *same* words (see first part of this chapter). In fact, *all meaning-related paronyms from the same root are denominatively analogous to one another.* Nevertheless, there are homonymous paronyms (merely equivocal ones), analogous paronyms, metaphorical paronyms and denominatively analogous paronyms but not univocal ones. However, paronyms can be *nearly* synonymous in a context, just as distinct words can be nearly synonymous. For example, 'prayers' and 'orisons' are distinct, non-paronymous words similar in meaning. And the paronyms, 'quote'/'quotation', 'concept'/'conception', 'percept'/'perception', 'move'/'movement', are sometimes nearly synonymous.

When I classify distinct paronyms from the same root as either merely equivocal, analogous by proportionality, metaphorical, denominatively analogous or figurative in comparison to one another, I apply the analogy *classification* to phenomena that do not satisfy a necessary condition ('same terms') for those technical labels (see Definitions in chapters 3, 4 and 5). (That would be enough, on Goodman's account to make that classification *metaphorical.* But not on the account of metaphor I have offered.)

On my account, the classification (except for 'univocal') applied to paronyms differentiates, adopting truth conditions closely related to, but not the same as, those given in chapters 4 and 5 for its various predicates, and serves an equivalent explanatory function. It is, therefore, analogous by *proportionality* (but is not metaphorical; see the other conditions for metaphor, chapter 4).

'To plow' is to 'a plow' as 'to wait' is to 'a waiter', namely, denominatively analogous, where the predicate 'denominatively analogous' is, itself, *analogous by proportionality* when substituted between the two pairs. Two proportional relations make up the above proportionality statement: the first between same words, and the second between morphological variants of a common root, yet both pairs are said to be 'denominatively analogous', thus differentiating that predicate. Similarly, the whole classification for the analogy theory applies to paronyms by analogy of proportionality.

The classification (and its component schemes) undergoes the minimal adjustment of affinities and oppositions that is required for acceptable utterances about the new realm of application.

For instance, to apply {univocal, merely equivocal, equivocal, analogous by proportionality, denominatively analogous, analogous by attribution, representationally analogous, simply metaphorical, figurative, etc.} to paronyms, 'univocal' has to be dropped from the classification and the 'same-term' presupposition is suppressed and replaced by an *explanatory equivalent*, 'is morphologically variant on the same root as . . . and differs in meaning in a law-like way from . . .'.

It is not that there cannot be univocal distinct paronyms because, by definition, distinct paronyms are not same words. For that would exclude 'merely equivocal', 'analogous by attribution', 'denominatively analogous' and 'analogous by proportionality' as well.

The reason there cannot be univocal *distinct* paronyms is that if *a* and *b* are *distinct* paronyms from a common root, then *a* and *b* differ morphologically and that difference is in law-like correlation with difference of *meaning*. That follows from the definition of 'distinct paronyms'. So, distinct paronyms differ from one another in meaning. Therefore they cannot be univocal. Yet they can be near synonyms on occasion, as illustrated above.

Are the other analogy phenomena paralleled among paronyms?

(1) There are merely equivocal paronyms. For instance, 'lay' and 'layer', according to *Webster's International Dictionary*, come from a common root, although in certain pairs of contexts there is no synonym of one that is substitutable as a near synonym of the other: (i) 'He *lay* upon the floor' and (ii) 'His music was constructed in *layers* of tones'. That is, 'layer' as 'levels' is unrelated in meaning to 'lay'. Of course, (iii) 'There were three *layers* of varnish on the painting' would be related to 'lay' in (iv) 'The painter *lay* paint on the walls'. A common expression, 'coat', denominatively differentiated, is substitutable in (iii) and (iv): 'The painter *lay* (coated) paint on the wall'; and 'There were two *layers* (coats) of paint on the wall'. The paronyms 'lay' and 'layer' in (iii) and (iv) do not satisfy the conditions for mere equivocation: there is at least one common near synonym (denominatively differentiated) that does not become merely equivocal or alter the meanings already in the context. The paronyms 'lay' and 'layer' in (iii) and (vi) are analogous by proportionality as well as analogous denominatively (paronymously, if you like). But 'lay' and 'layer' in (i) and (ii) are merely equivocal.

Further, 'action' is a morphological variant upon a common root

139

with 'act'. In 'Where's the *action*?', there is little overlap with 'act' in 'The clowns performed their act'. I do not know a substitutable near synonym. Similarly, if 'pen' and 'penned' morphologically have a common root, then in 'He wrote with a pen' and 'He penned the pigs', they would be merely equivocal paronyms.

(2) There are paronyms analogous by proportionality, as the lay/ layer example (iii) and (iv) illustrate. So too, in 'That man is *white*' and 'The victim *whitened*'. 'Whitened' is a paronym for 'white' (and vice-versa, because that relationship is symmetrical and the morphological differences indicate meaning differences symmetrically, as well), and is equivocal in that 'whitened' means 'turned white'. 'Turned white' is compatible with 'is white' in that a white man can turn white; but if *white*, the stem, had the same meaning in 'whiten' that it has in 'is white', nothing that is white could *turn* white. So we may conclude that because both statements might be true of the same individual, the predicate schemes for 'white' and 'whiten' do not have the same members. 'Whiten' is not, I think, metaphorical in relation to 'white' but is analogous by proportionality, just as 'white' in 'white man' is equivocal but not merely equivocal (rather analogous by proportionality but not metaphorical) with 'white' in a standard list of color names for painters' basic hues.

(3) Sometimes paronyms are denominatively analogous. Between 'light' and 'lighten', as between 'fly' and 'flyer', sometimes the one difference is that between 'to *be x*' (light) and 'to *make* something to be *x*' (lighten), or between 'to *F*' (fly) and 'to *be* a thing that *does F*' (flier), where (as in attributional analogy) the meaning of the one paronym is explicable in terms of the *significatum* of a distinct paronym.

(4) Thus many paronyms are analogous by attribution. One need only notice that meaning pattern to discover them everywhere in discourse. The fireplace smokes – so it is a smoker; the person drives a car – so he is a driver. Just as 'drive' and 'driver' are denominative paronyms and 'drive' can have metaphorical occurrences, so also can 'driver', in 'Smith is a driver'.

The manufacture of end-product, function, purpose, means, instrument, activity, disposition, characteristic, inclination, (and the like) expressions out of simple verbs, and the manufacture of verb expressions out of function (etc.) expressions is displayed virtually everywhere in extended discourse.

The *further* differentiation of such expressions e.g. 'driver' ('one who puts himself *under great pressure'* – another metaphor) is ubiquitous and has already been described in chapter 4.

Paronyms, denominatively analogous to a common word, can be merely equivocal. For example, 'fryer', a chicken that is suitable for frying, and 'fryer', a person whose activity is to fry foods, are both denominatively analogous to 'fry' but merely equivocal.

(5) Paronyms can be differentiated metaphorically, for example, 'fryer' for person whose characteristic way of cooking is to fry (rather than bake), and 'fryer' for a person who characteristically solves problems by castigating his subordinates. Thus, 'He's a fryer' (castigator) can be metaphorical in relation to 'He's a fryer' (a kind of short-order cook). And one could imagine ghoulish persecutors might refer to certain martyrs as 'fryers'. The metaphorical, analogous and denominative relationships of paronyms are analytically equivalent (see chapter 8 for a development of that idea) to the same-word relationships I have described. So, the analogy theory explains its own extension by analogy from same words to paronyms.

6

Figurative discourse

The meanings of salient words in figurative discourse can be hypothetically constructed as a shortest sequence of stepwise adaptations from typical same words in nonfigurative discourse. The steps of differentiation are those already explained: proportionality, metaphor, denomination and paronymy.

The 'double differentiation' cases that involve both metaphor and analogy (or paronymy) are characteristic of figurative discourse. They are its semantic signature.

'To be used figuratively' and 'figurative occurrence' have three different senses in various contexts that follow. A word is said to be used figuratively, (1) if its being used in a certain way is constitutive of some classical figure of speech, e.g. 'governed' in 'He governed himself and his province', to create zeugma; (2) denominatively, for every word constitutive in some figure of speech (e.g. alliteration) and (3) the technical usage developed in this chapter for 'occurring figuratively', 'is a figurative occurrence' and the like: a word occurs figuratively just in case it occurs constitutively in figurative or heightened (as identified by likeness to paradigms in poetry and literature) discourse and its shortest path of hypothetical construction (by meaning adaptation) from a typical, not-merely-equivocal same word outside figurative discourse involves both analogy (or paronymy) and metaphor.

Hypothetical construction is successive domination that generates one sense from another. Different frame-expressions, that do not cause mere equivocation, successively differentiate a word from non-figurative discourse (in a typical occurrence) until an occurrence univocal with the figurative occurrence has been generated. Such a sequence counts as a correct hypothetical construction provided there is no other typical non-figurative (and not merely equivocal) same word from which the figurative sense can be constructed by step-wise adaptation (a) without a metaphorical differentiation in the succession, or (b) without one of the other kinds of analogy or paronymy in addition to metaphor, or (c) in a shorter sequence of steps.

You may wonder why I ignore actual generation of meaning when we know perfectly well that figurative discourse involves diachronic derivation. Why ignore speaker intentions when figurative discourse is characteristically (but not always) the result of speakers' intentions? Perhaps even more puzzling, as I explain 'hypothetical construction', the origin of the hypothetical construction can be an occurrence that the figurative speaker would certainly not have in mind.

I am not concerned to explain the psychology of figurative discourse or to provide a technique for discovering figurative meanings. Rather, I show (1) that figurative expressions (whose meanings we know) stand in discernable, atomizable, meaning relations to equivocal (but not merely equivocal) same expressions occurring in typically non-figurative discourse; (2) that many standard figures of speech do not logically involve differentiation at all and that many others require only denominative analogy and that only one or two actually require metaphor as a logical element; (3) that it is the interaction of figures of speech with double differentiation (metaphor plus analogy or paronymy) that (semantically) typifies paradigm cases of heightened discourse.

The most complex figurative expressions, for which we do not even have names as far as I know, involve not only double differentiation but also various modes of reference (and supposition). Examples of complex reference are: (a) use of the word 'phoenix' not for the mythical bird but for the *idea* of such bird, and (b) the use of a person's name, Ulysses, for the adventure he had (*Odyssey*) while connoting the stationary adventure of the same kind in another story of that name (Joyce's *Ulysses*).

Reference, supposition and the ways verbal environments dominate the modes of reference are matters for a separate inquiry, theoretically subsequent to the present one. But I do point out that modes of reference, like modes of inherence, are regularly environmentally determined and are not simply creatures of intention. Mere intention cannot determine the reference of 'man' in 'Man has three letters'. In some respects reference is determined by meaning and, no doubt, in other respects, vice versa.

Because there is so much that needs to be said about reference and how reference can be differentiated and piggy-backed, analogously to the way that predicative meaning and predicate mode can be dominated and differentiated, there is an inevitable anemia to this sketch of figurative discourse. For the whole point of heightened discourse is to employ syntactic and semantic organization and reference and allusion to create rhythm and cognitive overtones that are discernably out of the ordinary, expressive of deep feeling and that evocatively affect the hearer's *understanding*.

Like music, figurative discourse has semantic dimensions and a metric-rhythmic dimension, connected with actual or potential sound, steps in thought, complexity of images or, in extreme cases, the visual appearance of words on a page. The total effect involves both the semantic and metric–rhythmic dimensions. Essential to the semantic dimensions are the complexities of reference as well as the complexities of scheme and mode adaptation which, alone, are examined here.

One of the reasons why I am not concerned with the authentic biography by which some figurative meaning developed from a non-figurative one is that such developments are usually unrecoverable, even in principle. First, there is no way to know which word occurrences a given author adapted; we would have to guess at the *type* of occurrence, when we can get along better without guessing at all. Secondly, the meaning relationships, like a pile of magnets into which one has been forcibly inserted, are rearranged into a structure from which the earlier structure may be unrecoverable because the system of oppositions and affinities of meaning may have adjusted.

That seems likely after a new figurative device is actually achieved by Shakespeare, John Fowles or Faulkner and has become widely understood. Retroactively it affects the way the 'prior' meaning relationships now appear to have been. The meaning relations of English words, their affinities, oppositions and unconnectedness form a dynamic system that, after inconsequential verbal oddities produced by careless and deviant speakers, and after significant wrenching of word affinities and oppositions by ambitious writers (like Patrick White) who put words together at the extremes of intelligibility, more or less suddenly metamorphose after a critical disturbance, so that intelligibility and regularity are achieved. *There may be no path left* from a recently invented figurative use of a word to the non-figurative occurrences that *actually* precipitated it. There will still be, in the basic semantic relations of analogy, metaphor, denomination and paronymy, *semantic pathways* from the figurative occurrence to non-figurative occurrences, pathways that are hypothetical linguistic constructions, simulations of adaptation by which the figurative meaning is related to one or more non-figurative tokens. These are not pathways of derivation but pathways of semantic circulation.

I use a conventional and typically loose list of classical figures of speech, classical not only in their antiquity but even their names. A person who can identify those devices can, by analogy, recognize newborn devices for which we have no names but from which we can construct even more complex figures.

When we take modes of reference into account, there is no discernable limit to the complexity of the meaning relation between a figurative occurrence and some nonfigurative same word. There is only a practicability limit, at any given time, to what degree of novelty is intelligible and accessible, (as is true with painting, sculpture, music, and architecture). And accessibility depends upon experience. For people used to watching television programs with background music while simultaneously listening to radio news or music programs, the compositions of Charles Ives may be less formidable than they were to his contemporaries.

Symbolic discourse 'Symbolic discourse' is a real, pragmatic dimension of communication that typically has figurative discourse as its vehicle but need not.

When I talk about utterances functioning symbolically, I have in mind something like what Tillich described as an important, indeed central part of religious communication.[1] In fact Tillich, with considerable justice, considered symbolic utterance to be an integral part of civic and political communication as well. I am not, therefore, talking about some universal but merely referential property of all symbol schemes, as Goodman (1968) employed the notion of 'symbol'. (Goodman's use of 'symbol' is merely equivocal with Tillich's.) To function symbolically discourse, or parts of it, has to *do* something (have a perlocutionary effect). That effect involves a different mode of thought, in which reactions to the arrangement, rhythm, sound, references and emotive associations of the utterance accomplish or *realize* something that Tillich calls 'the presence' of what is symbolized. Surprisingly, we can make sense in a pragmatic way of Tillich's notion that the symbols (words) *participate* in the reality symbolized:[2] They cause a reaction to the symbols

145

that is the same, counterfactually, as the reaction to the thing symbolized and thereby realize, subjectively, the *presence* of what is symbolized.

At the very least, we can consider the 'learned response' to the words, which is 'the same' as the response to the reality symbolized, to *be* the relevant participation of symbols in the reality. I do not think that kind of symbolic reality is necessary for or even characteristic of Judeo-Christian religious discourse, though it may be a sought after response to liturgy among some believers.

In any case, utterances sometimes do function symbolically in the sense that the reactions of the hearer-understanders are noticeably the same as their (expected) reactions to the things symbolized (just as sexual response to a picture may be 'the same as' one's response to the pictured and 'realizes' the 'presence' of what is pictured). But figurative discourse is not necessary for symbolic discourse, though it seems to facilitate that pragmatic effect. And discourse can be figurative without, in Tillich's sense, being symbolic.

Further analysis of the symbolic functioning of utterances lies, like the study of designation (reference and supposition), beyond the horizon of this book. Pragmatic functions are grounded upon pragmatic modes of meaning and in the *effects* words have upon emotions and thoughts. Certainly it is not unreasonable for utterances to realize the presence of the reality symbolized, (as the scream 'I am *furious*' can realize the fury it symbolizes) and that they can evoke responses to the *words* (to the understood utterances) that are 'the same' as those appropriate to the state of affairs (reality) symbolized. The screamed *words* may evoke a response of fear or aggression in a hearer which is the same as his appropriate response to the fury (the state of fury) the words report. As I have said, that is not unreasonable but it is beyond the scope of this book.

2   A HYPOTHETICAL CONSTRUCTION

I sketch a hypothetical, and perhaps artificial, construction, merely assuming that there is not a shorter adaptation pathway between the 'figurative' and the 'non-figurative' occurrences chosen. Let 'They *paddled* the canoe closer to the buoy' be the 'non-figurative' occurrence in a story about Grand Banks fisherman lost in a fog. And let 'The critics *paddled* the directors' be a figurative occurrence, in a poem about a play's closing (by a poet such as Auden or Eliot). One adaptation pathway would be as follows. Denominative differentiation of the name of a process (to paddle) to name an instrument (a paddle). The instrument name for a kind of tool (a paddle) is abstractively differentiated into an instrument not a tool (a ping-pong paddle). Then by metaphor an instrument name for a game (a ping-pong paddle) is made into a name for a *weapon,* so that 'initiates are paddled'. Next, a reverse denomination, where the name for the instrument is differentiated into the name for the process of using the weapon, 'to paddle the initiates'. Finally, by analogy the process name is differentiated abstractively to mean 'punish', in the sense of 'inflict deserved condemnation', so 'the critics paddled and directors' by inflicting deserved castigation. Through this somewhat fanciful sequence, we have adaptations that involve: denomination, metaphor, denomination, and abstraction.

A hypothetical construction that 'generates' one meaning out of another consists in such a pathway of simulated adaptations (to explicitly formulated dominating environments), each of which is one of the analogy, metaphor or paronymy steps.

My general hypothesis is that complex meaning-relatedness can be decomposed into step-wise atomic adaptations (proportionality, simple metaphor, denomination and paronymy) whose structures are ubiquitous and law-like in the corpus of natural language. Figurative occurrences can be similarly decomposed into step-wise adaptations whose salient semantic feature is double differentiation, at least one of which is metaphorical and the other of which often involves paronymy.

Once we construct such complex adaptations (by writing out a few decompositions into atomic adaptations), we gain insight into the infinite polysemy available in natural language and the unlimited expressive power that can be achieved by interplaying variations of reference (supposition, designation), sense, rhythm, predicate schemes, predicate modes and connotation. *No matter how complex the relatedness, if one understands the meaning of the 'final' occurrence, one can map out its step-wise adaptation from any not merely equivocal same word (whose meaning is also known).*

3 METAPHOR AND FIGURES OF SPEECH

Figures of speech are objective linguistic structures, just as analogy, mere equivocation, metaphor and paronymy are. The account of 'linguistically objective metaphor', provided in chapter 4, section 4, applies *mutatis mutandis* to the other phenomena mentioned. So it is natural to ask whether classical figures of speech always involve metaphor and, if not, whether any, other than metaphor, do.

We find different answers with different accounts of metaphor. For instance, Aristotle thought metonymy always involves metaphor (*Poetics*, 1457b, 7ff). Nelson Goodman (1968: 81–84) not only shared that view but also proposed a mapping of evaluative classifications which can be moved as a unit up or down a scale (created by a related classification used to range the phenomena 'normally') and can thus be 'literal' or 'normal' (as against 'figurative' or 'fanciful'), or 'hyperbolic', or 'overstated' (as against 'understated'), or can be distorted at one or the other end ('overemphatic') or otherwise a caricature, and can even be *inverted,* so as to create irony.

Indeed we do shift classifications relative to one another, in that way. But Goodman's alternative mappings, to create the modes of metaphor, do not usually satisfy my conditions for metaphor (though they do satisfy Goodman's conditions); some are, relatively to other 'normal' occurrences, merely analogous.

The difference from Goodman's account is not that I deny that a predicate schema acquires a new realm in such figures of speech, or that a schema may be reoriented (the realm remaining the same but the ranges being reallocated), or that there is a difference in the intra-predicate contrast relationships from one sort of application to another. The difference is that those features are not enough for metaphor; they do not exclude analogy. And regarding what I call 'analogy' to be the residue of 'dead metaphors' is unconvincing because it fails to explain the endless polysemy in natural language, of which metaphor is only one species. There has to be some asymmetrical meaning-relatedness for metaphor and Goodman's theory does not account for it.

I do not, of course, mean that hyperbolic predicates cannot be metaphorical; just the opposite: 'The mouse *trampled* his opponent in the dust.' Understatement and overstatement may similarly involve metaphor. But that there is metaphor is not assured merely by the shift of scale of evaluation (or grading) in comparison to a 'usual' or 'normal' application, as Goodman conjectures (1968:81). And that is because application of words to 'new' realms or to reallocated ranges in an 'old' realm is, as I have shown in chapter 4, incidental to metaphor and often common to analogy (for instance, abstractive analogy, as in the 'carry' examples).

Of the classical figures of speech only personification logically involves metaphor. Some of the others require analogy, particularly denomination. Some are indifferent to differentiation, sometimes have no differentiating effect and sometimes have such an effect, depending upon what words are involved. And others never have a differentiating effect (when compared with typical contexts where the same words occur and are not part of figures of speech).

In particular, Goodman (1968:81) mistakenly treats synecdoche, metonymy, and antonomasia as modes of metaphor. Those figures of speech can be realized by denomination, paronymy and proportionality, without metaphor. Goodman's account of 'expression' in art as 'metaphorical 'exemplification' will have a different (and I think more plausible) interpretation when 'metaphor' is differently conceived.

Consequently, I do not accept Goodman's classification of the modes of metaphor. Instead, in chapter 4 I suggested a different basis for a classification of modes of simple metaphor, namely, variation along two axes of simulation (the different 'exclusion' criteria and the different 'implication' relations).

Syntactical figures of speech Many of the standard figures of speech are syntactic devices: (a) *tmesis,* separating elements of a compound word by an intervening word, *'to us ward';* (b) *syncope,* the elision of a vowel or syllable for rhythmic reasons, 'e're'; (c) *synchysis,* interlocked word order, 'and having to the enemy lied, gallantly rearward deplaned'; (d) *polysyndeton,* the use of extra conjunctions, 'east and west and north and south'; (e) *inconcinnity,* deliberate unbalanced phrase rhythm; (f) *hyperbation,* the transposition of words from normal order, 'the hills among' for 'among the hills'; (g) *chiasmus,* repetition in reverse order for rhetorical effect, e.g. Pope's 'they all successive and successive rise'; (h) *asyndeton,* omitting ordinary connectives, 'Sighted sub sank same'; (i) *aposiopesis,* leaving a sentence incomplete as if unwilling or unable to complete it, 'I wanted, want to . . .'; (j) *antithesis,* the balancing of sentence structure with contrasted words, 'It was the best of times; it was the worst of times'; (k) *anaphora,* repetition of a word or phrase beginning successive clauses: 'The voice of the Lord', Psalm 29; (l) *anacol-*

uthon, violation of grammatical sequence to concentrate energy, 'Out he went', 'Home at last he came'; (m) *alliteration, 'perpetua pace possitis providebo',* 'malevolent minions of malice'; (n) *assonance,* repeated same sounds, 'home, tome, comb, moan'. None of those syntactical devices presupposes differentiation.

Most of the figures of speech that presuppose arrangements of *word meanings* are also independent of differentiation. I mean that although such figures of speech require arrangements of ideas or meanings (for instance in order of abstraction), they can be accomplished without differentiating any of their component words from typical non-figurative occurrences.

Prolepsis, anticipating questions or objections with answers, ('He shot him dead', 'He wrote himself famous'); *hendiadys,* using two words conjoined ('might and main') for a modified idea ('all his strength'), *crescendo,* using successive longer and mightier words for effect; *climax,* successive intensifying words ('He left, concealed himself, evaded observation and escaped'), need no differentiation. So also: *litotes,* double negative or understated assertion, 'fact of no small importance'; *hysteron–proteron,* hyperbation inverting normal thought order, 'Is your father well? Is he alive?'; and *praeteritio,* assertion under expressed intention to omit: 'I won't mention his execrable personal habits and unnatural affections'.

In fact, among the large traditional classification of figures of speech, only eight, or so, typically involve differentiating contexts; only a few of those *logically presuppose* differentiation and only one, metaphor. The typically differentiating contexts include: zeugma, personification, euphemism, antonomasia, paronomasia, oxymoron, hyperbole, metonymy and synecdoche.

Some of those figures of speech *require* differentiating contexts, compared to typical contexts which do not share the structure that constitutes the figure of speech. For example, *synecdoche* (part for whole, whole for part – 'roofs of the city were dark', 'marbles gleamed in twilight') and *metonymy* (attribute used to name thing, 'crown' for 'king', 'bigmouth' for 'indiscreet person') *at least* involve analogous denomination. (I think it was the obvious differentiation that misled Aristotle and Goodman to regard metonymy and synecdoche as inherently metaphorical.) Those figures of speech cannot be realized without differentiating words from the meanings they have in *some* typical contexts that do not satisfy the figurative structure and to which they are related by denominative analogy.

150

Hyperbole is differentiating but not necessarily metaphorical. For 'He's an Einstein' to be true, when the individual is not literally the bearer of that name, the predicate has to be moved downward on a comparative scale, just as Goodman explains, (1968:81). Yet that does not guarantee that 'is an Einstein' is metaphorical.

Antonomasia, using a title or epithet as a proper name, requires denominative differentiation. That is how such names as Carpenter, Smith, Driver, and even Pedersen, came about; and to turn 'thief' into a name, as in 'Look, thief, we want to escape' also requires denominative differentiation. A fine example of antonomasia is the name given a Morman by his four wives in different towns: 'Seldom Seen Smith'.

Personification requires metaphor. 'The cats figured out that I had fish'; 'Trees, tell me what you dream in winter'; 'With skeletal hands the trees wrote tales of terror on the slated sky'.

Zeugma, too, requires differentiation. But it does not require metaphor. It is usually explained as the kind of structure where an adverb modifies two verbs or a verb governs two nouns when it is directly only logically connected with one, 'the modifying or governing being conceded to *alter* meaning slightly' [italics added], as applied to the second. (Notice how someone had sensed the *dominance.*) That device allows more differentiated meanings than there are tokens of the word and allows pronouns to function in place of differentiated words: 'You have your way and I'll go mine', (the kind of examples John Fowles (1977) used, see chapter 2, section 5, above). Other examples, 'He opened his door and his heart to the homeless', 'He governed himself and his province'. You can easily see that zeugma logically requires differentiation because it is a relation *between* word meanings and requires the number of same-word meanings to exceed the number of actual word occurrences. (So, too, with syllepsis.) The way the differentiation is achieved is, of course, quite elementary under the general principles of the analogy theory. You simply surround a word with a pair of differentially *dominating* completion expressions in a frame where either would be acceptable alone (where there is no logical or semantic exclusion of both together had you repeated the differentiated word); then just leave out the second occurrence or use a pronoun. This figure of speech is an important part of the *proof* that verbal dominance exists and is an *explanatory* linguistic structure.

However, *oxymoron,* the use of 'contradictory' or 'incongruous' words in the same phrase, '*felix culpa*', 'proud humility', 'deceptive truth', 'laborious idleness', 'weary ease', 'mannered ugliness' (John Updike 1966: 403), need not differentiate and usually does not, but might. *Paronomasia* (pun) in the cases where it consists of 'the same word with different senses' logically requires differentiation, usually with more meanings than occurrences. In the cases where it consists of different words having similar sounds, used in opposition to one another (e.g. 'conceived conceits') to provide antithetical force, there is usually denomination but need not be differentiation.

Thus zeugma, personification, euphemism, antonomasia, paronomasia (in one sense), hyperbole, metonymy and synecdoche all require an environment that is differentiating from typical contexts that do not structurally realize the respective figures of speech. But not all require metaphor.

Most startling of all, *only personification requires metaphor. All other figures of speech can be realized without metaphorical differentiation,* despite the weight of opinion to the contrary. ('Personification' here also includes the reverse classification of persons as if they were machines, miscellaneous objects etc., and of the living as non-living, and vice versa.)

Why then do I propose that figurative discourse is inherently metaphorical and insist that there is something special that only double differentiation involving metaphor can explain? The answer is that 'heightened discourse', 'figurative *discourse'*, as contrasted with isolated figures of speech, involves iterated differentiation from which metaphor cannot be eliminated. Furthermore, it typically involves paronymy as well. Heightened discourse can be elementary, like Patrick Henry's 'I have but one lamp by which my feet are guided and that is the lamp of experience' (zeugma with 'guided' functioning metaphorically), or complex, like 'He doth bestride the world like a colossus and we petty men walk under his huge legs and peep about to find ourselves dishonorable graves.'

What we recognize as typically figurative in poetry and drama and dramatic oration is the interaction of metaphor, proportionality, denomination, paronymy, and the other syntactic and semantic devices, especially rhythmic ones, (and new ones invented for the occasion and lacking names) to induce *emotive intensity* both *expressively* and *evocatively*.

Not every part of figurative discourse involves figures of speech (even if you count simile as important); see the line from *Julius*

152

Caesar, i, ii, 224–273, 'If the rag-tag people did not clap and hiss him, according as he pleased and displeased them, as they use to do players in the theatre, I am no true man.' One might, though I do not, regard the *logical* structure, where the evident impossibility of the consequent – ignoring the pun on 'true' – is supposed to guarantee the falsity of the antecedent, as a figure of speech. It's like the Irish expression, 'If Smith is a saint, then there aren't any'.

In any case, not every part of figurative discourse is included in some figure of speech, nor does every figurative element involve metaphor. But the salient *semantic* feature of heightened discourse is metaphor combined with some other kind of differentiation (especially, paronymy). Typically figurative is, 'Your bait of falsehood takes this carp of truth' (*Hamlet,* II, i, 47–86). So also is this from *Othello,* 'And it is thought abroad that twixt my sheets he has done my office.' There is synecdoche of 'twixt my sheets', metonymy of 'my office', resulting domination of 'done', and 'done my office' is metaphorically understood for sexual acts usurped. And see *Coriolanus,* V, iii, 22–67, 'These eyes are not the same I wore in Rome.' 'Wore' is metaphorically differentiated, while 'eyes' differentiates metonymically.

It is not a few figures of speech sprinkled with metaphors that make discourse figurative. Deliberate (skilled) employment of the expressive and evocative *accomplishment* of the discourse (for which the various structures are the means, especially metaphor), makes 'heightened' discourse. Classical figures of speech are at most *indicia* not necessary conditions, for figurative discourse. Still, in the semantic dimension double differentiation is the salient, the semantic signature.

Previous accounts of figures of speech have confused denominative analogy and analogy of proportionality with metaphor and, thus, have described the semantic figures of speech incorrectly, a matter I hope is now clarified.

4   SOME EXAMPLES FROM POETRY

Typically, 'double differentiations' combine metaphor with paronymy. *Apostrophe,* addressing absent objects or persons as present, combines personification (which logically involves metaphor) with other differentiations, frequently paronymy, as in

153

Thomas Hardy's 'Hap', *Wessex Poems and Other Verses*, 1898:

> But not so. How arrives it joy lies slain,
> And why unblooms the best hope ever sown?

'Unblooms' is a paronym of 'blooms' and is used metaphorically of 'hope' as, also, is 'sown' which further involves an implied denomination because 'flowers' is used denominatively of *seeds*.

Combinations of personifications (which always involve metaphor) are very common. For instance, when the inanimate is characterized with predicates for persons whose behaviour it resembles: 'Nature is cruel . . . Nature is stubborn . . . Nature is fickle . . . Nature forgives no debt. . . .' from Matthew Arnold's '*In harmony with Nature . . . to a preacher*'.

Paronymy functions integrally in Matthew Arnold's *Requiescat*, 1853:

> Her cabined, ample spirit
> It fluttered and failed for breath.
> Tonight it doth inherit the vasty hall of death.

The spirit is metaphorically depicted as bird, candle and heart with 'fluttered' and as an animal which 'failed for breath'. 'Spirit' is used metonymically for 'life' and 'she'. 'Inherited' applies metaphorically in the sense of 'naturally succeeded to' and 'death' is personified and applied as a denomination to 'vasty hall'.

The paronym, by the way, is 'cabined' which of course is also metaphorical.

Outright punning (paronomasia) can be found in poetry (Auden):

> Freud did not invent the
> Constipated miser;
>
> Banks have letter boxes,
> Built in their facades,
> Marked *for Night Deposits*

Richard Murphy in the 'The Philosopher and the Birds, in Memory of Wittgenstein at Rosroe' (1974: 6–7), provides gems of paronymy and a number of the typical *double differentiations*. There are some referential devices that those who know Wittgenstein's life will identify.

'He became for a *tenebrous* epoch the stone' [italics added to call attention to the paronymy, 'tenebrous']. 'He clipped with February shears the dead metaphysical foliage'; 'Old in fieldfares fantasies rebelled though annihilated';

He was haunted by gulls beyond omega shade,
His nerve tormented by terrified knots
In pin-feathered flesh. But all folly repeats
Is worth one snared robin his fingers untied.

Undoubtedly particular references are integral to the poem,
'Rosroe' ('But at Rosroe hordes of village cats have massacred his
birds'), 'stone' (philosopher's stone?), 'birds' (He broke prisons,
beginning with words, and at last tamed, by talking, wild birds')[3]
But so are differentiated words, like 'He *becomes* worlds where
thoughts are wings', which, of course, means 'adorns' and not
'turns into'.

Sometimes prose includes phrases of remarkable evocative power
and obvious 'double differentiation': 'The opening Chapter of his
new novel, *Morning, Noon and Night,* cloudy as a polluted pond,
swarms with verbal organisms of his strange engendering' (John
Updike 1966: 403).

Gene Derwood's *Shelter* has these lines, with evident iterated
adaptations (metaphorical):

While people hunt for what can satisfy their wants
There is a watching and a sharp recording,
Both seekers and watchers are the palpitants
And much is said with no deep ferny wording.

'Palpitants' is a paronym for 'palpitate', used here metaphorically
to convey anxiousness and 'wording' a paronym for 'word' used
metaphorically for 'meaning'.

When you leave aside (1) *references* to fictional, legendary, mythical, historical and existing unstoried persons, (places and things),
(2) *structured responses* to other works of art (whether detectable imi-
tations or indetectable quotations, parodies, caricatures, inversions,
permutations, resonances, and the like), (3) the *interaction of the
symbols* (I mean organizing motifs and sensory phenomena) with
one another and from one work to another, and undoubtedly, (4) a
dozen other dimensions of meaning and association that are, in principle at least, within *the conscious control of the artist* (and therefore
form part of the meaning structure to be understood and explained
in literary analysis), we come at last to the veins of linguistic
meaning. And there the structures are quite simple.

When I say that the veins of *linguistic* meaning in figurative discourse have a relatively simple structure and that figurative meanings can be hypothetically constructed from 'typical, non-figurative ordinary meanings' of the same words, I am not offering to diagnose the meanings of passages we do not understand. The explanation discloses *continuities* among meanings we know.

5   CONCLUSION

The veins of linguistic meaning are the analogy structures. The meanings of the words are kept alive by their standing in affinity and opposition of meaning to other same words, relations that are 'circulated' by the analogy phenomena and can be hypothetically constructed as sequences of adaptation to context.

Some poetry presents considerable difficulty of access to the uninitiated. That is not surprising because new music, new novels and new philosophy present difficulties of the same kind, as do paintings, sculptures and even buildings. Although 'getting' the meaning is not easy, that is no difficulty for the present account. Its only function is to show how the meaning, once known, is hypothetically generated from other occurrences of the same word(s) by the analogy structure I have described.

> Altarwise by owl-light in the half-way house
> the gentleman lay graveward with his furies;
> Abaddon in the hangnail cracked from Adam,
> And, from his fork, a dog among the fairies,
> The atlas-eater with a jaw for news,
> Bit out the mandrake with to-morrow's scream.
> Then, penny-eyed, that gentleman of wounds,
> Old cock from nowheres and the heaven's egg,
> With bones unbuttoned to the half-way winds,
> Hatched from the windy slavage on one leg,
> Scraped at my cradle in a walking word
> That night of time under the Christward shelter:
> I am the long world's gentleman, he said,
> And share my bed with Capricorn and Cancer.

That is difficult enough to find one's way into and become at home in. The incomparable Dylan Thomas continues 'Altarwise by Owl-light' with, 'Death is all metaphors, shape in one history'. Impenetrable at first, that poetry eventually will be as lucid as Polly Garter's desires in *Under Milk Wood*. Realism is a matter of familiarity, of ease of access. Goodman (1968: 36) observed, 'Just here I think, lies the touchstone of realism: not in quantity of information but in how easily it issues.' The circulation of meaning from that poem to discourse more pedestrian than Dylan Thomas ever heard in Wales is as simple as the differentiation patterns I have already explained. (See the access provided by a critic's explanation in Tindall, 1966.)

The sketched 'hypothetical constructions' are intended only to illustrate (i) that the same semantic structures govern linguistic meaning, even in poetry and literature, regardless of the areas or subjects of discourse; and (ii) that the semantic (non-referential) dimension of figurative discourse is adequately described by the analogy theory and its salient feature, double differentiation, usefully clarified.

7

Analogy and religious discourse: craftbound discourse

1 RECONCEIVING THE PROBLEM

The central issues in the dispute about the cognitive content of Judeo-Christian religious discourse are not peculiar to religion. Metaphysical, ethical, aesthetic, legal and scientific discourse raise generically the same issues. They are all craftbound and their vocabularies are similarly embedded by analogy in other craft discourse and in unbound discourse.

The business discourse of plumbers, football coaches, mechanics, philosophers, physicists, physicians and lawyers is paradigmatically craftbound. That name, 'craftbound discourse', connotes that *skill in action* is necessary for a full grasp of the discourse. Ordinarily you master a craftbound discourse only if you become an 'insider' to the doing that the discourse is about.

The basic vocabulary of these kinds of discourse is similarly anchored to benchmark situations (legal cases, Scripture stories, scientific experiments, particular professional observations and responses) that structure and stabilize the central meaning relationships.

So, although the immediate subject matter of this chapter is the religious discourse of relatively orthodox Christianity, the forms of argument, the general strategy and the specific analogy claims apply to any craftbound discourse whose cognitive content is challenged and, in particular, apply to explaining the relationship of theoretical predicates in science to 'observational predicates in discourse that is independent' of the theory. To illustrate that generality, I provide some examples from legal discourse and refer to further discussion of jurisprudence in chapter 8.

At the core, the challenge that religious discourse is without cognitive content is that *there is nothing expressed by the utterances of such discourse that is worthy of any epistemic attitude at all.*[1] By an epistemic attitude I mean any attitude, whether of belief, doubt, withholding belief for more evidence, claiming to know, denying, qualifying, or rejecting, where mentioning *evidence* is relevant to justifying the attitude.

The noncognitivist does not claim religious utterances are worthy of no attitudes at all. Approval, disapproval, encouragement, reinforcement or even disgust or pleasure may be appropriate. But whatever their justification, it cannot be an *evidential* justification turning upon the content of the religious utterances.

Various and confused reasons have been offered for the noncognitivist's verdict. The most important stems from the objections considered by Aquinas and has had many later formulations. At heart, it is the claim that because we learn how to apply predicates and to justify them in particular cases from observation and *experience* (which is, in the last analysis, sensory and emotive), religious applications, where such experience is not even relevant as a justification, are *uncontrolled* by the experiences through which we originally learned the words and can only be merely equivocal. Whatever the words mean, they do not mean anything to which the original experiences are relevant and, therefore, do not mean what they meant where such experience was the only relevant justification. We have, then, no access to the content of such predicates. And because the religious uses are discontinuous in meaning with the occurrences we understand, we ought not to acknowledge that they have any content at all.

That is the equivocation challenge in, I think, its most coherent form. The underlying proposition, that all knowledge arises from experience, is ambiguous. And the overall argument rests upon a false implicit premise: that if a certain kind of experience is indispensable to justified application of a predicate in one statement and utterly irrelevant to justified application or withholding in another, the two occurrences are merely equivocal. That is manifestly false. For 'is not a man' is a predicate that I can use my eyes to deny of my neighbor and to apply to a stone; but seeing is irrelevant to justifying that 'is not a man' applies to God and to the number one. Nevertheless 'is not a man' is univocal in these cases. Therefore, the missing premise is false.

The fact that a certain kind of experience is indispensible to justifying the application or withholding in one case and utterly irrelevant in another has nothing directly to do with the meanings. Lest one think only negative predicates are counterexamples, I can apply 'is a human' to the last person born of woman who will ever exist. Experience is irrelevant to justifying the predicate in that case but is relevant to applying it to a figure seen at a distance. Yet the predicate is univocally applied to both.

Revised formulations of the basic challenge and of the key reason for the noncognitivists' position are not more successful. The original challenge should be sharper about exactly what is denied. And reasons have to be provided why (a) mere equivocation must occur in religious discourse, relative to 'ordinary discourse' (I, of course, regard religious discourse as 'ordinary discourse'), and (b) *why* equivocation in religious discourse, in comparison, say, to family talk, will evacuate cognitivity when it rarely does so elsewhere. Being merely equivocal might make talk of God inaccessible, like an undeciphered language, but why inherently without meaning? Of course, one might rejoin that there is no relevant distinction here; if the meanings are inaccessible, that is functionally the equivalent of being without content. Yet that is misleading. For the alleged functional equivalence is acceptable only if the challenge is that there is no *access* to the content and therefore no way of justifying one predicate over another. But if the objection is a linguistic one, that there is *no content*, then inaccessibility is not equivalent to absence of content (as an undeciphered language shows).

Nevertheless, I will for the sake of argument grant that (a) terms applied to God and to other things are frequently but not always equivocal; (negative predicates have to be univocal and so do certain affirmatives, like 'is eternal'); (b) being merely equivocal with every other same term would defeat access to the content, if any; and even (c) if there is no access to the content there is no inherent meaning. (That, of course, is manifestly false: the undeciphered language.)

Still a vast fissure mars the argument. One cannot pass immediately from 'equivocal' to 'merely equivocal'. It has to be proved that the God-predicates are *merely* equivocal with every same word where experience (perceptual construal) is the only relevant justifi-

160

cation for applying the words. No one has even attempted that. And there is no point in attempting it, for the simple reason that the predicates of religious discourse do not on the whole pass the mere equivocation test, as I will show below.

We could, I suppose, count the language-gone-on-a-holiday and language-broken-loose-from-its-moorings objections as trying to establish that religious predicates are merely equivocal with their 'ordinary' applications. For the 'linguistic discontinuity' hypothesis contends that religious occurrences are fraudulent meaning-pretenders, whose pretense is negated by the lack of proper ancestry in meaningful discourse. Nevertheless, I will consider the discontinuity challenge separately.

The equivocation hypothesis has another false premise: that when there is a meaning carryover from one realm of discourse to another, there must be a carryover of relevant experiential justifications for applying that predicate rather than an opposite. And because there is no carryover of 'ordinary' experience as a relevant justification for divine predicates, there can be no carryover of meaning either. That exposes the notion of experience that characterizes noncognitivism and tacitly premises that predicates are not applied to God on the basis of experience. If we free ourselves from narrow positivist conceptions of experience, experience, especially self-construal, is indeed relevant to justifying predicates in religious discourse, even predicates of God: e.g. 'God *loves me*', 'God *provides* for me', 'God *cares for me* as a father'.

I merely mention the logical positivist's argument which has the defects of the equivocation hypotheses along with further deficiencies of its own. At least positivism was clear and definite that non-analytic meaningful assertions have to be, in principle, conclusively verifiable or falsifiable through immediate sensory experience. Because no version of the position has survived the scrutiny of philosophers of science (Hempel 1950 and Urmson 1956) and because the position could not pass its own test and so has to be itself a defective test for meaningfulness, it can be dismissed. It is regrettable that so many religious writers accepted the positivist outlook and then conceded that religious utterances are not cognitively meaningful[2] or wasted ingenuity showing how religious utterances can be verified or falsified.[3]

With the demise of positivism, noncognitivism took a Wittgensteinean turn, it urged a *linguistic* discontinuity reason for the noncognitivist verdict. In religious discourse, language has 'broken away from its moorings',[4] language has 'gone on a holiday'.[5] The idea is that words in religious discourse do not interlock with one another in the same meaning-creating way that they do in most other kinds of discourse. In fact, the words of religious talk do not interlock in any way the protesting writers can understand.[6] There is no distinguishable difference between 'God forgives sins' and 'The seawall cooled monthlies'.

It was argued that although 'God loves all men' looks like 'Lincoln loved his country', the conditions of implication, paraphrase, disavowal, objection, and the like, are of quite different kinds and, in the first case, are far more uncertain than in the latter (Alston 1964b). That words in religious talk have 'broken loose from their linguistic moorings', is manifested by that uncertainty. Sometimes it is said that all religious predicates are symbolic or figurative and non-literal[7] rather than merely meaningless.

The critics say that they are uncertain what would count as paraphrases, implications etc., of religious utterances, whereas they are not uncertain about the same words in non-religious discourse. Perhaps that is because they have not examined many non-religious cases and do not understand religious talk from the inside, as participants in the craft. Perhaps they have 'outgrown' a childlike connection of such words with one's interior states and one's actions and are now unable to *use* the discourse for self-construal. It is not surprising that discourse you no longer have a use for should seem meaningless. Perhaps they have underestimated the uncertainties in non-religious talk as well.

Uncertainty of implication, paraphrase, qualification and the like, will not display a cognitive infirmity in religious discourse because similar uncertainty exists in non-religious discourse where there is no reason at all to suspect cognitive evacuation, e.g. 'That legislation was *wise*', 'Smith has a *right* to be here'.

Many words of God-talk were originally learned in other environments where perceptual construals were the basis for applying them. In religious discourse experience of that sort is typically not relevant. So, it is urged, there is nothing to assure continuity of meaning from the non-religious experiential contexts to the religious non-experiential contexts. Skepticism, at least, about cognitive content is justified and, some think, outright denial is as well.[8]

The argument assumes that continuity of meaning between equivocal occurrences of a word requires continuity of the relevant experience for applying it. But we have already seen that that is not true even for univocal occurrences. Asymmetry in the relevance of sensible experience to the justification of a predicate cannot by itself cause mere equivocation. So we still have no rational basis for the 'mere equivocation' hypothesis.

To establish that some religious predicates are equivocal with typical non-religious applications is not, I repeat, to prove anything all believers would deny. Many cognitivists think the divine attributes are equivocal with non-religious applications of 'is powerful', 'knows', 'wills', 'forgives', 'judges', 'creates', etc. St. Thomas Aquinas systematically espoused that view, a view that has prevailed among theologians for centuries. Equivocation for at least some divine predicates is a logical consequence of the fact that religious discourse is craftbound discourse. (I shall explain why, later.) Yet, the non-cognitivist attack fails because it cannot establish *enough* of a meaning difference to constitute *mere* equivocation.

The most decisive consideration comes from the analogy theory itself. *Same words are merely equivocal just in case there is no non-homonymous near synonym of one that can be substituted for the other to yield a sentence approximately the same in meaning as the original.* It is evident that there are meaning-relevant, non-homonymous near synonyms of divine attributes that are thus substitutable for non-religious, equivocal, same words. 'Parents *forgive* their children'; 'God *forgives* his people'. We can substitute 'does not store up remembered wrongs against'. The two tokens of 'forgive' are clearly not unrelated as bank/bank.

If that substitution feature really does identify words that are related in meaning and never picks out merely equivocal ones (and I have shown in chapter 4 that it *cannot* do so) then, beyond any doubt, the relations of religious predicates to non-religious same words is not always mere equivocation. The 'discontinuity' hypothesis simply collapses along with the 'mere equivocation' hypothesis.

I could stop there, having established that no version of a 'discontinuity' thesis based upon claiming mere equivocation between divine predicates and non-religious same-term occurrences can succeed. But one really wants a positive explanation besides. What corresponds in the present theory to the account offered by Aquinas of how the meaning of religious predicates is embedded in the wider fabric of non-religious discourse? A brief word about Aquinas first (See Ross 1958 and 1961).

In Aquinas' theory the community of meaning between the two kinds of same words was founded upon the proportional similarity of the objects designated by the terms. The relationship between a divine being and being wise is proportionally similar to the relationship between being a human being and being wise. So divine wisdom is *proportionally* (not directly) the same as human wisdom. In other words, 'being wise' names relations that God stands in to His actions that are similar to relations Socrates stands in to his own actions. For instance, both are perfections, both imply understanding and will, both concern things known to be done, both concern the correct disposition of means to ends, and so forth. So too, when a number and a stone and a quality are all said to have being and to be, the words 'have being' and 'to be' have just that sameness of meaning and just that difference of meaning that the referents have as sameness and difference of being. How is that possible?

Concepts are abstracted from things and are limited to the being of the things from which they are abstracted. Thus a difference of *modus essendi* of a referent corresponds to a difference of *modus significandi* of a predicate; for the concept *is* the meaning of the predicate that signifies it, and the concept differs as the being differs. When the *res significata* of same words is the same and the *modus significandi* is different, we have analogy of proper proportionality. Aquinas reasoned (*In I Sent.* 22, 1, 2 c.):

So the creature fails to be a perfect representation of the exemplar because of the different mode in which the perfections are received. And because of that, there is a scale, as it were, among creatures. And because of this, there are two aspects of the terms to consider: *the thing signified and the mode of being signified.* Therefore we must consider that when we, who know God only from creatures, employ a term, we always fall short of a representation of God with respect to the 'mode of being signified' because the term signifies the divine perfections through the mode by which they are participated in by creatures. If, however, we consider *what* is signified by the term, what the term is used to signify, we find that some terms are used primarily to signify the perfections exemplified in God alone, not being concerned with any mode in their signification, and that some terms are said to signify perfection received according to a given mode of participation. For example, all knowing is an imitation of divine knowing and all knowledge of divine knowledge. So, the term 'sense' is used to signify knowing through that mode by which knowledge is materially received through the power of the conjoined organ. But the term 'knowledge' does not signify a particular mode of participating in its principal signification. Hence it must be said that all those terms which are used to signify a perfection absolutely are properly used of God and primarily used of Him with respect of what is signified, even though not with respect to the mode of signification, such as 'wisdom', 'goodness', 'essence' and others of this type.

Aquinas replied to a linguistic discontinuity claim with an account of *meaning continuity* by analogy of meaning, based metaphysically in the real analogy among the things referred to (*analogia entis*) and causally mediated by conceptual abstraction (*analogia rationis*) where the concepts, which *are* the meanings of the words, reflect the similarity and difference of the beings.

I do not follow the same steps because I reject the idea-in-the-mind conception of linguistic meaning, even the very sophisticated version that Aquinas employed, and I emphasize that on linguistic grounds alone the continuity of meaning can be established.

3   RELIGIOUS DISCOURSE IS EMBEDDED IN UNBOUND AND OTHER CRAFTBOUND DISCOURSE

(a) *Craftbound discourse and unbound discourse*

The distinction of craftbound from unbound discourse is contrast-dependent and employs the preanalytic notions, 'acceptable utterance' and 'craft', 'profession', 'art', etc. Unbound discourse is discourse that does not share the salient features of craftbound discourse.

Craftbound discourse has five distinguishing features. (1) Part of its vocabulary has affinities and oppositions of meaning which are detectably different from those of the same words in unbound discourse. (2) Although one might already know how to speak the language, one has to *learn* to use the craft discourse (medicine, law, farming, Christianity, plumbing, tree surgery, metaphysics); and learning the discourse is not the same as learning the vocabulary, but involves learning to make *justified construals* e.g. 'We are on course', 'The floor is level', 'There's no platter for that turn-table'. (3) Usually a craft discourse has, in addition to differentiated words that occur in other crafts and unbound discourse (bridging words), a vocabulary of its own that is internally interdefined and is merely equivocal or metaphorical with the same words outside that craft ('strike' in baseball and 'strike' in unbound discourse and in law) or, perhaps, some of its words do not occur outside the craft at all, 'negligence *per se*', 'collatteral estoppel' in law. (4) The discourse functions often to motivate and characteristically to modulate human behavior in the pursuit of craft-identifying objectives. (Philosophers talk philosophy in order to do philosophy; doctors talk medicine to facilitate medical practice.) Now I do not mean that each particular utterance is behavior-modulating, but rather that the function of such discourse, talking carpentry, talking plumbing, talking metaphysics, is to modulate what we think, say and do, see or perceive or conclude, in the course of doing carpentry, plumbing or metaphysics or related things. (5) There are *conditions upon the acceptability of utterances for communication in pursuit of craft-objectives that are more stringent than (additional to) those of unbound discourse.* There are correlated restrictions on paraphrase, qualification, modification and utterance presupposition, which do not apply to discourse in general or wholesale to discourse in other crafts. That means that sentences that would be acceptable English, even though perhaps vague, in other environments will be unacceptable when one is doing metaphysics, medicine, explaining salvation or talking with plumbers who are doing the job. 'My husband is crazy!' is not acceptably formed for psychiatric diagnosis. It is like saying to the helmsman of a sailboat 'Turn right', or 'Go up to the front of the boat'. (New navy-talk allows some formerly 'unnautical' expressions.)

I think that is the core feature of craftbound discourse: there are conditions for the acceptability of expressions, and therefore of paraphrase, qualification, and even of presupposition, which do not apply wholesale throughout the language and have to be learned along with the vocabulary and, usually, cannot be learned without participatory experience in the craft. For example, you do not *send* a complaint to the court and the defendant, you *file* the complaint with the court and *serve* the defendant. Sometimes we say, 'But you can't say it that way' when we *understand* what is said but find the expression unacceptable because of the linguistic practice of the craft. Fussy people nag others that way.

Unbound discourse, on the other hand, is marked by the absence of acceptability conditions that result from the practice of a distinguishable skill, craft or profession.

'Ordinary discourse', whatever that is, is not the same thing as unbound discourse. People can and do talk 'ordinarily', as opposed, say, to academically, professionally, publicly, using both

166

unbound and craftbound discourse, for instance, surfer-talk, C-B-er-talk.

(b) *Religious discourse is craftbound discourse*

Philosophers tend to obscure the intimacy between religious discourse and human action. They persist in talking as if parents, ministers, priests and teachers of religion told stories (Scriptural, historical and of the saints) and taught catechism and creeds and explained liturgy and ritual without any tie to human behavior.

Yet anyone who knows the Christian or Jewish religion will recognize instantly that bible stories, credal teaching, stories of saints, and all the religious talk (even sermons when properly done) are designed to modulate one's conception of oneself and of one's relationship to other people, to modulate one's judgments about the physical world, about the goals and values of life and one's judgments about God (who is to be encountered through faith, in obedience to moral law and in the pursuit of holiness). The discourse is inherently action-oriented, response, self-construal and judgment oriented.

Religion is taught in order to modulate living. And the connection between words and action, e.g. examining one's conscience (appraising one's inner states), is so intimate and inextricable that liturgy (the *enactment* of religious mysteries with words, stories, song, poetry, physical movement and physical symbols) is considered an indispensable religious reality. In addition to anything efficaciously achieved through the enactment of the mysteries (the sacramental theory of liturgy), there is communication, there is teaching. That is why the liturgical year is constructed to model the economy of salvation and the sanctification of the world: *lex orandi, lex credendi*. The teaching is directed to Christian living, not merely charity to others, but personal development and integration of one's life and basic desires.

Living in God, in the spiritual Word, is the object of the craft of Christian doing; and Christian talking functions to prompt and modulate it. One has to make well-informed judgments about oneself, judgments that apply religious predicates and either explicitly attribute or imply divine attributes. Thus, 'I am *saved* not by my merits but by His *mercy*; I have been *redeemed*; I have *sinned*; I have been *forgiven*; Christ died for me and *rose* again; I too will *rise* from the dead'.

Experience is essential to applying such predicates to oneself. Such judgments are products of self–construal. Any account of religious discourse, denying that judgments based upon experience have any evidential role in justifying statements about religious realities and about God, is manifestly in error.

There can be no question that religious discourse satisfies the conditions for craftbound discourse just as well, say, as does legal discourse or the discourse of physicians, musical performers and abstract scientists. Salvation is as much a craft objective as is health or the peaceful resolution of controversy. You practice religion as you do law, medicine, or philosophy, through judgments, justified through one's *construal* of reality, and directed toward action.

(c) *Religious discourse is embedded in unbound discourse by meaning-related same words*

Unbound discourse has a logical priority over any craftbound discourse. An expression can be acceptable in English but not if you are, say, talking law. So, 'being in English' is prior and independent. Moreover, when you learn a craft, you learn more than a vocabulary but less than a language, and when you learn a language, you do not learn a craft.

The deepest and most direct rooting of religious discourse in experience is by common words that also occur in unbound talk about experiences that characterize the human condition and are psychologically prior (for humans as a group) to religion: the experience of losing someone in death, of pain, of loss of well-being; the experience of depression, of failing to understand, of being lost, endangered, and frightened; the experience of some meaning larger than the meaning of single events, a pattern glimpsed and a plan unknown; the sense of there being another, watching, not human; the feeling or experience of law, of demand from outside oneself, the vertiginous attraction of what is forbidden, of wanting what one cannot name, of feeling loved, favored, privileged but not by any human; one's feeling of irresistible progression, transitory moments; the feeling that all material promise is delusion, the feelings of being punished or deserving to be; being aided, enlightened and cherished; the experience of mysterious powers in individuals, as if they communicated with an over-mind; the insight, from artistic reorganization of experience, that what *we* see cannot be all that reality is. These are a few of the human experiences that are *construed with religious talking*.

Religious talk *construes*, often with different words ('grace', 'sin', 'salvation', 'redemption'), those characteristically human experiences and puts them into a story. The common words become terms in religious discourse and are often univocal with such non-religious occurrences. The unbound description of the human condition in experience-predicates like those mentioned above is correlated with a religious story, with story-predicates: creation, fall, exile, sin, sickness, promise, covenant, violation, recovenant, incarnation, death, resurrection, redemption, salvation, repentance, *metanoia*, life, light, fulfillment and glory. The basic meaning patterns of the story-predicates are established by the way they are used to explain and resolve the human condition through the telling of the religious story. Key religious predicates (sin) are tied, as construal words, to experiences (guilt, transgression, disobedience) that are universal and *demand* construal in a rational life.

At this point I repeat the argument against mere equivocation, presented in section 2, above. First, I emphasize that since 'religious predicates' must not be restricted to 'divine attributes' but include all those unbound experience-predicates I mentioned along with the correlated religious vocabulary that I illustrated, there is a significant overlap of *univocal* words between religious discourse and discourse not directed to religious objectives.

Secondly, key words of the religious story occur analogously elsewhere:

(a) A pair of equivocal same words is meaning-related by *analogy* if there is a meaning-relevant near synonym of the first that can be substituted non-homonymously for the second to yield a replacement sentence approximately the same in meaning as the second sentence.

(b) For any occurrence in religious discourse of such key religious predicates as:

is perfect		born
really exists		suffered
is really present		died
died for you		was buried
lived after death		rose again
will rise from the dead	and	will judge
will come again in glory		giver of life
is almighty		forgives
creator		sin
his only son		life everlasting

there are non-religious occurrences (that is, occurrences not part of re-

169

ligious discourse, not part of discourse directed to modulting action toward holiness, guided by Scripture) such that condition (a) is satisfied.

(c) Therefore, religious discourse as a whole is meaning-related to unbound same words. Sometimes the relatedness is by metaphor, sometimes by analogy and frequently even by univocation.

(d) *The divine-attribute words are embedded in unbound discourse by analogy of proper proportionality*

Typical descriptions or characterizations of God include predicates like 'forgives all who repent', and 'loves all sinners', 'knows all things', 'is all-powerful'. Those words also occur unbound, 'forgives anyone who owns up', 'loves the retarded', 'knows all about baseball'. And the principle of connection is this: every predicate used to characterize or describe God has typical unbound occurrences that (i) satisfy condition (a) for analogy or univocity in section (c) just above, and (ii) have discernibly similar meaning matrices (patterns of affinity and opposition to other words.)

Of course, some divine-attribute words are merely equivocal with some unbound same words; for instance, 'grace', (divine) and 'grace', (physical.) But analogy and metaphor are the general rule. There are *always* meaning-related unbound occurrences of divine-attribute words, *always*! The mere equivocation hypothesis and the meaning discontinuity hypothesis are completely baseless.

The idea of similar meaning matrices was explained in chapter 4. I summarize it here. First, put roughly, the meaning matrices for a pair of same words are similar just in case the patterns of their affinities and oppositions of meaning to other words are similar.

Put more formally, the matrix for a word, T^1, consists of its oppositions and affinities (such as 'is a determinable of', 'is part of the definition of' 'is the contrary of',) to its predicate scheme members, and of their oppositions and affinities to the other words that frequently co-occur with any of the scheme members occurring univocally (that is, occurring in the sense the scheme members would adopt on being substituted for T^1). Same words with differing but markedly similar predicate schemes and similar meaning matrices are analogous by proportionality. Because a meaning matrix is, in effect, only a pattern of meaning relations, T^1 and T^2 are analogous just in case their patterns of meaning relationships are similar.

When craftbound and unbound same words are not merely equivocal, there is typically a striking similarity in their patterns of affinity and opposition to other words, whether the relatedness is by analogy alone or by metaphor.

'God *loves* all men' has 'loves' analogously to 'A parent *loves* all his children'; it is *also* analogous to the differentiated 'A bride usually *loves* her bridegroom' and 'A proud man *loves* praise'. That is, it is analogous to *every* occurrence that is not merely equivocal or univocal with it. So one must not think the analogy relations hold only for one pair of occurrences. The analogy holds among *all* the same words, taken in pairs, that are neither univocal nor merely equivocal. *Meaning nuances* of an analogous token *result from its samenesses and differences with a wide range of tokens* that are not merely equivocal with it. And it is, by its relatedness to such tokens, *embedded* in the meaning relations of words in unbound discourse.

An admonition: we must not confuse saying that all or most divine-attribute words are used analogically of God in comparison to typical applications of those words to humans with saying that *all* predicates in religious discourse are analogous, or merely equivocal, with *all* typical non-religious occurrences of the same predicates. The latter is manifestly false. The former, properly understood, is no more than is to be expected when words from unbound discourse acquire craftbound employment.

Part of the embedding of religious discourse in unbound discourse consists in the carryover of *univocal* words that I mentioned, e.g. 'My heart is *restless* till it *rest* in thee.' A second part consists in the carryover, analogous in some cases and univocal in others, of the experiential predicates that are used pre-religiously to describe elements of the universal human condition, terms around which the technical vocabulary of a religion develops. Thirdly, even for religious judgments like 'I have sinned', 'I have been forgiven', statements that imply divine attributes, experiential judgments are evidentially relevant: 'I know I did what I was forbidden to do', 'I know I did not do my best', 'I give in to my impulses', and so forth. Thus, empirical judgments and self-construals function to ground judgments about God, e.g. 'He will forgive all my sins'.

4   FINAL ASSAULT: ANALOGY GENERATES NONSENSE

The noncognitivist will try to appropriate the analogy defense and turn it around for a final assault. He will argue that systematic cognitive evacuation of religious discourse is caused by (i) successive abstraction (analogy), (ii) denominative analogy that makes substantives out of abstractions ('grace', 'atonement', 'redemption', 'indwelling'), and (iii) maladroit metaphors (e.g. 'The Spirit *dwells within us*'.) To confirm that there is such nonsense one need only look at typical sermons and religious disputes. Religious talking is shot through with nonsense, but so is a large part of all talk.

Even granting that nonsense is rampant, is that enough to *evacuate* creeds, liturgy, catechism and other proclamations of the faith? I think not.

(a) *Meaninglessness has to be induced*

A grammatically well-formed sentence will make whatever sense it can. (See the basic principles mentioned in the Introduction.) It will have whatever meaning(s) its environment permits. Inconsistency, which is meanful, takes priority over senselessness. But inconsistency, unless it is well entrenched (e.g. 'Bachelors are married') or reinforced or caused by a stand-off of dominance, will give way to ambiguity. Meaninglessness occurs only when meaning is environmentally *prevented*. And that can happen in two ways (at least): (a) through *conflict* of dominance that produces linguistic nonsense and (b) through *lack* of enough dominance to give the sentence a syntagmatic backbone.

'Saturday follows Mary' could have a computable meaning. But if the environment negates a 'haunts' sense of 'follows', and requires the day-of-the-week sense of 'Saturday', it prevents the sentence from locking together. That is linguistic nonsense, *meaning prevention by environment*. That's not the same as the *learned nonsense*, vacuity, that we find in philosophy and religion and in many so-called sciences, too.

Linguistic nonsense cannot, therefore, occur without a discourse environment that *prevents* what would elsewhere be plausible readings of the sentence. Equivocation caused by conflicting dominant environmental factors generates nonsense because it can prevent sense. Effective prevention needs conflicting dominators of the same words, operating in opposed directions. Then the words can join together in twos and threes but not *all* together while the elements stay in the same predicate schemes by which they hook to

172

their neighbors. That is, A hooks with B ('Saturday follows' . . . e.g. Friday) if the schemes for A and B are S and S^1, but B hooks with C ('*follows* Mary' . . . e.g. Fido) only if the scheme for B is S^2 (for example, metaphorical to S^1). Thus there is no one scheme pattern in which the *whole* sentence can be linked together, even inconsistently, because one of the words behaves like a duck-rabbit picture, jumping to one scheme as it hooks to one word and to another as it hooks to the next. Because dominating words *capture* a common word, the sentence is torn apart. (See discussion of linguistic nonsense, chapter 3, p. 81–2.)

Such environmentally conflicting dominance was unreflectively supposed, I think, for the familiar examples, 'Green ideas sleep furiously' and 'Relativity eats quadratic equations'. If we construct a discourse environment that dominates so that 'green' *has* to be a color and not the same as 'new' or 'fresh', and 'sleep' *has* to mean to 'be asleep' and not 'gestate', and 'furiously' *has* to mean 'in wild anger' and cannot mean 'as it were, boiling', (where 'has to mean' implies actual domination), then overall sense is effectively prevented in that environment; the schemes *cannot interlock* to create an overall meaning. That's *linguistic* nonsense. And it is relative to an environment.

There is a second kind of meaningless sentence, the *exsanguinated* sentence, the vacuous utterance: 'Thingness evokes essential being', 'Time is imperfect double negation'. Here there is no resistance to overall concatenation. There is no resistance to any possible reading of the words. Each word is a mere blur of dots, no configuration at all. The words have bled to death.

Vacuity is at an extreme from linguistic nonsense. The sentence can go together in virtually any of the meanings of any of its terms and the environment provides no 'use' for any of those readings. There is no 'friction', no dominance to make something the other words have to adapt *to*. One way to create vacuities is to make abstract substantives, denominatively, out of other words ('thingness' out of 'thing', 'invisibility' out of 'invisible') and combine them with metaphorical predicates ('evokes', 'invites', 'surpasses') to produce nonsense: 'Thingness evokes essential being'; 'Analytically, deontology invites comprehension of the logic of reality'; 'The everpresence of God, the overwhelmingness of His intimate interpenetration of the innermost being of things, surpasses even the union of being and essence'. This is the kind of nonsense one usually finds in religious discourse. It is the nonsense that has evacuated religious talk of its content, says the noncognitivist.

Abstractive analogy consists of the differentiation of a word by the suppression, relatively, of a meaning affinity or opposition (in effect, a presupposition) of another occurrence. Thus:

(1) Minds are *invisible* (embodied but not material or capable of stimulating senses).
(2) God is *invisible* (not embodied).
(3) Atoms are *invisible* (too small to see).
(4) Stars are *invisible* in the daytime (background too bright).

The expression: 'cannot be seen' combines analogously with each. There are common co-applicable contraries: 'is perceptible', 'is visible', 'is visually detectable', and there are also disparate contraries that are not co-applicable with the four subjects, 'differentially stimulates the visual receptors', 'reflects light'. So 'invisible' is analogous. *Meaning-relevant near synonyms that reflect a sufficient condition for the truth of the whole statement, are different.* (That's another test for analogy.)

We can use 'invisible' where *none* of those contraries is even relevant and none of the specific near synonyms applies. For instance, (5) 'He walked around in broad daylight, his eyes moving over the objects, but the city was *invisible* to him'. In some sense 'He can't see it', but not in any of the senses of the other occurrences. A manic philosopher could move denominatively from (5) to (6): '*Invisibility* is the product of incomprehensibility'. Out pops utter nonsense. Intellectuals and bureaucrats dilute thought into speech, like a drop of blood into a gallon of water. They don't have to face the blank stare the pump repair man would give the householder's diagnosis, 'Well, the centrifugal switch succumbed to gravitational facticity'. (How can we know there is no 'gravitational facticity' when we don't have any idea *what* it is?)

Nonsense can be created through the mechanisms of meaning-differentiation, through the very factors that cause analogy. Conflicting dominance and absence of entrenched dominance can yield linguistic nonsense; vacuous nonsense is produced by exsanguinating abstraction, metaphor, and misplaced denomination.

174

A speaker can respond to indifference–dominance relations to produce nonsense, just as a manufacturer can respond to the laws of physics to make bombs. But the analogy laws do not make nonsense by themselves. A sentence will make sense if it can: if it falls within the dominance conditions I have described and has a use in its environment from which to get a semantic backbone. Lots of grammatical sentences have no 'use', though poets (Dylan Thomas) and novelists (Patrick White) characteristically write such roles. For instance, 'Admissions have orbited throughout the metropolitan area' has no use I know of (in any environment) but quite obviously it could be given one.

Nonsense, whether linguistic or vacuous, is an incidental by-product of underlying meaning structures with other causal roles, other functions, in view: infinity of expressive capacity within a finite vocabulary. Nonsense results from the structures of natural language the way wrong-doing results from free will.

That means, of course, that one can produce nonsense within any kind of discourse in natural language. The fact that vacuity is common in religious discourse, in pseudo-science and even in psychotherapy is not the fault of the language but the result of limited understanding and of there being a (social, pragmatic or personal) value on speakers' letting words fit together as they happen to and regarding the *result* as their thought. (One ought not to ignore the fact that the general run of talk that is not stories or greetings or signals is a combination of feckless falsehoods and vacuities.)

(c) *Cognitive content cannot be evacuated from an anchored, embedded and practised craft*

The key words of a craft discourse are attached to *fact stereotypes*, clinical cases in medicine, bible stories in Christianity and recorded appellate cases in law. Such situations, rigidly correlated with the words, are stereotypes for what *counts* as such and such. So, the words can undergo endless differentiation within the craft discourse without ever losing the definite meanings needed for telling and interpreting the story. 'Malice' has undergone substantial development from 'ill will' to include 'reckless disregard for the truth or falsity of one's published speech' in the law of libel. Yet each of the extensions from the older idea of 'ill will' is fixed in a chain of cases whose *facts* are stereotypes for what *counts* as malice.

175

In the authoritative tradition of Fathers, Councils and Liturgy one finds institutions functioning equivalently to the judiciary and to Putnam's 'experts' in science (Putnam 1975). The central doctrines are constantly proclaimed in the same terminology, sometimes with new terminology correlated (Vatican II), and key words are deliberately correlated with Scriptural events.

No matter how one differentiates religious words, one cannot evacuate the words used for the canonical statement of the faith because they get their meanings from the events reported in Scripture. Whatever 'sin' means elsewhere, in the context of the Adam and Eve story its range is restricted by the reported knowing disobedience of the command of an acknowledged lawgiver, followed by discovery, judgment, guilt and punishment.

Similarly, one cannot read 'love' in 'One should love his neighbor as himself' as 'show carnal love for'. The originating story where Jesus summarized the Law and told of the good Samaritan, the explanations by St Paul, the practice of the early church, the comments of the Fathers of the Church, the way love is enacted in the Liturgy – all these anchor the meaning of 'love' against any such interpetation. The senses of key words like 'love', 'sins', 'redeem', 'adopts', 'life everlasting', and so forth, cannot just drift away on tides of thoughtlessness. When religious talk is actually being used for its craft objective, the modulation of living toward holiness, the words are engaged with the Scriptural stereotypes and anchored to those *cases* of what is meant.

To propose, as Paul Van Buren did, that 'Jesus rose from the dead' is some kind of moral appreciation of Jesus is a hopeless attempt to force words to state what they cannot express. The sense of 'rose from the dead' is fixed by the Scriptural account of what the disciples *believed*, that Jesus had died and then was with them *in person* and not by illusion, dream or magic. In telling and interpreting the stories of Easter, of Lazarus, of the Widow of Nain, words like 'rose from the dead' become captured and dominated by the rest of the narrative. Their meanings are restored and renewed, regardless of their exsanguination in other environments.

5 CONCLUSION

A final broadside to the noncognitivist. To get either the discontinuity version or the mere equivocation version of noncognitivism onto the debating agenda, the noncognitivist has to *assert* a key premise of the analogy theory: that words adapt in meaning to their verbal environments. He has to affirm that because the frame 'is wise', according to him, is meaningful in 'Socrates is wise', surely has a different meaning in 'Fasting is wise' and has no meaning at all in 'God is wise'.

Now what could account for the differences of meaning of 'is wise' *except* 'Socrates', 'Fasting' and 'God'? But once he has conceded that one expression may affect the meaning of another which co-occurs, he *too* needs an analogy of meaning theory because he sees (how can he not?) that not all equivocation is *mere* equivocation. Yet an adequate general theory of analogy of meaning is not compatible with the claim that *all* predicates in religious discourse, or even all divine attribute predicates, are merely equivocal with all their typical non-religious occurrences.

And so, he is driven to accept more of the analogy theory and to argue that even if it is true that religious predicates, and even divine attributes, are often analogous to non-religious occurrences, still cognitivity has been *lost* because they have been bled to death by abstraction, denomination and metaphor: they are cognitively evacuated. But that leads the noncognitivist to the final defeat. For some words in religious discourse are anchored to Scripture stories and cannot be dislodged. And other words are common to pre-religious descriptions of universal human experience. There is simply no way to get the creed to come out vacuous as long as its words are understood so as to tell the stories of Scripture, and tell how those stories were understood in tradition (Creeds, Councils, Liturgy, Fathers of Church, etc.).

The fact that some philosophers cannot understand religious talk seemed important at first. They thought there must be something wrong with the talk. Now we see the talk is craftbound, that you cannot fully understand it unless you learn it, and its making sense to you is connected with your having or imagining a use for it to modulate living. The philosophers who cannot understand the discourse have forgotten or abandoned or never knew its *use* for getting certain *results*: they have disengaged the discourse from the *practice* it functions to modulate. No wonder it is vacuous for them. People who *use* religious discourse in their living, learning and self-construals are cognitivists even if they talk nonsense; noncognitivists are outsiders to the forms of life, the practices, modulated by religious talking.

Noncognitivism, which is essentially an *argumentum ad ignora-*

177

tiam, invites its own crushing refutation because it has to employ elements of the analogy theory, particularly the meaning-differentiation principle, even to be stated. So the only issue then becomes: have they got the facts straight about meaning? The answer is no.

8

Analogy and analysis

Most philosophers think truth-conditional analysis tends to fail. From the paradigm itself, the Russellian contextual analysis of 'The author of Waverly was Scott' that treated ordinary proper names as definite descriptions, through Ayer's criteria of meaningfulness and verifiability, Lewis' analyses of modes of meaning, Hart's model definition for jurisprudence, Grice's analysis of speaker meaning, Hempel's analysis of explanation and Chisholm's (1966) analyses of knowledge, truth-conditional analyses founder on counterexamples and, when repaired, typically show more anomalies than did the originals. Besides, analyses that set out to clarify often become so complex (Schiffer 1972: 165; cf. Coady 1976: 102–9), abstract or artificial that they cannot convince. For example, Goodman's analysis of musical notation (1968:177–92); Field's (1978) and Fodor's (1975) account of beliefs as 'language-like internal representations' that are, or correspond to, 'sentences or sentence analogues'. See also Harman (1974b: 57). Is the fault in our performance or in our expectations?

Truth-conditional analysis is misunderstood. Attention to the analogy phenomena will correct some misconceptions. Others persist from confusions about the inter-relationships of sentences, statements, propositions and truth conditions, from confusions about the notion of same logical form and from unrealistic expectations about what is to be accomplished by analysis. I touch incidentally on the latter matters but my main interest is in showing how analogy and equivocation place constraints upon the process of analysis.

I conclude that truth-conditional analysis is an *articulation* device, instrumental to encompassing strategies (like explanation, conceptual realignment, auditing a reasoning process, hypothesis establishment or rejection), that determine the units of appropriate logical and conceptual decomposition. There are many ways to state, decompositely, truth conditions for statements expressed sen-

179

tentially. Which among such articulations is to be preferred depends upon what the result is to be used for. Most widely useful is an articulation of jointly sufficient and individually necessary conditions each of which is 'meaning-relevent' (see below) to a key word(s) in the analysandum.

One cannot provide truth conditions without providing sentences to express them, even though the truth conditions are the states of affairs whose obtaining is sufficient and necessary for the truth of what one states.

Truth conditions for *s* are conditions under which and only under which what is *stated* is so. To say a *sentence* has truth conditions is not, therefore, to say that sentences are true or false independently of statements or propositions expressed. In fact, sentence meaning, antecedent linguistic meaning, affects truth-conditional analysis. For it is through the sentence, rather than the statement expressed, that equivocation and analogy affect expressive capacity. An analysis that provides 'meaning-relevant' truth conditions is one where the conditions given are individually necessary and jointly sufficient for the truth of the analysandum and where each is such that its *not* having been a condition would have required that some word (or words) of the analysandum have had a different meaning.

1 WIGGINS' FREGEANISM: KNOWING MEANING AND KNOWING TRUTH CONDITIONS

The account of 'knowing the meaning of a sentence', attributed to Frege, that says it is 'knowing under what conditions the sentence is true', is grossly misleading and encourages blindness to the constraints of analogy.

David Wiggins (1971a: 14–34) offered a Fregean account, an interpretation influenced by Dummett's *P. A. S.* commentary: (1958; see also his 1973): 'if we will simply take the notion of "true" as clear enough for the purpose – not for all purposes, but for this one – then we can say that, for arbitrary sentence *s*, to know the meaning of *s* is to know under what conditions the sentence *s* would count as true'.

If *s* is ambiguous, do we have to know 'under what conditions *s* would count as true' for each meaning? If to know 'under what conditions the sentence is true' is exactly the same thing as to know what it means, then one might know what it means without ever having encountered the sentence, e.g. a lot of French sentences; moreover, I know such a truth condition for any sentence: that God asserts it.

But if to know what it means you have also to know something *else*, namely under what conditions it is true, then *why*? Either what *s* means is *the same thing as* 'under what conditions *s* is true' and *that* is why one has to know the latter in order to know the former,[1] or the truth conditions are *not* the same thing as 'what *s* means'. In that case, we need a reason *why* to know the one thing (what *s* means) one has to know some other thing either about *s* or about something else.

Wittgenstein was not caught in that dilemma. For him, to know the meaning of *s* one usually does have to know something else, namely, how to use *s*.[2] Craftbound discourse provides many examples where one does not know the meaning of *s* if one does not know how to use *s*. For instance in law, 'That's hearsay' has a complex role in the admission of evidence; if you do not know how to use it, you do not really know what it means. Wittgenstein's linking meaning to forms of life is surely a recognition that craftbound discourse modulates activity (see *P.I.*, 19 and 23 and Pitcher 1964, 'Speech Activities', p. 239).

One of Wiggins' more qualified and articulate formulations of the 'Fregean' claim treats 'knowing its truth conditions' as necessary for 'knowing the meaning of a sentence'. Wiggins says:

However many concessions the objector succeeded in wresting from a defender of the Fregean doctrine it is difficult to believe that they could imperil the following minimal contention – that any satisfactory theory of meaning (whether or not exempt from the allegedly crippling descriptive fallacy) must entail the following proposition:
To know the sense of an indicative sentence s, it is necessary to know some condition p which is true if s is true and which is the designated condition for s.

Either 'is true', occurring twice in the italicized formula, is a predicate for sentences or it is equivocal. If equivocal, then because we have no anchoring occurrence for 'is true', we cannot assign a definite meaning to Wiggins' formula. So, the formula is *not* entailed by every adequate theory of meaning.

But if 'is true' is a predicate for sentences only and is used univocally here, then *p* is a sentence, as is *s*. In that case *p* is either the same sentence as *s* or a different one. If *p* is the same sentence as *s*, then to know what *s* means it is necessary to know *s* is true just in case *s* is

181

true. But no such metaproposition has to be known at all to know the meaning of s.

But if p is a distinct sentence from s, why, to know what s means, do I have to know some other sentence p which is true just in case s is true? Or, on another reading, why do I have to know *about* some other sentence that it is true just in case s is, in order to know what s means? In fact, to know about some other particular sentence p that it would be true just in case s is true, I would already have to know what s and p both mean. So p cannot be a sentence and 'true' must be equivocal.

If p is *not* a sentence, why would I have to know that p is true just in case s is true, in order to know what s means? And in what *sense* of 'true' is p supposed to be true? (No account of the conditions of truth for propositions or statements has been provided; but one thing is certain: they cannot both be true in the same sense of 'true'.)

Wiggins adopted a *polarized* conception of sentence meaning where there is a meaning bearer, the verbal token, and the meaning it bears (a judgment or proposition, like the meaning attached to symbols in a code), the meaning being attached to the token by a complex social convention. The candidates for the meaning that is expressed, that s bears, are propositions and statements.[3]

Mine is a different conception: the well-formed sentence is inherently meaningful (whether a written or spoken token). To be a well-formed and acceptable sentence is to be meaningful, to have expressive *capacity* that the evacuation and nonsense factors can defeat, but only superveniently upon what would otherwise (in some hospitable environment) be linguistically meaningful.

Regardless of what statement s is used to express, s (in a given environment) has a logically *antecedent linguistic meaning* (or range thereof if it is ambiguous) (i) that is not the same as what is stated but is the medium within which the expressed statement is realized, (ii) that restricts what can be expressed, (iii) that is not the same as what some philosophers call the 'truth conditions for the sentence', (iv) that can be known even by one who does not know what is stated or otherwise expressed, and (v) that one who knows what is stated may still not know (foreign language). Knowing the antecedent linguistic meaning is sufficient for knowing the meaning of s even though it is not sufficient for knowing what is *meant* by s on a particular occasion.

The *consequent sentential meaning* is what is stated or otherwise expressed, e.g. the question, command, hope, doubt, and the like. It is what is *meant-by-s* on a particular occasion. It is achieved through thinking in those words, asserting, say, by writing or uttering *s*. (It can misfire, too, when what the sentence means is not what the speaker means to say.)

Antecedent sentential meaning has a life of its own, resisting thought, advancing it, and having expressive capacities realized by the adaptation, to one another and to environment, of the component words. The *language* is a medium in which we think, verbalizing thought, and sentences that we *use* are *outputs* of verbalized thought. (There are other kinds of thoughts, realized in images, actions and movements.)

No satisfactory theory can be committed to the identity of sentence meaning with the statement expressed. For *s* can have the same linguistic meaning when a different statement is expressed. Without antecedent linguistic meaning there would be no restriction upon what can be expressed. But we know there are restrictions. 'The boy stood on the burning deck' *cannot express* that grapevines can be damaged by the winter.

W. Stegmuller (1970: 431) attributes a similar view to Wittgenstein, (*P.I.*, 176) where Wittgenstein's emphasis is upon discrediting the idea that meaning something is a kind of intending or attending. There is a common principle: that what you *can* mean, if your thought is realized in the words you use, is not independent of what the words *do* mean – something not dependent upon what you think or intend at the time.

'The boy stood on the burning deck' can *encode*, 'Grapevines may be damaged by winter'. But in the same sense of 'mean' in which that sentence means that some boy stood on a burning deck, the sentence cannot mean that grapevines can be damaged by winter. There's no possible world where a given sentence of English *means* anything you like independently of what any other English sentence means in that world. I do not articulate what explains the limited expressive possibility of English sentences, though *limited* expressive capacity is a necessary condition for *any* expressive capacity at all.

Meaning is inherent in English sentences, not attached, as to a code. That is why, if you concatenate words acceptably in some environment, they will *have* a sentential meaning whether or not that is what you intend. It won't necessarily be unambiguous, or even very definite, of course, but it will be restricted in its range of acceptable interpretations.

Antecedent sentential (linguistic) meaning cannot be the same thing as truth conditions or statements because *s* can have the same antecedent linguistic meaning whether or not it expresses a statement at all (e.g. it expresses a question, command), and when the expressed statements differ, 'The men were late for work today', reported daily for a week. The antecedent linguistic meaning is the *capacity* of the sentence to express many things but not just anything.

Linguistic meaning is not attached by intention, it is only modulated intentionally (and then, not directly). The dominance relations explain that. That is why you can fail to say what you mean and happen to say what you did not mean and, in a word, find yourself in a battle with your words to get them to obey.

Whether your speaker meaning is conveyed is dependent upon the linguistic meaning of the sentence (its capacity for expression), upon the sentence token whose linguistic meaning is a consequence of environment and upon the dominance–indifference relations. Thus, important meaning elements of individual sentences lie outside the intentional control of the speaker at any given time but are in David Lewis' (1969) way conventional.

I do not presume that these remarks refute Grice's (1957, 1968, 1969) account of speaker meaning. For, of course, it is quite a different matter to analyse 'Jones meant that *p*' and 'The sentence *s* means "boys will be boys"' and 'That utterance "Get out all of you" *meant* that we should all leave'. These are distinct but analogous senses of 'meant' and 'means'. There is something to be *learned* from the fact that ordinary words differentiate (and form paronyms that are more than denominatively related).

Schiffer (1972), provided amendments to Grice's account, sharing Grice's background assumption that 'linguistic meaning is a species of timeless meaning and timeless meaning is generated out of speaker meanings on occasions via habits, policies, conventions, etc.' (Coady 1976: 103). Even if Grice were right in his conjecture about the origin of linguistic meanings, he would still need to show that linguistic meaning does not now exist independently (in the ways supposed here) of speaker intentions on given occasions.

The chief contemporary contending accounts of sentence meaning, Grice's constructions from speaker meaning, Davidson's identification of knowing the truth conditions with knowing the meaning, and Quinean–Skinnerean behaviorism, all fail to account for the inherent, antecedent linguistic meaning of sentences in natural languages and, in particular, for the dominance–indifference phenomena that underlie equivocation and exert their causality independently of what we intend or believe the words to mean.

As Richard Cartwright (1962: 92–3) showed, (a) 'variations in what is asserted are *not* always accompanied by corresponding changes of meaning'; (b) 'knowing' what the words 'It is raining' mean, is not 'to know what (one and only) statement is made by assertively uttering those words. There is no such statement'; (c) and from the fact that 'what a *person* means may be a statement, it by no means follows that the statement is what his *words* meant – even as used by him on that occasion'.

To recapitulate, to know a set of truth conditions for what is stated is not the same as to know the antecedent linguistic meaning of the sentence (which can be the same when what is stated is different) or vice versa. Besides, I can know a set of truth conditions (say, 'true in all possible worlds') for a sentence whose meaning I do not know (e.g. a sentence in an undeciphered language), and I can know the antecedent meaning of a sentence that does not have a consequent meaning because it is only mentioned and not used. Therefore, to know the linguistic meaning of a sentence is not the same thing as to know under what conditions it is true. So, the key assumption of the 'Fregean' position is false. Consequently the role of truth-conditional analysis has to be reconceived.

2   INTERSECTIONS BETWEEN ANALYSIS AND ANALOGY

(a) *Benchmarks and univocity*
One cannot trust the following *transfer* of analysis: (1) 'Smith does *F*'. (2) In order that (1) be true, the following *a–n* is sufficient and necessary. Therefore, (3) for any *S*, for '*S* does *F*', to be true, than *a–n* is sufficient and necessary, *mutatis mutandis*.

First, 'Smith' and other proper name substituends for *S* may be in sufficient contrast to differentiate 'does *F*' so that one or more of the conditions (*a–n*) fails to hold or additional conditions are required: 'Buridan does logic' does not have the same truth conditions as 'Univac does logic'. Hart (1953: 18) fell into that trap.

185

Secondly, sentences with the same subjects, surface grammar and predicates may have different truth conditions because *completion* words (his brother/happiness) differentiate the predicates. For instance 'Smith *knows where to find* his brother' and 'Smith *knows where to find* happiness' differentiate 'knows where to find' and have different truth conditions. To discriminate whether sentences, with the same word as a predicate and of same surface grammar, are subject to the same truth conditions, we have to have *independent* access to the linguistic meanings of their component words. For we have to determine whether the same words in similar sentences are univocal with the benchmark occurrences. (Benchmarks are complete sentences disambiguated in a discourse environment.)

Consider this situation:

(a) *Benchmark occurrence:* 'John *knows* that cheating is forbidden. But he does it for excitement.' (Environment: discussion of expulsion of student by academic disciplinary board.)

(b) *Analysis:* '*S* knows that *p*' if and only if '*S* believes *p*, *p* is true, and *S* is justified in believing that *p* and *S*'s being justified in believing that *p* is suitably immediately caused by *p*'s being so'. (Please ignore the crudity of the statement of the 'causal' condition and the fact that *it* is not 'meaning-relevant' but is a general place-marker for the kind of condition that *would* be meaning-relevant.)

(c) *New case:* 'The Internal Revenue service *knows* that less than one percent of taxpayers falsify income.'

(d) *New case:* 'Jones *knows* that he hasn't the courage to buy that building but he still believes he has.'

(e) *New case:* 'When the computer's light goes on, the auditors *know* that the accounts have been posted.'

Do (c), (d) and (e) have to satisfy the conditions of (b) in order for (b) to be a correct analysis of the truth conditions for (a)? That depends upon whether the latter are *of the same form as* (a) and on whether 'knows' in the new cases is *univocal* with 'knows' in (a). Needless to say, we would beg the whole issue of whether the analysis is correct if we tried to settle the univocity issue by saying the truth conditions are or are not the same. Wittgenstein's 'reading' examples (*P.I.*, 156–71, 475) illustrate that one has already to grasp the different senses of 'read' in order to see that the truth conditions for statements involving 'read' in those senses could not be 'the same'.

Thirdly, when a philosopher analyses 'knows' in the frame '*S* knows that *p*', he tacitly assumes that his conditions will hold for instances of the same form in which 'knows' occurs univocally with 'knows' in 'S knows that p'. But that puts the cart before the horse. What determines the meaning of 'knows' in 'S knows that p'? That cannot be settled by semantic contagion (dominance) because 'S knows that p' is not acceptable as an English sentence. It has no environment. There must be a *benchmark*, an actual sentence disambiguated in a discourse environment, to fix the class of univocal occurrences whose sentences, of the same form as the benchmark, have to satisfy the expressed conditions of the analysis. A benchmark must be provided explicitly because it negatively determines whether the analysandum-frame correctly articulates the logical and semantic form to be analysed, and positively determines the sense of the predicate under analysis. Without a benchmark, analysis of 'knows' in 'S knows that p' is arbitrary.[4]

Fourthly, which occurrence of 'believes' should be chosen as a benchmark in which 'S believes that p' is a truth condition for 'S knows that p'? Perhaps the substitution of constants from the benchmark into the stated truth conditions will differentiate the *implied* predicates? For instance, 'believes' in the sense in which 'America believes that there must be justice for all' is surely not intended. A mere sentence schema, 'S believes that p', fixes no sense for 'believes'.

Can we avoid most of the difficulties I mention if we say that only *statements* have truth conditions, not sentences? No, that is false; the analogy structures of English cause 'have truth conditions' to differentiate when applied to sentences. The result is acceptable, though its interpretation or *reading* is disputed. We could say that the truth conditions for the sentence are the same as for the statement expressed plus one: *that* the sentence does express the statement whose truth conditions we, supposedly, will give. But that bypasses the intimate relationship of the *words* of the analysandum to the phrasing of the analysis.

Fifthly, the vacuity about being 'of the same logical form' has to be exposed. 'The truth conditions hold for all statements of the same form, with the same predicate.' That falsely assumes that the predicate cannot be equivocal when the form is the same.

The degree to which the logical grammar of the benchmark is made explicit and formally articulated with quantifiers, individual variables, predicate variables, relational predicates, modalities (logical, epistemic and deontic), specification of structures of clauses in indirect discourse etc., is a consequence of one's strategic objectives. There is no absolute standard.

Two examples of 'knows' above, (a) and (d), have the same surface grammar if schematized as 'S knows that p'. But if they are schematized in detail that distinguishes the *reflexive* structure of (a) from the non-reflexive structure of (d), and if the proper name in (a) is distinguished from the definite description in (d), then the two sentences will not be of the same form. Certainly it is not true that if s^1 and s^2 contain a univocal predicate and are, under *some* description, 'of the same logical form', then s^1 and s^2 have the same truth conditions. So under *what* description do s^1 and s^2 have to be of the same logical form to be subject to the same truth conditions? Is 'He knows where to find happiness' of the same logical form as 'He knows where to find lodgings'?

For the five reasons given, then, it would be rash and unjustified to expect the truth conditions, *a–n*, formulated for 'Smith does F' to hold for every sentence that is of the general form 'S does F' or even for those that are not *also* instances of a relevantly different form of which the benchmark is not also an instance.

(b) *Relations of analysandum and analysis to benchmarks*

'Knows' in 'S knows that p' is neither univocal, equivocal nor analogous with 'knows' in 'Mary *knows* that John is a cheat' because metalanguage predicates like 'is univocal' are restricted by the definitions of chapters 1 to 6 to same-word occurrences in English sentences (and certain analogous extensions already mentioned). I could, of course, apply that classification analogously to include English sentence frames as well, but that might obscure the stipulative relationship of analysandum-frame to benchmark. It is *stipulated* that the predicates in the analysandum-frame have the sense (meaning) of the predicates in the benchmarks, to the extent permitted by the logical form articulated by the analysandum-frame. One might even select his benchmark from the verified quotations of *O.E.D.*, specifying that they are to be read in the environment from which the compilers selected them.

Stipulation guarantees nothing about other instantiations of the analysandum-frame. If the logical form is loosely delineated, for instance 'S knows (adverbial clause)', then even if the benchmark occurrence, 'John *knows* where to find novels in the University Library' fixes the sense of 'knows' in the analysandum-frame, other adverbial clauses will differentiate 'knows', for instance, 'knows where to find happiness', 'when to stop arguing', 'how to fly airplanes'.

Furthermore, every difference of sentence meaning can, in principle, be represented as a difference of logical form. For instance, the difference between 'John' and 'Mary' *can* be represented as male vs. female proper names. So, some less stringent notion than 'is of the same form and no other' has to be used, something like 'is *sufficiently* the same in logical form' where there must be some form, articulated in the analysandum, which the new case instantiates and *no relevantly different form that it instantiates and the benchmark does not*. That is the only way to extend truth-conditional analysis to sentences that differ in meaning, like 'John *knows* that it is raining' and 'Harry *knows* that he is late'.

'Relevantly different logical form' is determined by the necessities of the encompassing task. Whether a distinction of the forms of (a) and (d) (in the second reason, above) is relevant depends upon how decompositely we need to state truth conditions to achieve the explanatory, descriptive, or other objectives we pursue. In any case, I know of no way to articulate the form of some benchmark so as to prevent its key words from occurring equivocally as predicates in sentences of the same form.

So at least three conditions have to be satisfied by new cases that extend truth-conditional analyses beyond the single benchmarks for which they are fashioned. (a) The new case must be like the benchmark, as formally schematized in the analysandum-frame, and not of any relevantly different logical form from the benchmark. (b) Terms common to the new case and to the benchmark must be univocal. (c) Substituting constants from the new instance for variables in the condition-frames must yield sentences that have to be true when the new instance is true and which are meaning-relevant (see 3b, below).

(c) *Having to justify benchmarks*

No occurrence of a word is philosophically 'central' or 'focal' in a way that a differentiated same word is not. No one class of sentences of the form 'S knows that p' (or of statements expressed by sentences of that form) is inherently more important, or involves what is *really* or *primarily* knowing, or whatever, in a way that differentiated occurrences do not.

189

Any notion of 'basic', 'really', 'primarily' F, will have to be theory-relative. Thus priority of words with a certain meaning over others with analogous meanings has to be relative to some descriptive, explanatory, evaluative or classificatory objective. That is to say that what really knowing is, as against derivatively or secondarily knowing, is not any more than relatively, really so.

The consequence is that benchmarks have to be justified, partly in terms of their efficiency. When a cluster of analogous same words ('reads' in Wittgenstein's examples, *P.I.*, 156–71) has been identified, one selects a benchmark that is easy to contrast, truth-conditionally, with analogous occurrences. That need not be the only or even a consideration, but some consideration is needed to avoid futility.

Analyses of 'S acted freely in doing F' that yield conditions like 'S could have done otherwise than F under the circumstances that surrounded his doing F', that are tacitly supposed to hold for all instantiations of S and F, or even for all that do not make the key predicate merely equivocal, are misguided. It is an empirical matter whether instances of that analysandum-frame do or do not have such a necessary condition. In some contexts 'S did F freely' is not in semantic opposition to 'S did F by nature'. (For instance, Aristotle thought men seek happiness by nature but voluntarily. And Aquinas thought God loved Himself and chose the good freely but could not do evil.) So a philosophical argument that supposes there are no contexts where the key predicate differentiates so that the expressed statements (in sentences of the same logical form) have different necessary conditions, simply ignores the empirical facts of analogy.[5] (See Chisholm 1976: 52–69, for a sensitive exploration of the 'avoidability' conditions.)

Philosophers conclude from such analyses of 'S acted freely in doing x' that 'no one could act freely when he could not have done otherwise than as he did'. But all they are *entitled* to conclude is the weaker, if 'He acted freely' occurs *univocally* with the benchmark, then the former sentence cannot be true when 'He could have done otherwise than as he did' is false. It is arbitrary to dismiss the other cases as 'Well, not in *this* sense', as if they were merely equivocal and unrevealing. For the general notion, say of responsible action, will be illuminated by our understanding the contrasting functions of analogous expressions of the form, 'S acted freely in doing F', which have *different* truth conditions. For instance, I think 'Jones stayed all night in the building freely' could be true when, unknown to Jones, who had chosen to stay all night and had fallen asleep in his office, the security force had locked and barred all feasible exits, so that he could not have left if he had chosen to.

There has to be independent access to univocity, to sameness of logical form and to the truth conditions of a pair of statements in order for one to determine whether difference of truth conditions constitutes a counterexample. So, it would be hopeless to *define* univocity in terms of sameness of truth conditions. Further, one cannot authenticate an analysis by what one can do with the product, for it need not be substitutable for the benchmark or 'have the same meaning as' the original, either. What meaning relationship is the analysis to bear to the analysandum, then?

3 ANALYSIS AS ARTICULATED RESTATEMENT

(a) *Does analysis have a function worth its cost?*

Some writers speak very clearly without the apparatus of quantifiers, variables, modal operators and the like. And some have no interest in reductive or eliminative ventures that typically display such apparatus, like Russell's logicism and phenomenalism or Quine's nominalism. There is no philosophical objective that cannot be pursued with adequate discipline and reliability without truth-conditional analysis.

Stating truth conditions is supposed to *articulate* – 'to put together with joints or at the joints' (*Webster's International*) and, in the obsolete sense, 'to draw up or write in separate articles' (corresponding to the logical and conceptual components of its meaning) independently necessary and jointly sufficient conditions for the truth of what is analysed. It is supposed to achieve a restatement that is sufficiently articulated to facilitate disciplined argument or inquiry and somehow elucidate meanings.

Articulation depends upon some kind of decomposition into elements with joints as visible as the whole (like a skeleton). Component states of affairs, each independently necessary and jointly sufficient, are usually sought for that purpose. But there are always alternative decompositions both logically and conceptually. And commonly accepted standards for satisfactory articulation, e.g. a

191

statement of *all* the independent necessary conditions for truth and an explicit representation of the logical form, cannot be met.

David Wiggins (1971a: 26) remarked that difficulties about certain dictionary entries have serious consequences for analysis:

Indeed it is part of what is a much larger flaw in the programme of philosophical analysis, *the unremitting search for analysis by intersubstitutable equivalents*, which has taxed the ingenuity of a whole tradition, Plato (*Theaetetus*), Aristotle, Leibniz (*Characteristica Universalis*), Frege, Moore, Wittgenstein (*Tractatus*), early and middle Carnap and even some Oxford philosophy. When Goodman, Quine and Carnap lower their demands to some looser equivalence I think this smacks more of *disappointment* (and of Goodman's and Quine's dissatisfaction with the idea of *a priori* necessity) than any fundamental reappraisal of what is involved in giving an adequate explanation of sense. Once we revise our ideas about what this really involves it is possible again to see Goodman's merely extensional requirement as much too permissive. And a number of other problems are transformed too [italics added]. (Lewy (1976) nicely expounds the traditional paradoxes of analysis.)

Elsewhere in his paper, Wiggins indicates (1) that the enterprise of truth-conditional analysis is not properly understood; (2) that 'not all meaning specification can be by provision of an intersubstituend' (p. 28); (3) that some equivocal terms cannot be defined disjunctively because 'actually true statements would be converted into false'; (4) that we do not yet know 'what exactly is involved in a satisfactory specification of the intended truth conditions for a sentence' (p. 25); (5) that 'satisfactoriness in an explanation is relative to an interest' (p. 25) but that we do not have 'a very clear idea' ... 'what is the best formulation of the theoretical interest one should have' (p. 25) in providing truth-conditional analyses.

Wiggins (p. 31) thinks, as I do, that 'the existence of non-interchangeable paraphrases for 0^1 and 0^2 is not sufficient condition of ambiguity'. (I think Wiggins uses 'ambiguity' the way I use 'equivocation'.) But that is, I think, because paraphrase differences may represent sentence differences that are not locatable as particular word differences.

Acknowledging Aristotle's insights, Wiggins recognizes that ambiguity and equivocation are related to focal meaning and to analogy of meaning (p. 32). But he does not grasp the importance of analogy of meaning to truth-conditional analysis. Even with Alston's (1971: 40) perceptive remarks that some 'other word ... in the sentence frame ... *shifts its meaning* in the course of these substi-

tutions'. . . [italics added] 'using the substitution test we are assuming that the rest of the sentence holds fast semantically',
Wiggins does not propose that there is a meaning adaptation structure that would explain differentiation. Instead, he stops with the
observation (p. 33):

The generalizable point is that when we distinguish senses we do not
necessarily condemn a word to *pun* status, and that it is part of the equip-
ment of the nature speaker of a language that he possess some principles
(e.g. extension by analogy, extension of senses from a focus) which enable
him to invent or 'cotton on to' new uses of a word and see their rationale.

Then Wiggins commits himself to a 'semantic structure' account
of truth-conditional analysis which, I conjecture, he thinks will
obviate structural analysis of equivocation (1971a: 19):

The truth condition must have been produced by the operation of a systematic, general, and uniform procedure competent to analyse any sentence in
the language into semantic components drawn from a finite list of such
components (i.e. a vocabulary or dictionary). And the procedure must
account for the semantic structure of the sentence by showing how it could
be generated by a finite number of semantically interpreted modifications
or steps from one of the finite number of semantically basic sentence-forms
of the language.

Although Wiggins saw that the intersubstitutability project fails
because the product cannot be substituted, he was distracted by the
generative semantics ideal and offered an impracticable proposal,
see above quotation, for producing truth conditions, which has the
effect of dismissing as unjustified every prior analysis whether or
not it stated truth conditions correctly. Further, it *assumes* that differentiation is not constant and that the vocabulary is finite. And so,
he overlooked the import of Alston's qualifications, that meaning
differentiation is ubiquitous, regular, explicable, and deep in the
chain of accounting for the difficulties with analysis.

There are, indeed, reasons to be disenchanted with truth-
conditional analysis. But they are different. First, many philosophers wisely doubt that 'to know the meaning of *S*' is 'to know the
conditions under which the *statement* expressed by *s* would be
counted as true.'

Secondly, no one stated the relationships between truth conditions and analysandum-frame and benchmark sentences even
plausibly before now, nor did anyone explain what it means to say

193

that sentences with different meanings satisfy the *same* truth conditions.

Thirdly, such analyses fail so often and, apparently, inevitably that there seems no point to the enterprise. Where are conspicuous examples of success?

Fourthly, the compromise to mere equivalence (Goodman and Quine) deflated expectations below our threshold of 'cognitive advance', while the synonymy and substitutability demands of Frege, Moore *et al.* superheated the expected output. Thus no acceptable and achievable performance level has been identified (cf. Wiggins 1971a: 26, note c).

Lastly, the complications now introduced by the analogy phenomena are dismaying. Benchmark sentences, the need to justify such selections, the difficulty of certifying counterexamples, the theoretical difficulty in stating relationships of truth condition frames to benchmarks, the difficulty in specifying whether two sentences are of the same form, the demand for independent tests of sameness of logical form, sameness of meaning and sameness of truth conditions, like unpaid creditors, threaten to expose the technique to be an intellectual chain letter.

But suppose we deny that there is or will be a unique decomposition into basic elements.[6] And suppose we acknowledge that, usually, each condition we state is intended to be *included* in what is meant and that the whole analysis is supposed to express a sufficient and necessary condition for truth but as a whole is *not* required to 'have the same meaning as' or 'be substitutable' for the original but only distinctively to reflect the linguistic meaning of the original expression.

Suppose we become sensitive to the regularity of analogy and to the fact that classifications are often typically differentiated analogously to encompass things that approximate one stereotype better than any of the others, while failing to satisfy any stereotype exactly and failing to satisfy the truth conditions for prior applications of the terms.

Then we can ask again, 'What is the function of analysis?' The answer emerges: '*Articulate restatement of what is meant is the whole function of analysis.*' The degrees of logical and conceptual articulation and the standard of relevance for stated conditions and even the classifications within which conditions are to be expressed are dependent upon the nature of the encompassing philosophical task.

(b) *Identifying meaning-relevant truth conditions*

One cannot practicably state all the logically independent necessary conditions even for a contingent truth and there are none for necessary truths. So one needs to specify a subclass of conditions usefully and practicably to be listed. The natural selection would be 'meaning-relevant' conditions, as I will explain. Nevertheless, other selections can be as well justified, depending upon the kind of inquiry. For instance, one might wish to state the conditions for a crime in terms of the elements that have, independently, to be proved. Any selection of individually necessary and jointly sufficient conditions that reformulates the benchmark and yields a cognitive advance through the decomposition it achieves may be adequate for one or another purpose.

Even where one is presenting meaning-relevant conditions, decomposition and articulation (relative to some larger objective) are necessary for a cognitive advance. And each articulated condition is 'something meant' by the benchmark, 'something meant' in the sense that if the benchmark did not mean that (given its complete environment) then one or another of its component words would have had a different linguistic meaning. (That's what 'meaning-relevant' means here.) Thus, if '*S* believes (assents) that *p*' were not a necessary condition for '*S* knows that *p*' (as 'knows' is meaning-determined in some benchmark sentence), then 'knows' would have had a different meaning.

There is a direct connection between truth conditions for a benchmark and the *antecedent* linguistic meaning of the benchmark. For given another occurrence of the same words in the same sentential form, if *C* is not a necessary condition for *whatever* that sentence is used to state, then some word in that sentence is equivocal with the same word in the benchmark under analysis (and, presumably, correctly analysed). That, I hope, delineates the close connection of equivocation, and therefore, analogy, with providing truth conditions. (I bypass consideration of reference here.)

Even though each stated condition is meaning-relevant, still there is no requirement that the result of analysis must be substitutable for the benchmark sentence or that it 'have the same meaning as the benchmark', although each part of it is something the benchmark means (in the sense specified).

In fact the conjoined conditions *cannot* have the same antecedent linguistic meaning as the benchmark. That follows from the requirement that in some respects the analysis must be a decomposition of the benchmark. So, the conjoined stated conditions do not have to have the same consequent meaning as the benchmark either. That does not rule out that the state(s) of affairs and only that (or those) that make(s) the stated conditions true make(s) the benchmark true.

In brief, truth-conditional analysis for a certain benchmark is likely to make a cognitive advance if: (1) there is joint logical equivalence of the stated conditions and the consequent meaning of the benchmark; (2) each stated condition expresses a 'differentiating' element of what is linguistically meant by the benchmark (see explanation of that as 'meaning-relevance' above); (3) the form of the stated truth conditions articulates the form of the benchmark; and (4) the conceptual units of the stated conditions are (relative to one's philosophical objectives or to ordinary language relationships) conceptual components of the benchmark.

Mere equivalence of analysandum and analysis is too weak; synonymy is too demanding. But decomposition and articulation of what is meant both semantically and logically, along with joint equivalence of conditions and individual meaning-relevance (in the way suggested) are feasible objectives offering substantial cognitive advances.

That test turns out to be eminently useful where there is, in effect, one key word, e.g. 'acted freely', 'intended', 'knows' in a simple benchmark sentence. *For each condition is differentiating just in case the key word would be equivocal (not necessarily 'merely equivocal') in any other occurrence in which that condition did not hold.* For instance if 'being so' were not a necessary condition for 'knows' in some other benchmark, then 'knows' would be equivocal with the given occurrence, as in 'Smith knows everything'.

Further, truth-conditional analyses can be given for a necessary truth. One takes a benchmark expression of it and sententially states those conditions that are necessary and differentiating for key words in the benchmark and jointly equivalent to what is stated. Two different necessary truths will not have the same *complete* sets of differentiating conditions. (A satisfactory analysis does not require a complete set of such conditions to be stated.) And the same state of affairs differently stated (e.g. 'Five times five is twenty five' and 'Five squared is twenty five') may have different analyses.

There is something else to be learned from the suggestion that truth conditions should be 'something meant' by the benchmark. If we regard the first three conditions for 'knowing' – '*S* believes *p*', '*p* is true' and '*S* is justified in believing that *p*' – as being part of what is *meant* by a particular statement of the form 'Jones knows that he owes Smith money', then we also know that *more* is meant, *along the lines* of 'and *S*'s being thus justified is not haphazardly related to *p*'s being so'. That is, something else is meant that precludes accidental coincidence of truth, evidence and belief, though we don't know how to state, in many cases, what else is meant. With respect to the fourth condition, 'knowing' is analogous. That is why some statements of the missing condition cover some cases and others cover others but none fully captures what we mean in all. And a disjunction of such conditions is not what we mean either. (The same is true of the 'believe' condition and the 'justified' condition as well.)

Because cases differ from one another in the *way* that haphazard, unreliable and justification-defeating gaps between one's believing and *what* one believes are *avoided*, there are various functionally equivalent conditions (relatively to the policy of avoiding such gaps). For instance, in some cases 'it is not possible that *S* believe that *p* for the reasons *S* has, when *p* is false' provides such a condition. Because those conditions cannot be *disjoined* to make a *meaning-relevant* condition for either benchmark (above) containing 'knows', it follows that the class of occurrences of 'knows' that satisfies the first three conditions and the *policy* for the fourth condition is analogous. (Again, the same things are true of the 'believe' condition.)

Differentiated same words, say 'knows' (with non-disjoinable fourth conditions but the same first three conditions), just as appropriately classify diverse things, like knowing that I am awake when I am awake and knowing I have a philosophical problem to solve and knowing that it is cloudy, as do three different words like 'intuit', 'recognize' and 'perceive'.

The reasons analysis is thought to have failed conspicuously are to be traced about equally to (a) thinking analyses are *absolute* (stating *what* meaning is, what believing is, or what knowing is) rather than merely instrumental, and (b) thinking that all those things that are *really* knowing, believing, lying, doubting, promising, being justified in believing etc., satisfy the *same* truth conditions – when the very opposite is the fundamental truth.

197

Generally, *if an analysis is supposed to apply to every case that is really F, and if the analysis consists of a single set of truth conditions (even formulated disjunctively), it must be erroneous.* There is nothing designated by any commonly used expression, *T*, in English such that all cases that are *really* cases of *T* satisfy the *same* set of truth conditions (in the sense of 'same' in which two univocal tokens, 'Henry *knows* philosophy', 'Ryle *knows* philosophy', can satisfy the same conditions for knowing).

Once we deflate analysis to its proper instrumental role and reformulate what the conditions are supposed to express, there is no scandal about the failure of analysis; there are successful instrumental analyses (e.g. Chisholm 1976).

There cannot be conspicuous successes at analysis because the conditions for such a success are the very conditions the analogy phenomena *causally* preclude. How can you 'succeed' in saying what 'believing' *really* is, when as soon as you have 'said' it, the analogy phenomena permit the classification of something not satisfying those conditions under the very predicate you have just analysed?

4   DIFFERENTIAL ANALYSIS AND DISJUNCTIVE DEFINITION

(a) *Putnam's lemon*

Distinct truth conditions for benchmarks with analogous predicates can be *analytically equivalent. That is, distinct truth conditions can fulfill, equally well, some principle or policy guiding the application of a common predicate to diverse situations.* Thus the fourth condition for 'knows' may, as noted above, differ equivalently. What about disjoining such conditions into a single analysis? Putnam (1975: 143) provides an example of the 'slightly crazy' results of such disjunctive analysis:

One possible use of a natural kind term is the following: to refer to a thing which belongs to a natural kind which does not fit the 'theory' associated with the natural kind term, but which was believed to fit that theory (and in fact, to be *the* natural kind which fit the theory) when the theory had not yet been falsified.

To analyse '*x* is a lemon' *disjunctively* as '*x* belongs to a natural kind such that *y*, *or* belongs to a natural kind whose normal members were formerly believed to . . .' is 'slightly crazy', he says. He is right because those are distinct conditions correlating with analogous meanings of 'is a lemon'. It should not be surprising at all, to a person who knows about analogy, that 'lemon' might mean 'normal thing of a natural kind with typical properties such as . . .' and also mean 'thing that *used* to be thought to be a normal instance of a natural kind, having the formerly stereotypical properties . . .', but not at the same time and not disjunctively.

Putnam does not say that we deal here with more than one sense (meaning) of the same term ('is a lemon') as I do, but he does say (1975: 143): 'But the fact that a term has several possible uses does not make it a disjunctive term; the mistake is in trying to represent the complex behavior of a natural kind word in something as simple as an analytic definition.'

Putnam is right. The fact that a term has 'several possible uses' cannot be sufficient to make it a disjunctive term, a term that means '*x or y*'. For every term has 'several possible uses', as I have shown, and yet not every term is disjunctive in meaning, as is 'sibling'. In law, as section 6 indicates, terms do come to have disjunctive meanings as a diachronic consequence of analogous extension (to be explained). But not all words that have been extended analogously over time come to have disjunctive meanings, in fact, very few do.

So far, so good. But Putnam describes the mistake awkwardly Some analytic definitions *are* too simple in structure to 'represent the complex behavior of a natural kind word' (1975: 143). Undoubtedly. But the trouble is not that the disjunctive definitions are too simple. It is that they have to represent as univocity ('"bank" means "verge or depository"') what is, in fact, conceptual plurality, equivocation (p. 143; see also 'The Meaning of Meaning', 1975: 215–71). The meaning of 'expected' in 'He expected a fight' is not a disjunct of the meaning of 'expected' in 'He expected a friend'; it is analogous to it. So also with 'action' and 'act' in the phrases 'physical act', 'mental act', 'physical action', 'mental action'. 'Lemon' is used analogously, not only by proportionality but also denominatively in the various meanings Putnam illustrated. Analogous terms do not have their meanings disjunctively; then they would not be analogous but univocal.

(b) *Analogous terms cannot be defined disjunctively*

Suppose someone truth-conditionally analysed various benchmarks containing a word ('game', 'play', 'understand' or 'reflect') that occurs analogously in them. And suppose he proposed now to

199

disjoin the sets of truth conditions into a single disjunctive definition or analysis.

If the truth conditions are supposed to provide a definition, then the enterprise is self-refuting. For the meanings of the predicates are *ex hypothesi* different, analogous, but the proposed truth conditions are the same. Such disjoined conditions cannot 'give' the meaning, the particular sense the term has in either of its supposed contexts.

What then of analysis? The disjoined truth conditions cannot be an adequate restatement of what is stated by any one benchmark because the conditions of the analysis can be satisfied when the benchmark is false. For instance if 'T' occurs analogously in s^1 and s^2 and one analyses the term as 'A or B', then, when s^1 is false because 'T' does not apply in sense 'A', the disjunction 'A *or* B' can be satisfied, namely when 'B' applies. Thus 'Jones can play the piano' would be true if Jones is physically able, whether or not he has the skill. So the analysis would deny the very distinction we make when we talk, in an environment that concerns hiring musicians (say, violinists), about Jones' additional skills.

Furthermore, the very claim that there is a correct disjunctive analysis amounts to a denial that the occurrences are analogous. The proposal to provide disjunctive truth conditions is therefore self-contradictory.

Supporting considerations for the important claim that analogous terms cannot be disjunctively defined (and thereby reduced to or eliminated by univocity) follow.[7] One cannot create disjunctive meanings for equivocal terms because some sentences (in their consequent meanings) already true would have to be false on such readings. Consider Wiggins' example (1971a: 28) of 'bank' defined as 'verge or depository'. On that reading, 'All United States banks are supervised by state and federal bank examiners' is false, whereas in fact it is true. Similarly, 'All banks on major waterways and along the coast are inspected by the Army Corps of Engineers' would have to be false, when it would, or might, otherwise be true. Because analogous terms are equivocal terms, I could apply the argument to them by instantiation. But illustration is more persuasive.

Imagine various senses for 'read' in truth conditions for sentences of the form 'S read the x'. In one sense a person reads only if he extracts a meaning from inscriptions having meaning inherently, 'S read the letter'; in another, he reads if he extracts *the* meaning even if the inscriptions are not inherently meaningful, '*S* read the morse code signal, deciphering'. In a third meaning, a person reads even if he extracts no meaning at all but only says the letters or the words or makes the sounds (reading nonsense words or the eye–chart). Now if '*S* reads *X*' is true if and only if '(a) *S* extracts meaning from inherently meaningful inscriptions via visual perception (etc.) *or* (b) *S* deciphers and extracts a meaning from a code signal *or* (c) S sounds out words, *or* sounds out letters, etc., or (d) . . .', then, when a contract to teach reading, not otherwise defined, is signed, it could be fulfilled by teaching letter sounding alone.

While it is obvious that in various contexts 'read' can mean either (a) or (b) or (c) or (d), there will be few contexts indeed in which it means '(a) or (b) or (c) or (d)' and in every one of those it is *equivocal* with each of the others. Otherwise, when asked 'Can you read French?' one could reply affirmatively without knowing a word of French because one could read the letters.

Another example, although 'scholars' can mean either 'serious students' or 'established researchers', or even the disjunction of the two, a library rule 'Rare manuscript collections open to scholars only' would have its exclusion of students defeated if read disjunctively. The simple fact is that a term that means both (a) and (b) in different occurrences does not on that account mean '(a) or (b)' in any particular occurrence. Disjunctive analysis would conflict with that fact.

(c) *Counterexamples and analysis*

Let me distinguish positive counterexamples of two kinds and negative counterexamples. Positive counterexamples bear the predicate being analysed and (a) are not subject to one or more of the stated truth conditions proposed for the benchmark, or (b) require additional necessary conditions for joint sufficiency. Negative counterexamples satisfy the truth conditions stated and do not bear the predicate under analysis.

There is no positive counterexample unless the predicate in the example is univocal with the predicate in the benchmark. Thus if a counterexample to an analysis of '*S* acted freely in doing *X*' which has '*S* could have done otherwise than *X*' as a truth condition, is supposed to be expressed by 'God acted freely in being just to Jones', which does *not* entail 'God could have done otherwise than have been just to Jones', it must be independently determined that 'acted freely' in the latter is univocal with the benchmark.

One can challenge a purported positive counterexample for sameness of logical form and univocity. But, without making the whole inquiry circular, one cannot base one's assertions about absence of univocity exclusively or mainly upon the countercase's not satisfying the stated truth conditions for the benchmark. Considerations for and against univocity have to go outside the circle of truth conditions (further evidence against Davidson's theory of meaning).

The same requirements hold for negative counterexamples except that the predicates of the stated truth conditions for the proposed counterexamples must, in case of doubt, be tested for univocity with the predicates in the stated conditions for the benchmark. Furthermore, the force of the negative countercase depends upon our being certain that we would *not* characterize the situation with the benchmark's predicate applied univocally. It is, further, erroneous to conclude that something that does not satisfy the truth conditions for some benchmark 'is not a case of F' (e.g. of expecting), where all that is justified is 'is not a case of F (of expecting) where F (expecting) is univocal with the benchmark occurrence'.

5   ANALOGY AND ANALYTIC JURISPRUDENCE

In his famous Inaugural lecture, Hart emphasized two central ideas: (1) that analysis of legal concepts should be *truth-conditional*, 'the cardinal principle that legal words can only be elucidated by considering the conditions under which the statements in which they have their characteristic uses are true' (1953: 28); and (2) that common expressions central both within legal (craft-bound) discourse (say, about corporations) and within non-technical, non-legal (unbound) discourse, e.g. 'wills', 'knows', 'resides in', 'exists', are *analogous*, 'when words used normally of individuals are applied to companies, as well as the analogy involved, there is also involved a radical difference in the modes in which such expressions are now used and *a shift in meaning*' [italics added] (1953: 26).

The reasons he gives for each of these claims err markedly, though the claims themselves approximate the truth. For instance, it is not true that 'legal words can *only* be elucidated by . . . conditions under which the statements . . . are true' [italics added] (1953: 28). Such words are elucidated in legal decisions (see examples below) and in the Socratic method of the law schools where the technique of truth-conditional analysis would be inefficient. Even for philosophical purposes, the kind of explication Hohfeld employed (Hohfeld 1923 and Radin 1938), has considerable elucidatory value.

Truth-conditional analysis is an instrument to achieve conceptual decomposition and logical articulation. Like coronary arteriography it has inherent dangers risked for strategic necessities. Lapse of attention or confusion can introduce novel errors, e.g. Hart's fatal ambiguities of quantification in analysing 'X has a right' in terms of the obligations of (some, all, certain?) others to forbear or conform (1953: 16) and the futile attempt to find a single set of truth conditions for analogous terms.

Hart's observations about the 'shift in meaning' in legal discourse not only indicate his awareness of analogy of meaning but provide for an easy illustration of the way analogy and analysis interact.

Hart offers a perceptive reason for thinking there is a 'shift in meaning' (1953: 26–7):

Hence any ordinary words or phrases when conjoined with the names of corporations *take on a special legal use*, for the words are now correlated with the facts, not solely by the rules of ordinary English but also by the rules of English law much as when we *extend words* like 'take' or 'lose' by using them of tricks in games, they become correlated with facts by the rules of that game [italics added].

. . . the word 'will' *shifts* its meaning when we use it of a company [italics added].

Analogy with a living person and *shift of meaning* are therefore of the essence of the mode of legal statement which refers to corporate bodies [italics added].

The 'shift in meaning' for 'ordinary words' when applied to corporations is explained, first, because the words are applied or withheld under an additional set of rules, 'the rules of English law' (an approximation of the idea of craftbound discourse), and secondly, because the words are applied to a non-human by analogy with living persons. At least four times he speaks of 'actions analogous' (p. 20), 'analogous' circumstances (p. 21), 'analogy with a living person' (p. 27), and 'analogy is not identity' (p. 27).

Those two reasons are quite different in their effects. That words are applied or withheld under the rules of English law at least intimates that legal discourse is craftbound and has its own predicate schemes. Hart's saying we apply the word 'person' to what are,

203

outside the law, not persons (corporations), by analogy to real persons, is an intimation that *within* legal discourse words differentiate; for instance, 'person' in voting laws under which corporations and trusts are not persons, and 'person' in the law of jurisdiction under which corporations and trusts are persons. Mixed with these two facts, Hart touches upon a third: that same words occur in both legal discourse and unbound discourse (he says, 'ordinary words and phrases . . . take on a special legal use') and in doing so are differentiated, but not merely equivocally.

Throughout Hart's lecture the three phenomena interweave. But they have to be disentangled here because important consequences for jurisprudence attach to each: (a) that legal discourse is craftbound – that was explained in chapter 7; (b) that *within* legal discourse there is analogy of meaning – that is the basis for the discussion of judicial decision in section 6, next; and (c) that legal discourse is embedded by similarity of meaning matrices in unbound discourse – that is the basis for the cognitive continuity of the craftbound talk of lawyers with their other craftbound and unbound discourse.

Although there has been no serious challenge to the cognitive continuity of legal discourse, its embedding in natural language should be kept in mind as an exemplar for the embedding of religious, scientific and ethical discourse in unbound and other craftbound discourse.

It is the analogy of meaning *within* legal discourse that has destructive effects upon Hart's proposed analysis, and yet contains the material for a significant advance in analytic jurisprudence, one that I illustrate in section 6 with an account of judicial characterization problems.

Hart recognized, but described differently, the following fact: *all predicates differentiate when used as craftbound legal expressions in contrast to some unbound occurrences.* Some terms of art are entirely craftbound, like certain expressions in religious and scientific discourse, having their meanings entirely from the contrasts within craft discourse ('collateral estoppel'); others are incidentally craftbound, differentiating when dominated by craftbound terms ('is the cause of'). And, of course, some words, not terms of art, are univocal in legal and non-legal contexts, such as the words used to describe the facts that generate the need for legal classification, 'Smith hit Jones with the ax'.

But Hart did not distinguish and remark upon a fundamental fact for analytic jurisprudence: *Terms of art* (like 'possession', 'signature', 'consideration', 'promise', 'payment', 'judgment', 'right', 'liberty', 'duty', 'knows', 'intends', 'wills', 'complains', 'defends', 'caused' and thousands of others) *differentiate in contrasting LEGAL contexts.* Legal discourse is shot through with analogy of meaning. Hohfeld, distinguishing 'right' as a correlate of 'duty', as approximating 'liberty', 'power', and 'immunity' in various contexts, incidently shows us that 'right' is often equivocal and yet not merely equivocal in legal discourse.

The 'meaning shift' of 'acted knowingly and wilfully' applied to Smith and to Smith Corporation is only the tip of an iceberg, titanic to Hart's analysis. For we are told that '*X* has a legal right' may be truth-conditionally analysed by the following sufficient condition (1953: 16):

(a) There is in existence a legal system.
(b) Under a rule or rules of the system *some other person Y* is, in the events which have happened, obliged to do or abstain from some action.
(c) This obligation is made by law dependent *on the choice* either of *X* or some *person* authorized to act on his behalf so that either *Y* is bound to do or abstain from *some action* only if *X* (or some authorized person) so *chooses* or alternatively only until *X* (or *such person*) chooses otherwise. [italics added].

A sufficient condition elucidates but does not analyse. For a merely sufficient condition could be entirely irrelevant, for instance, '*S* has a legal right to *p*' if '*S* has a liberty, power, immunity, privilege or other claim to *p* that is enforceable at law'. Why isn't that just as useful as Hart's proposal? (It does make clear that '*S* has a right to *p*' does not always entail '*S* has a *right* to *p*.')

Chopping up Hart's analysis would be cruel sport were its instruction not indispensible. Either Hart's analysis does not capture a sufficient condition for '*X* has a legal right...' in the vast class of legal assertions of that general form or the words *within* the stated condition must differentiate exactly covariantly with equivocations in the analysandum sentences. How could anyone not suspect so unlikely a covariance? By overlooking its necessity, by not attending to the fact that many instantiations of '*X* has a legal right...' are equivocal; and furthermore, by not having noticed that you cannot define equivocal terms disjunctively.

There is nothing to indicate why Hart regards his chosen units of

205

logical and conceptual decomposition to be atomic (appropriately simple). Why take 'bound to do', 'authorized', 'obliged', 'conform' and 'forbear', and the like, as units for analysis rather than *their* conceptual components? Whether the analysis is to be a reduction to non-legal discourse has to be decided; whether the units of decomposition are appropriate to the larger philosophical enterprise has to be decided; and whether logical form is suitably articulated (e.g. why not use deontic modal logic for 'obliged', 'authorized', etc.) has to be determined.

'Action' and 'chooses' differentiate when the substituend for '*Y*' is 'Smith Corporation' rather than 'Smith'; that may cause *'has a right'* to differentiate. (One cannot provide analyses without complete benchmarks in actual discourse.) Hart wants simultaneously to acknowledge the differentiation and keep the *same* statement of truth conditions.

The need for benchmark occurrences of legal words (that have the effect of rigidly designating the facts) has been systematically recognized in Anglo-American law by the characteristic anchoring of legal analysis to the facts and judicial rationales of particular *cases* and in the warning, 'you cannot understand the rule of the case apart from its facts'.

This is an appropriate place to mention that in *some* cases where we do not know how to provide an analysis for the specific senses in which a common word like 'is alive' applies analogously to various kinds of things, we can provide a single set of truth conditions that is satisfied by analogously differentiating the predicates in the analysis, in each of the cases. Aristotle defined 'to be alive' as 'to be actively self-moving' and held that both the definiendum and the definiens apply analogously over the same range of predications, plants, animals, humans, intelligences, God. No doubt this can be, and must be, done with a great many words, like 'cause', 'explain' and 'determine'. The fact that we cannot say just what the differences are among such cases (of being alive, for instance), may be of the greatest metaphysical importance.

But for the purposes of this work, I do not want attention bemused with the fact that, if we are resourceful as Aristotle was, we can give something *like* a truth-conditional analysis with predicates differentiating over a range of analogous applications. Whether that is always so with (proportionally) analogous (but not metaphorical) words, I am not certain, but I think it doubtful. And

206

so we need to explain *why* it is sometimes possible and sometimes not. The matter will have to be investigated separately and need not detain us now. But it does suggest that philosophical analysis can be applied to fashioning *analogous* definitions and to test for the *range* of contexts over which they articulate what is meant by the analysandum.

There is a cognitive advance from the point Hart had reached in grasping the 'meaning shift': namely, analogy of meaning is a *direct result* of the kind of predicate projection the legal system uses appellate courts to achieve.

6 ANALOGY AND JUDICIAL DECISION

Here is a final illustration of the practical consequences of the analogy phenomena for philosophy. There is a class of judicial decisions that involve *characterization* problems. Such decisions frequently result in the differentiating (analogous) projection of legal predicates. I call the activity 'projecting' in order to associate it with problems of induction (Goodman 1965: 57–8, 81–3, 84–9); but it is distinguished from simple induction by the fact that such classification of new cases under old labels differentiates the labels analogously.

Not all appellate cases, by any means, involve decisions of that sort. But a significant number do, when the facts differ markedly from those stereotyped in precedent, yet the judicial rationales of prior opinions seem applicable. In such cases the argument *against* applying a certain predicate is the evident and relevant distinguishability of the instant facts from the stereotypes given by precedent. The argument *for* applying the predicate is that the general legal policies and principles that demanded application of the contested predicate to the fact stereotype (the precedent) in the first place would be violated or ill-served by denying the predicate to the present case.

I distinguish cases that involve decisions of legal *principle*, as Dworkin (1977) explains in his discussion of 'hard cases', from cases that as a result of prior decisions of principle present problems of analogous classification. The latter, too, can present hard cases.

For instance, in the earliest *scienter* cases, competing *principles* were of the sorts: (a) buyers, unable to check out all materially relevant facts for themselves, should be indemnified for harm suffered when they are induced to rely to their detriment on knowingly false claims of a seller; (b) 'buyer beware' is enough protection; (c) any material falsehood, whether or not knowing and whether or not accessible to checking, should make the seller liable to indemnify the buyer. The first principle was held to govern, so that damage through *knowing* falsehood was made the basis for holding the seller liable. And principles of strict liability (c), and of no liability (b), were rejected. Thus the *scienter* condition for fraud was created at common law. Those cases settled matters of legal principle.

A later case, where the seller did not lie, but without any effort to find out the truth assured the buyer of what was false (e.g. that a house has a cellar), and induced him to rely to his detriment upon those material misrepresentations, falls under the same general considerations: to protect buyers from the reprehensible misrepresentations of sellers. The facts of the second are with respect to the general *principle*, equivalent to the first: whether there was lying or merely utter disregard for truth, the misrepresentation is reprehensible because accompanied by lack of belief. But, argued the opponent, the public policy was to protect the buyer from *knowing* misrepresentation. Now one proposes to make the defendant *retroactively* liable in a situation that clearly does *not* involve lying (saying what one knows to be false), just utterance, *without belief*, of what happens to be false. The court had to decide whether reckless disregard for whether what is said is true, given the public objective of protecting the buyer from culpable misrepresentation, is enough like a knowing falsehood to satisfy the '*scienter*' condition. In effect, under governing principles are the situations equivalent? *Scienter* was found in that case, and the *meaning* of '*scienter*' was altered by analogous projection to be 'misrepresentation through false assertion accompanied by *lack of belief* in what is asserted', rather than 'accompanied by knowledge of falsity'.[8]

Projection of predicates to characterize new circumstances is frequently differentiating and often has the effect of altering a single sufficient condition, e.g. 'knowing misrepresentation', to a disjunctive one, 'knowing misrepresentation or reckless disregard of the truth', or 'false and known to be' to 'false and known to be *or* false and not believed or false and believed unreasonably'. See, for instance, 'malice' in libel law; *Times* v. *Sullivan*, 376 US. 254 (1964).

Similarly, the precedent that defined common law rape described situations with legal rationales involving stereotyped forced sexual entry of a woman, not the defendant's spouse, where resistance and/

or unconsciousness were evidence for the force. What then of a doctor who told a rural, mildly retarded sixteen-year-old girl that unless she accepted his 'medical treatment' she would certainly die? She co-operated. Is that 'sexual entry by force' sufficient to support a charge of rape?

Judicial decision in such cases is a matter of construal, in consciousness of various principles and policies of law and of the analogous developments in the law of assault and battery ('unwanted touching', 'fraud that turns touching into assault'), so that when the predicate, 'entry by force', is applied, it is applied analogously to the line of precedent in the law of rape.

With conservatism characteristic of the law, a term T, used analogously in cases 1 (the earlier precedent) and 2 (the new projection that is now precedent, too), often becomes a disjunctive term whose meaning is 'either T as in 1 *or* T as in 2', like 'sibling' that means 'brother or sister' or 'cousin' that means 'offspring of either parent's siblings'. T may further differentiate when applied in some new case that satisfies neither stereotype 1 nor 2, giving rise to disjunction at a later stage. For instance, a *'scienter'* case might involve statements of one who misrepresents the material facts by assertions in which he lacks belief, who is not *reckless*, but only *negligent*; for instance, he does not hold his tongue when he should.[9]

The sub-areas of law employ words analogously, too. What is property in law of jurisdiction is not always property for inheritance law, again for very good reasons of legal principle and public policy. Whether something or another counts as being *an F* or being *G*, or counts as being *of the same sort as* some other thing in a certain area of the law, is a matter either of statutory determination (subject to judicial interpretation) or judicial construal. (An apt illustration of the differentiation through time and across different areas of law of one representative word, 'issue', may be found in Dorothy Sayers' story *Unnatural Death* (1944: 141–3).)

Judges are the only relevant 'experts'. I have in mind here the way Putnam (1975: 139–52) explained the *extension* of natural kind words from stereotypical instances, via scientific theories, to cases that on the surface do not satisfy the stereotypes. 'Asking an expert is enough of a test for the normal speaker; that's why we don't give a test in an ordinary context.' Judges fulfill the role of 'experts' in determining the extension of legal terms, often possessing an articulated *theory* of what 'fraud', 'malice', 'intention', 'issue', 'easement', 'adverse user', 'reliance' or 'consideration' consist in. *They* tell, about the cases that can't satisfactorily be classified by simple application of stereotypes (precedent facts), how they are to be labeled. (See amplified discussion by Putnam 1975: 215–71, especially his summary at 271 and also 146: 'The problem in semantic theory is to get away from the picture of the meaning of a word as something like a *list of concepts*; not to formalize that misguided picture.')

It is even an exercise of judicial construal to determine that a question raises an issue of fact rather than an issue of law. No expert is allowed to settle whether a heifer is a cow or, under the Interstate Motor Vehicle Act, whether an airplane is a motor vehicle,[10] or whether railroad engines are railroad cars under a federal statute providing that brakemen injured by cars without automatic couplers are to be indemnified.[11]

On all such matters where statute or prior decision does not already provide descriptive conditions that the new case directly satisfies, judicial construal determines what are the relevant stereotypes and whether under the controlling principles and policies the new facts are equivalent to the old and bear the same predicate.

Analogy of meaning, even within narrow areas of the law, is so obvious, once one has learned to discern it, that proposals like Hart's for a single set of truth conditions for expressions of the form '*X* is a *motor vehicle*', '*S* acted with *malice*',[12] '*S*'s saving *Z* and being injured in the process was *consideration* for *Z*'s later promise to support *S*',[13] or 'The parents of *S* *neglected S*' [in not providing him access to free medical care needed to correct a hare-lip and cleft palate[14]] are plainly abortive.

Truth-conditional analysis can effectively apply to legal discourse. One can group differentiated words into clusters of related meanings to look for analytic equivalences. Such clusters undoubtedly reflect the values and principles that guide the development of law, just as differentiations of 'action', 'free', and 'act' can reveal important truths about our understanding of human action. Analysis can be even more effectively accomplished when relevant co-occurring distinct expressions are similarly compared, for instance, 'knowingly', 'materially relevant', 'matter of fact', 'reliance', and 'detriment' in a body of law concerning fraud.

Finally, it cannot be said that philosophers applying such analysis to law will be doing anything vastly different in substance from what is already done, less formally, by legal theorists. If there is not an explanatory, descriptive or critical objective that requires the articulateness afforded by the truth-conditional analytic device, the apparent precision will be superfluous.

Notes

INTRODUCTION

1 The expression 'same words', without 'the', is used throughout the book to substitute for the cumbersome 'different tokens of the same word' and similar phrases. It cannot be replaced by 'polysemes' or 'homonyms' because same words can be either. Thus, I use expressions like 'meaning relationships among same words are regular and law-governed' instead of 'among tokens or occurrences of the same words'.

2 Other writers have remarked on some of these points. For instance, H. L. A. Hart (1953) and W. P. Alston (1971) both talked about shifts of meaning for the same word when concatenated with different surrounding words. George M. Miller (1971:569–85) remarked that 'nouns may have a relatively stable semantic character, but the words that go with them, adjectives and verbs, are much more dependent upon context for their classification'. Eric H. Lenneberg (1971:536–57) said, 'the static dictionary meaning of words does not appear to restrict speakers in their cognitive activities'. Uriel Weinreich (1971:322) recognized that there may be *infinite polysemy* in the language and that a Fodor-Katz dictionary would thus be thwarted. An ideal dictionary that had to have an entry for each sense would not be ideal at all. Just the opposite: any sense should be generable from some given dictionary paradigm in a few steps that take account of the semantic features of the 'completion expressions', the other words in the environment.

In any case, Weinreich saw that there is a linguistic *differentiation* structure and even used the same word for it ('differentiation', p.322) that I do. Further Kurylowicz's analysis of 'two subpaths' for 'dictionary entry' (see Weinreich 1971:323) is similar to (but the converse of) my analysis of mere equivocation. See also 'Where do noun phrases come from?' by James D. McCawley (1971:217–31) and Howard M. Maclay's fine 'Overview' (1971:57–81). I delay detailed comment upon the excellent Wiggins and Alston papers (Steinberg & Jakobovits, 1971) until chapter 8, acknowledging their approximation of some of my observations.

3 A *benchmark sentence* is a sentence in a complete discourse environment that determines, fixes, unambiguously, the linguistic meaning of some word or expression one wants to analyse. It makes all the difference whether 'knows' has the sense of 'Plato knows philosophy', 'Fleabrain knows everything', 'Charlene knows men' or 'Chisholm knows there are physical objects'. Thus a benchmark is a sentence whose environment fixes the meaning as far as the analysis will require.

A *benchmark situation* (see chapter 7) is an experience or observation or story that provides a stereotype, a paradigmatic case, that fixes the sense (linguistic meaning) of a predicate (or predicates) used to construe it. The facts of a case in law, clinical observations in medicine, a bible story, are examples. For instance, the experience of pressing a patient's abdomen while the medical teacher says 'Now that's what we call distended'. Benchmark situations are fact stereotypes of what counts as a such and such (explained in chapter 7, 4c).

4 Some might want to deny that I've formulated *laws* of differentiation. In part that represents a disagreement about how particular and how quantified data has to be for generalizations that hold for it to count as laws. I do present universally quantified propositions that hold counterfactually and exhibit some kind of necessity. One might look at the generalizations on pages 82, 92 (a and b), 95, 99, 102, 104, 117, 119–20, 128, 129, 130, 131, 137, 138, 147, 174.

CHAPTER 1

1 For some things are called beings, or are said to be, because they have being of themselves, as substances which are called beings in the primary and proper sense. Others are called beings because they are the affections or properties of substances, as the proper accidents of any substance. Others are called beings because they are processes toward substance, as generation and motion. And others are called beings because they are the corruptions of substances; for corruption is the process toward non-being just as generation is the process toward substance. And since the corruption terminates in privation just as generation terminates in form, the very privations of substantial forms are fittingly called beings. Again, certain qualities or certain accidents are called beings because they are productive or generative principles of substances or of those things which are related to substance according to one of the foregoing relationships *or any other relationship*. And similarly, the negations of those things which are related to substances, or even the substance itself, are also called beings. Hence we say that non-being *is* non-being. But this would not be possible unless a negation possessed being in some way [italics added]. Aquinas, *In Met.*, IV, l. 1, n. 539. (see Aristotle, *Meta.*, 1003b, 5f).

As regards analogous terms, however, *the things which are the foundation of the analogy* (say, quantity in so far as it is related in this way to its 'to be') are diverse in number, species and genus; nevertheless, they are the same in nature, not absolutely, but proportionally; for the notion of one is proportionally the same as that of the other (Cajetan, *De Nom. Anal.*, ch.6, no.65.) [italics added].

2 Cajetan, *De Nom. Anal.*, ch. 4, no. 36: 'in analogous names, on the other hand, the foundations of analogous similitude are of a different nature absolutely, and of the same nature to a certain extent, i.e., by proportion. Hence we must distinguish a twofold mental concept of the analogous name – one perfect and the other imperfect – and we must say that to the analogous name and its analogates there corresponds one imperfect mental concept, and as many perfect concepts as there are analogates.'

The 'one imperfect mental concept' is not a disjunction of the 'perfect' concepts and *they* are not determinates in relation to a determinable (the imperfect concepts) either. See Wittgenstein, *P.I.* 70, 71.

3 Norman Kretzmann (1967) cogently stated the characteristic scholastic (Aristotelean) view that concepts are the meanings of words, causally deriving from the quiddities of things, with conceptual modes (modes of signification) that parallel the modes of being (*modi essendi*) of the things known. A more intricate analysis of Aquinas' notion of the 'mental word', *verbum mentale*, is provided, particularly in the first two chapters, by Bernard J. Lonergan (1967).

4 Distinctions occur in our utterances which are not the result of our deliberate intention but are part of our expressed thought. When such distinctions have been provided as a result of linguistic structure, the language has done some of our thinking for us. Thus the grammar can provide elements of our thought by

making singular–plural distinctions, or verb–adjective distinctions ('clear') to which we often do not even advert. So too, semantic structures make distinctions of thought so subtle that not only do we not consciously formulate them in advance of speaking, we often cannot satisfy ourselves upon how to describe the distinctions that have been made: 'An accidental fall is non-voluntary and also involuntary.' See John Austin's *How to do Things with Words*, (Oxford, Clarendon Press, 1962). See also chapter 4, pp. 99–100, below.

5 Palmer (1973) says reasoning that employs analogous terms equivocates, which, in syllogistic reasoning, creates the fallacy of 'four terms'. In a romping and irreverent way, Palmer exploits the weaknesses of traditional explanations of analogy to accuse it of illogicality, agnosticism and nonsense. Needless to say, he does not grasp Bochenski's argument and does not understand the classical analogy theory as it has been interpreted here. And he is entirely unaware of the importance of analogy and equivocation to philosophy of language.

Patrick J. Sherry (1976a) criticizes both Palmer's negative account and Burrell's (1973) positive account insightfully and trenchantly. Sherry (1976b) also relates 'modern linguistic philosophy' to Aquinas on analogy, giving apt examples of analogous predication: 'rich', 'flourishing', 'sound', 'strong,' 'life', 'intelligent', 'thoughtful', and p.439, 'Blackpool is healthier than any complexion'.

Yves Simon (1960: 1–42) offered what still seems to me the most profound recent account (see pp. 41–2) of the way analogous predication functions to extend understanding. Note Simon's discussion of 'Classification by Stereotype', at pp. 1–2, a subject of recent inquiry by Putnam (1975).

6 Aristotle, *Meta.*, 1071a, 5; 1070b, 18: 'one might say that there are three principles – the form, the privation and the matter. But each of these is different for each class. . . . Therefore, analogically there are three elements and four causes and principles.' 'There must be three kinds of movement – of quality, of quantity and of place' (1068a, 9). And, 1070a, 31: 'The causes and principles of different things are in a sense different, but in a sense, if one speaks universally and analogically, they are the same for all. . . .' 'What then will this common element be? For there is nothing common to and distinct from substance and the other categories'; (1070b, 18) 'but all things have not the same elements in this sense, but only analogically'; (1070b–25) *'therefore, analogically there are three elements, and four causes and principles'*; (1071a–5) 'Analogically identical things are principles, i.e. actuality and potency; but these are not only different for different things but also apply in different ways to them.' Cf. also 1093b, 18: 'For they are accidents, but the things that agree are all appropriate to one another, and one by analogy. For in each category of being an analogous term is found – as the straight is in length, so is the level in surface, perhaps the odd in number and the white in color.'

7 See *Meta.*, 1003a, 31–5 (cf. Aquinas' comments in *In Met.*, IV, 1. 1, n.535–6) and 1003b, 1–18; also 1016b, 32–1017a, 5. *N.E.,* 1096a, 17–30; 1096b, 28–30. Aristotle also remarked that the representation and the exemplar bear the same name equivocally, *Cat.* 1a, ff. 'Thus a real man and a figure in a picture can both lay claim to the name "animal"; yet they are equivocally so named, for, though they have a common name, the definition corresponding with the name differs for each.'

See analogy *'pros hen legomena'*, *N.E.*, 1096a, 17ff; *Meta.* 1003a 33–1003b 10; 'attribution' in *Meta.* and *Top.*, where Aquinas' examples of the 'cause' and 'sign' relational analogies originate; proportionality' in *Meta.*, e.g. 1048b, 5–8, 'But all things are not said in the same sense to exist actually, but by analogy – as A is in or to B, C is in or to D; for some *are*, as movement to potency, and others as substance to some sort of matter.' See also *Phys.*, 249a; 'what is clearness in a voice is not the same as what is clearness in water'. And, finally, *Poet.*, 1457b, 5–33.

214

8 Aristotle, *Meta.*, 1070b, 16–25; 1071a, 5; 7–17; 1048b, 5–9 and 1048a, 37. See Muskens (1943). Aquinas, *In Met.*, III, 10, 465; XII, 4, 2483–86; XII, 4N. 2480n; 'for as man's mind is related to its known object so God is to his' *Ia IIae*, 3, 5 ad 1. Also, *De Ver.*, 2, 11, c.

CHAPTER 2

1 I am particularly grateful to Dr Rose Ann Christian who, while a graduate student in Religious Thought at the University of Pennsylvania, told me about the Aristotle passage.
2 One Englishman had just explained that 'he felt a perfect ass', when he confused his hostess with a guest, saying, 'It's a pretty dreary party isn't it?' Another replied that once at a dinner, he too had felt a perfect ass, but that happened when his hostess' pearls slipped down her backless evening gown and he thoughtlessly reached after them.

CHAPTER 3

1 Adrienne Lehrer kindly lent me a prepublication manscript of her book (1974a) that provided some of the examples here and gave me some first ideas about lexical fields. John Lyons' discussion (1966) was the source of others.
2 A near synonym for a given word (in a complete environment) is a distinct word that, when substituted in the otherwise unaltered sentence frame, creates a sentence approximately the same in meaning as the corresponding original, without newly differentiating any of the frame words.
3 The difference between syntactic (nominal) key and semantic (harmonic) key is explained rather fully in W. E. Webster, *A Theory of Diatonic Musical Scores,* 1971 (University Microfilms, Ann Arbor, Mich.) See also: 'A Theory of the Compositional Work of Music', *The Journal of Aesthetics and Art Criticism,* Fall 1974. I thank Professor Webster for helping me with the examples in this section.
4 I am indebted to John Ruane, S. J., for raising the issue and to Chris Bache, who I think suggested the word 'entrenchment' to describe the *bias* some words have to one rather than another scheme. Entrenchment in schemes provides support for Goodman's observation that vital metaphors involve 'submission while protesting'.
5 This statement of conditions for dominance has, I think, benefited from Jonathan Malino's, Ladd Sessions' and Edward Weirenga's criticism of an earlier version.

CHAPTER 4

1 Aristotle, *Categories,* 1a: 'things are said to be named equivocally when, though they have a common name, the definition corresponding to the name differs for each'. That is often interpreted as 'things named equivocally have nothing in common but the name'. See Anton (1968 and 1969). Philippe (1969) traces the text of Aristotle for 'analogia' and its cognates. This is a rich source of textual information. It has a less detailed parallel for Aquinas in Meagher (1970). On Aristotle see also Dubaile (1969).

Apparently Boethius (*In Categorias Aristotelis,* Migne Patrologia Latina, vol. 64, col. 164b and 166) introduced the distinction between equivocation 'a casu' and 'a consilio', which I take as 'fortuitous' or 'haphazard' as against 'conventional' or 'law-governed'. '*Aequivocorum alia sunt casu, alia consilio, ut Alexander Priami filius et Alexander Magnus.*' (Quotation and citation taken from McInerny 1961:72.)

2 If x and y are both correctly said to be alive, but 'alive' is analogous as applied to the pair, are all more general terms that apply to both, say, 'physical object' or 'thing', also analogous? (See Maurer (1955) for a parallel discussion of Aquinas.) I conjecture that if the dominating expressions are not categorially distinct (see section 5 of this chapter), then when a common completion word is analogous (by proportionality), all the commonly *implied* predicates are also analogous (including 'to be' or 'exists') and all predicates that *logically imply the analogous common one* are also, but not more general predicates that are logically independent of the common one. However, this matter needs a separate inquiry.

3 I infer that from what they said about genus and species. (See Owens 1951 and Maurer 1955.) Maurer seems to think some kind of analogy is involved in predicating the genus of members of the species, but a different kind of analogy from proportionality, because the 'logical intention' of 'animal' is the same but, in effect, what *makes* a dog an animal is different from what makes a human one. That corresponds to questions that are generated by reflection on the Kripke–Putnam talk about natural kinds: there may be a 'nominal' or 'analytic' specific essence, the essence of the kind, such that 'men are rational animals' is analytically true and there may be a *real* or empirical essence of the kind, formulated in *a posteriori* necessary truths, such that 'men are carbon-based molecular structures organized in the following way ... DNA ...'. And so, the *real* organization (like a program) that makes a dog an animal is different from that which makes a human an animal. That would support hypotheses that 'analogy of inequality' really does have something to do with meaning.

4 Having given the same name to different things (e.g. 'an attack and an accusation are both called "charges" '), one tends to find communities among them. 'Do we see analogies between things because there are similar forms for referring to them in our language?', John C. Calahan (1970: 406) asked. See Cajetan's interesting discussion of the 'bone, spine, pounce' case at no. 117 and no. 118 of *De Nom. Anal.* (1498). And Calahan refers to Max Black (1962) who espoused what Goodman later described as 'reducing simile to metaphor'. Wittgenstein (P.I. 104) was puzzled by related phenomena: 'We predicate of a thing what lies in the method of representing it.'·

5 Cajetan, *De Nom. Anal.*, no. 25; and *Comm in S.T.* I, 13, 3 (I); Aquinas, *Ia*, 13, 3, ad 3; *In I Sent.*, 45, 1, 4 c; *In IV Sent.*, 45, 1, 1, qa. i, ad 2; *De. Ver.*, 2,2, ad 2. Meagher (1970) contains comprehensive metaphor citations. See also Boyle (1954 and 1957).

CHAPTER 5

1 'Derivative' is used in *Basic Works of Aristotle,* Random House, 1941: 'Things are said to be named derivatively which derive their name from some other name but differ from it in termination.' The Greek word being thus translated as 'denominative' in Latin and 'derivatively' in English is παρονωμα.

2 D. P. Henry (1972: 57, and 1967: 31–116).

3 Aquinas observed: '*Omnia quae habent ordinem ad unum aliquid licet diversimode, ab illo denominari possunt*' *IIIa* 60, 1 c. Other passages where denomination is mentioned or explained include: *Ia*, 6, 4 c; *Ia*, 33, 2 ad 2; *C.G.* IV, 74; *Ia*, 37, 2 ad 2; *C.G.* II, 13; *Ia IIae* 111, 1; *IIIa* 22, 6; *Phys.*, III, 1. 1; *Phys.*, V, 1. 3; *De Ver.*, 21, 4 ad 2.

4 I thank my colleague, Ruth Mattern, for indicating the passages where Locke preserved the medieval 'denomination-absolute naming' distinction.

5 See the note at no. 10 of Cajetan's *De Nom. Anal.*, Bushenski and Koren translation, for illuminating citations from Cajetan's *Comm. in S.T. Ia* 6, 4, explaining denomination. There is also a third translation of the second paragraph above, in

Truth, Schmidt (1954: 20). The second translation offered above is from page 18, note 10 of the Bushenski and Koren translation of Cajetan's work (1498).

6 Although Cajetan (1498: ch.2) talks of substituting the definition, it is clear that the bank can be filled only with the *significatum* of the definition.

One should not confuse 'denomination' with 'denominative analogy'. Some denominations do not involve analogy because they do not require more than one word occurrence. For instance, the names 'a clinician', 'a physician', 'a musician' and 'girlfriend' are denominations, relational namings. Denominative analogy requires denominative differentiation.

7 For example, see the definition used by James Cornman (1975:31) in discussing Chisholm's theory of perception: 'e.g., (D^2) X is (secondary-quality) white = def. X has a capacity to cause normal perceivers to white-sense under normal conditions'.

8 *De Nom. Anal.*, no. 14. The definition requirement is Cajetan's Third Condition. Aquinas recognized the great variety of such differentiations in Latin, *IIa IIae*, 57, 1, ad 3, and *Ia*, 37, 2. These pairs, e.g. *moral* man/*moral* act, also have occurrences where they are related not with 'sign of' or 'cause of' relations but in the second mode of denomination, where the meaning difference is between productive properties and resultant properties, as mentioned above.

9 Supposition doctrines common in the thirteenth century are described by William and Martha Kneale (1962) and I. M. Bochenski (1961). Alan R. Perreial (1971) explains how varied the interpretations of supposition theory have been by Bochenski, Boehner, Matthews, Moody, Turnbull, D. P. Henry, Geach, Kneale, and others. These have to be reinvestigated for the contributions they offer to a new theory of reference needed to complement what we are now finding out about linguistic meaning.

10 Plato, *Phaedo,* 103b 2; *Cratylus,* 389b–390; *Parmenides,* 131; *Republic,* 596a 6–7.

11 Aquinas, *Ia* 13, 10 ad 4; Aristotle, *Cat.* Ia, 3. Cajetan, *De Nom. Anal.*, no.19, and *Commentary in Pred. Arist.*, cited at note 23 by Bushenski and Koren.

12 Boethius, *Commentary on the Categories of Aristotle,* quoted by D. P. Henry (1967:46).

13 Margaret MacDonald (1937–8) said, 'Whatever is correctly called a man or a horse is just a man or a horse, not something else to which properties are ascribed.' So, to be *really* a hat is not to be something else besides, while to be *representationally* a hat *is* to be something else besides.

I emphatically do *not* endorse the general principle that there is a different sense of a term *'T'* for every different way a thing can be *T.* That is a crude application of a platonic principle to my examples. In particular, whether two tokens of *'T'* have two senses or not is *linguistically* determined and the different sense of 'hat' is a result of the different sense of 'is', plus the larger discourse environment: It has nothing directly to do with 'different ways' to be a hat, or anything else, even a lemon (see chapter 8). There are many ways to be a fool and not different senses of 'fool' for each of them.

CHAPTER 6

1 Santoni (1968:136). Santoni provides illuminating explanations and criticisms in his Introduction. See also Tillich, *Systematic Theology,* 1951, 1957, 1963; *D.F.,* 1957; 1961a, b; 1968 and Hick, ed. 1964.

2 Tillich, *Dynamics of Faith,* 1957, 'The Religious Symbol' and 'The Meaning and Justification of Religious Symbols', in Hook (ed.), 1961. See critique by William P. Alston, same volume, 'Tillich's Conception of a Religious Symbol'.

3 Geoge H. Von Wright reported (Fain 1967:25), 'It is said that Wittgenstein became a legend among his neighbors because he had tamed so many birds, they used to come every day to be fed by him.' He refers to Wittgenstein's 1948 stay in Galway, Ireland.

CHAPTER 7

1 There are three distinct cognitivity attacks: (a) Religious discourse has no content worthy of an espistemic attitude (that is the one I consider here). (b) Even if religious discourse has content worthy of such attitudes, still there is no interpersonally reliable *access* to the content expressed. That is the *inaccessibility* challenge, that religious discourse is like a foreign and undecipherable language, that one cannot find out what has been said. (c) Even if there is cognitive content and cognitive access to the content of religious discourse, there is no way of *finding out* whether what has been said is true or even likely to be true. That is the skeptical position about religious knowledge. I do not address the second and third issues here because they are beyond the scope of this book.

2 See Flew and MacIntyre (eds), *New Essays in Philosophical Theology* (1955). F. Ferre (1961) and W. T. Blackstone (1963) provide informative surveys of the positions, Ferre from a cognitivst and Blackstone from a noncognitivist vantage. The Flew, Hare, Mitchell, Crombie debate, found in *New Essays*, is reprinted in Hick (1964). Braithwaite (1955), along with John Wisdom's 'Gods' (1944–5), precipitated the cognitivity debate that raged until the late sixties. That debate has more or less died out, accompanying a general lack of interest in issues of verification and falsification. Santoni (1968) provides a highly informative Introduction and a representative collection. See also strong statements of non-verifiability: Ronald Hepburn (1958) and F. Gerald Downing (1964), Antony Flew (1966), C. B. Martin (1959), T. R. Miles (1959), F. P. Schmidt (1969), Kai Nielsen (1963 and 1966).

By 1970 (see note 2, of Ross 1976:726, for citations from Nielsen, Martin, Norman Malcolm and G. E. Hughes) the cognitivity problem had taken a definitely Wittgensteinean turn, becoming a linguistic discontinuity hypothesis. My notion, 'linguistic discontinuity', is adapted from John E. Smith's (1958) description of the Barthian 'discontinuity thesis' that there is no epistemic pathway from the world we know to the knowledge of God. A very useful bibliography up to 1969 is contained in Heimbeck (1969).

3 See I. T. Ramsey (1957, 1965), John Ballie (1962), K. Bendall and F. Ferre (1962), William A. Christian (1964), I. M. Crombie (1955), Frank Dilley (1964), F. Ferre (1967), F. B. Fitch (1948), and A. Boyce Gibson (1956). John Hick (1957) presents his 'eschatological verification' proposal, together with I. M. Crombie; see also Hick (1960, 1963), Ninian Smart (1958, 1961) and John Wisdom, 'Gods' (1944–5).

By deprecating efforts to show that religious discourse satisfied the defective positivist tests I do not mean that the labor was without useful product. Two results of importance emerged from a line of inquiry triggered by Wisdom's 'Gods'. (a) That knowledge of the truth of certain claims, and even justified true belief, is often structurally dependent upon one's having the right (efficient or effective) *perceptual* and *conceptual* sets. See Ross (1969, 1972, 1977) and Heimbeck (1969). (b) A second and complementary strand of inquiry emphasizes the role of models (which function in science the way conceptual sets function in thought and perceptual sets function in perception) to *disclose* patterns within a body of data so that one thing bears evidential relationships to others. These writers link inquiry about religious knowledge to our developing understanding of scientific thinking. See F. Ferre (1963 and 1967) and Ian Ramsey (1967). Heimbeck (1969) tried an apologetic synthesis: insofar as verifiability is an acceptable test for meaningfulness, G-statements are directly or indirectly verifiable and the 'sets' through which religious knowledge is acquired, acting like models to organize experience, produce *configurations* of evidence within which verification or falsification is possible.

The similarity of the 'configuration' discussion and the 'foundationalist' discussion in epistemology to the pre-deductive and pre-inductive pattern-projecting reasoning investigated by John Henry Newman in his *Grammar of Assent* is striking and should lead (when all the strands are interwoven) to a new conception of religious knowledge.

4 See discussion of the 'linguistic turn' in note 2 above (cf. Rorty 1967) and W. P. Alston (1964b: 429–43). It is obvious that the verification form of cognitivity challenge was just a particular manifestation of a more general challenge that something is 'funny with the words' in religious discourse.

5 See references given in Alston (1964b) and High (1967).

6 An *argumentum ad ignorantiam* has less force than the authors have modesty in writing it. What probative weight does it have that a certain writer does not grasp the linguistic continuity or the conditions of implication or the conditions of paraphrase for expressions in religious discourse? That is like the argument that materialism is the best vindicated of mind–body accounts because all others that the *writer* understands have worse defects (where the author did not understand, and said so, the only theory that explicitly pretends not to have the defects on which the vindication was based, the Aristotelian one).

7 Paul Tillich, *Systematic Theology,* regarded all divine-attribute predicates as symbolic and not literal. See also his 'Existential Analyses and Religious Symbols' (1964). Further, see his *Dynamics of Faith* (1957) and his 'The Religious Symbol' (1961a) and 'The Meaning and Justification of Religious Symbols' (1961b) and W. P. Alston's critique in the same volume, 'Tillich's Conception of a Religious Symbol'.

8 For instance, Flew (1966), Blackstone (1963), Braithwaite (1965), Gerald F. Downing (1964) and D. R. Duff-Forbes, (1961), Ronald Hepburn (1958) and Kai Nielsen (1963, 1966). Of course, Hick (works mentioned), and MacIntyre (1957) do not accept the inference from non-falsifiability to non-cognitivity as Flew and others do.

CHAPTER 8

1 Any version of the truth-condition theory that *identifies* truth conditions with meaning will encounter paradoxes of analysis. See Lewy (1976: 69f) for a revealing discussion of the paradoxes of analysis. Harman (1975:286) trenchantly states the difficulties facing Davidson's 'knowledge of truth conditions' analysis of 'knowing the meaning of'.

2 Wittgenstein, *P.I.,* 43. 'For a *large* class of cases – though not for all – in which we employ the word "meaning" it can be defined thus: the meaning of a word is its use in the language.' Nevertheless, Wittgenstein did not *identify* meaning and use. See Stegmuller (1970:452–72) and Pitcher (1964).

3 Wiggins (1971a:22–3), acknowledges the complexity of providing a 'retrieval' device by which the appropriate statements are correlated with the sentences that express them. Certainly, in one sense of 'means', a sentence means whatever statement it expresses. But I do deny that *what a sentence means is the same thing as the statement it expresses.* 'He's asleep' often means the same thing despite the different occasions on which it is used to express different statements. See Cartwright (1962:92).

219

4 Wiggins (1971a:23) acknowledges this: '*s* confers an initial purport on *t* which it enjoys in abstraction from all the circumstances of its utterance, but in working out its meaning there is also the context in which it is lodged to take into account'. The antecedent linguistic meaning is *not* the same regardless of the context (environment) of *s*'s occurrence but is antecedent (as determined in its environment) to whatever *s* states. ('States' in that sentence is denominatively differentiated from 'states' in 'Aristotle *states* that form is distinct from matter'.)

5 Ziff's (1960:202–46) is a case in point. He denies that 'good' is 'fundamentally ambiguous', cf. 202, (which I take to be 'equivocal'), and concludes at 247, 'that apart from certain minor, derivative or deviant cases, "good" in English means answering to certain interests'. That is like Mavrodes' (1970) suggestion that 'unsound' for melons, buildings, ships and arguments, might mean 'unfit for its purpose'. The fact that a single expression is substitutable for the apparently equivocal one, and truth is preserved, is not competent evidence that the one means what the substitute means. That there are *common considerations* detectable over the range of apparently differentiated occurrences of a word does nothing to show that they are not analogous. See Wiggins' (1971a:28–31) effective criticism of Ziff's proposal and see Aristotle's warning in *Topics* 107b, 7.

Nevertheless, there is a theoretical loose end here. Sometimes a single definition, 'life is self-movement' (cf. Aristotle), can be substituted over a set of occurrences of an analogous word. Why does that not make the word univocal? See comments later in the chapter.

6 As Wiggins supposed (1971a:18): 'We understand fewer things than we need to understand about either the theoretical constraints on, or the canonical form for, the truth conditions which our defining procedure will mate with the English sentences whose sense they explain. But it is evident that . . . such conditions can only be produced by a method of systematic decomposition of the given English sentences into the basic structures and components from which they were built in the first place.'

7 The medieval discussion of the univocity of 'being' rejected a disjunctive definition. Scotus said the concept of 'being' is 'one by the unity of a distinct *ratio*' (*'Conceptum entis est unum unitate unius distinctae rationis'*), and is not disjunctive. Peter Aureoli objected to the view of Gerald of Bologna and Herveus Natalis 'that many objective *rationes* corresponded to the concept of being' and 'being' 'expresses different *rationes* when predicated of the different categories, but these rationes have a connection which overcomes the diversity to a certain extent' (Fitzpatrick 1971:218). Fitzpatrick reports: 'Aureoli asserts that according to this opinion the concept of being is disjunctive not copulative.' That was, apparently understood to be a decisive objection. This article also covers the views of Chatton and Ockham. Brown (1971:5–40) explains Robert Cowton's view that being is 'imperfectly equivocal'. (Both papers provide ample useful text.) Everyone in the analogy debate recognized why 'being' is not a disjunctive notion.

8 *Derry* v. *Peck*, 14 App. Cas. 337 (1888, House of Lords) set out the condition: 'a false representation . . . made (1) knowingly or (2) without belief in its truth or (3) recklessly, careless whether it be true or false'. Thus the *scienter* condition came to be understood as the requirement that the plaintiff *show* the misinformant's *lack of belief* in the truth of his statement. That is a rather unexpected sense of 'knowingly' (*scienter*).

Weston v. *Brown*, 82 N.H. 157, 131 A. 141 (1925) held the principle that 'negligent words as well as negligent deeds may constitute actionable fault', but because the case was brought on 'fraud or negligence' it does not stand squarely to broaden the *'scienter'* condition. But *Pulaski* v. *Levin*, 176 Pa Super. 370, went a little further by stating the *scienter* condition as 'actual knowledge of falsity or

220

reckless disregard' of truth or falsity 'or conscious lack of knowledge on which to base an honest belief'. Needless to say, distinctions in law between 'overreaching', 'trickery' and 'misrepresentation' need not, and probably will not, track the way those words are used in unbound discourse. (The passage from Dorothy Sayers (1927) illustrates my thesis.)

9   Clarence Morris (1953:258–68) provides a characteristically lucid survey of the *'scienter'* rule and of its relationship to negligence in these and similar cases. In 1980 the U.S. Supreme Court counted negligence as sufficient to satisfy the *scienter* condition for fraud under the *Securities Act of 1933*, if the negligent assertion is material and false and relied on to the customer's detriment (*New York Times* 6/3/80, D1).

10   In *McBoyle v. United States*, 283 U.S. 25 (1931), Justice Holmes determined whether 'motor vehicle' defined with a disjunct, 'or any other self-propelled vehicle not designed for running on rails', includes 'airplane' under an Act making it a federal offense to transport a stolen motor vehicle across state lines. He admitted that ordinary usage would permit 'motor vehicle', defined with that disjunction, to include airplanes, 'but in every day speech "vehicle" calls up the picture of a thing moving on land'. Holmes applied the rule that statutes imposing criminal penalties should 'give fair warning' and concluded that this one, not mentioning airplanes anywhere or being designed for the purpose of deterring such thefts, does not include airplanes.

11   *Johnson v Southern Pacific Co.*, 117 Fed. 462 (C.C.A. 8th, 1902): are railroad engines (equipped with automatic couplers which did not, however, couple automatically with the other train units) 'railroad cars' under a statute imposing liability in damages on the railroad company when a train crewman is injured coupling by hand 'cars' that by statute are required to have automatic couplers? 'To promote the safety of employees and travelers . . . by compelling common carriers . . . to equip their cars with automatic couplers, and their locomotives with driving wheel brakes, . . . and for other purposes.' That was the Act's stated purpose. Did that mean that locomotives did not have to be so equipped because they are not 'cars'? Or are locomotives 'cars' for one purpose and something else for another purpose, as bishops are people for one purpose and sole corporations for another? The court found that because the locomotive *was* equipped with an automatic coupler (even though it would not couple automatically because incompatible with those on the cars), the locomotive did satisfy the requirement for cars, and by implication was a car, but that no liability fell on the railroad because it had complied with the statute.

12   See 'Malice' in *Black's Law Dictionary,* with citations, where in criminal law it ranges over 'specific intent to kill' (which is the required form of malice for second degree murder), 'cruelty and hardness of heart', and 'a heart regardless of social duty and fatally bent on mischief' (*Crockrell* v. *State,* 135 Tex. Cr. T. 218, 117 S.W. 2d 1105, 1109, 1110). 'It includes not only anger, hatred and revenge, but also every other unlawful and unjustifiable *motive*' [italics added], *State* v. *Scherr,* 243 Wis. 65, 9 N.W.2d 117, 119. That may be confusing enough, but *Regina* v. *Muddarubba*, Australia, Supreme Court, Alice Springs 2 February, 1956 (Reported at 692–6 of Donnelly, Goldstein and Schwartz, *Criminal Law*, The Free Press, Collier-Macmillan, New York, 1962), says '"Malice aforethought" is a lawyer's expression. It doesn't mean "malice" in the sense of spite and it doesn't mean "aforethought" in the sense of premeditation. It simply means that *there must be an intention to kill or to do great bodily harm*' [italics added].

So far we have malice defined in terms of *motive*, then *intention*; now finally, in terms of *knowledge:* 'If, when the appellant did the act which caused the death of the child, *he must as a reasonable man have contemplated that death or grievous bodily*

221

harm was likely to result, he was guilty of murder' [italics added]. The case, *Regina* v. *Ward* (1.Q.B. 351, 1956) involved a man, 'admittedly of subnormal intelligence', frantic from a child's crying and from ulcer pains, who 'shook the child full force' to quiet her but 'certainly did not want the child to die and had no intention of hurting her in any way'; 'there was no thought in his mind except to make her be quiet'. And the connecting rule of law here was this: 'in law a man is presumed to intend the natural consequences of his act'. Notice too, that the 'admittedly subnormal' man was held to the standard of 'a reasonable man' and that if the jury should find, as they did, that counterfactually a reasonable man would have known that shaking the baby full force would have caused death or grave bodily harm, then the requisite malice is present for murder.

Commonwealth v *Drum,* 58 Penn. St. R. 9, 14–17 (1868), reported in Donnelley, Goldstein and Schwartz, 1962: 575–7: 'Malice is a legal term . . . It comprehends not only particular ill-will but every case where there is wickedness of disposition, hardness of heart, cruelty, recklessness of consequences, and a mind regardless of social duty, although a particular person may not be intended to be injured.'

13 For opposed 'expert' judicial construals see the following two. *Webb* v. *McGowin,* 27 Ala. App. 82, 168 S. 196, (1935), holds that where a person saved from great harm, recognizing a moral obligation to the savior, promises to support him for the remainder of his life, the prior service rendered by the rescuer is sufficient consideration for a binding contract; 'for an express promise to pay appellant was an affirmance or ratification of what appellant had done, raising the presumption that the services had been rendered at [saved persons's] . . . request'.

But *Harrington* v. *Taylor,* 255 N.C. 690, 36 S.E. 3d. 227 (1945), decided that where defendant's wife knocked him down with an ax 'and was on the point of cutting his head open' and 'plaintiff intervened, caught the ax as it was descending', 'saving defendant's life but having her hand mutilated', and where defendant subsequently 'orally promised to pay plaintiff her damages' but 'stopped after paying a small sum', 'a humanitarian act of this kind, voluntarily performed, is not such consideration as would entitle her to recover at law'.

Needless to say, the problems of 'natural kinds' that Putnam and Kripke addressed and related problems about analogy, definition, the role of policy in predicate projection and whether there is a kind of induction by 'pattern projection' in these sorts of cases, lurk unsolved within the body of law.

14 *In re. Seiferth,* 309 N.Y. 80, 127 N.E. 2d 820 (1955). The majority in New York's highest court found that the parent's refusal to order surgery, (opposed by the 14 year old child on peculiar religious grounds taught by the child's father, including a belief that spirits would have to *undo* the operation) did *not* constitute 'neglect' under the appropriate statute. The statute defined 'neglect' as refusing necessary 'surgical, medical and dental service'. Despite the child's badly deformed appearance and unintelligible speech, there was no medical *emergency* from a harelip and cleft palate. 'Necessary' was understood as a 'need creating an emergency'. An indignant minority wrote, 'If the parents are actually mistreating or neglecting a child, the circumstance that he may not mind it cannot alter the fact that they are guilty of neglect and it cannot render their conduct permissable.'

Whether to project the predicate 'neglected' upon these facts involves a subtle construal and could very well alter the meaning of 'neglect' from its conditions of application in prior cases. Analogy, governed by general principles and policies, is the very sinew of legal discourse.

222

Bibliography

Alston, W. P. 1961. 'Tillich's Conception of a Religious Symbol' in S. Hook (ed.), *Experience and Truth*. New York: NYU Press.
1964a. *Philosophy of Language*. Englewood Cliffs: Prentice Hall.
1964b. 'The Elucidation of Religious Statements' in W. L. Reese and E. Freeman, *The Hartshorne Festschrift: Process and Divinity*. Lasalle, Ill.: Open Court.
1971. 'How does one tell whether a word has one, several or many senses?' in D. D. Steinberg and L. Jakobovitz (eds.), *Semantics,* Cambridge: Cambridge University Press.
Anton, J. P. 1968. 'The Aristotelian doctrine of *homonyma* in the *Categories* and its Platonic antecedents', *Journal of the History of Philosophy* **6,** 4, 315–26.
1969. 'Ancient interpretations of Aristotle's doctrine of *homonyma*', *Journal of the History of Philosophy* **7,** 1, 1–18.
Aquinas, St Thomas. (Citations omitted are those of Vernon Bourke, *Encyclopedia of Philosophy*, P. Edwards (ed.), 1967, vol. 8, 114–15).
Commentary on Sentences of Peter Lombard (In Sent.)
Summa Contra Gentiles (C.G.)
Commentary on the De Anima of Aristotle (In De An.)
Commentary on Metaphysics of Aristotle (In Met.)
Principles of Nature (P.N.)
On Being and Essence (B.E.)
Summa Theologiae (Ia; Ia IIae; IIa IIIae)
Questiones Disputatae De Veritate (De Ver.)
Compendium of Theology. (C.T.)
Aristotle, *The Complete Works of Aristotle Translated into English,* W. D. Ross (ed), 12 vols. Oxford, 1908–1952.
Categories (Cat.)
De Interpretatione (De Int.)
Posterior Analytics (Post. An.)
Sophistical Refutations (Soph. Ref.)
Physics (Phys.)
Metaphysics (Meta.)
Nichomachean Ethics (N.E.)
Poetics (Poet.)
Topics (Top.)
The Basic Works of Aristotle, R. McKeon (ed.), 1941. New York; Random House.

Austin, J. 1961. *Philosophical Papers* (2nd ed. 1970), London and New York: Oxford University Press.

1962. *How to do Things with Words.* Oxford: Clarendon Press.

Ballie, J. 1962. *The Sense of the Presence of God.* New York: Charles Scribner and Sons.

Beardsley, M. 1976. 'Metaphor and falsity', *Journal of Aesthetics and Art Criticism* **35**, 218–22.

Bendall, K. and Ferre, F. 1962. *Exploring the Logic of Faith.* New York: Association Press.

Black, M. 1962. *Models and Metaphors.* Ithaca, New York: Cornell University Press.

Blackstone, W. T. 1963. *The Problem of Religious Knowledge.* Englewood Cliffs: Prentice Hall.

Bochenski, I. M. 1948. 'On analogy', *The Thomist* **2**, 424–47. Reprinted and corrected in *Logico-Philosophical Studies*, E. Menne (ed.), 1962. Dordrecht; 1959. Freiburg: K. Alber.

1956. 'The problem of universals', *The Problem of Universals, A Symposium*, pp.35–54. Notre Dame, Indiana: University of Notre Dame Press.

1961. *A History of Formal Logic.* Notre Dame, Indiana: University of Notre Dame Press.

1965. *The Logic of Religion.* New York: New York University Press.

Boethius. *Commentary on the Categories of Aristotle (In Categorias Aristotelis).* Migne, Patrologia Latina, vol. 64 (col. 165b and col. 166).

Boyle, R. 1954, 'The nature of metaphor', *Modern Schoolman* **31**, 257–80.

1957. 'The nature of metaphor: further considerations', *Modern Schoolman* **34**, 283–98.

Braithwaite, R. B. 1955. *An Empiricist's View of the Nature of Religious Belief.* Cambridge: Cambridge University Press.

Brody, B. A. 1967. 'Natural kinds and real essence', *Journal of Philosophy* **64**, 431–46.

Brown, S. F. 1971. 'Robert Cowton, O. F. M., and the analogy of the concept of being', *Franciscan Studies* **31**, 5–40.

Burrell, D. 1962. 'Religious language and the logic of analogy: apropos of McInerny's book and Ross' review', *International Philosophical Quarterly* **2**, 643–58.

1972. 'Beyond the theory of analogy', *Proceedings of the American Catholic Philosophical Association* **46**, 114–21.

1973. *Analogy and Philosophical Language.* New Haven: Yale University Press.

Cajetan, Thomas De Vio, Cardinalis Cajetanus. 1495. *Commentary on Aquinas' De Ente Et Essentia.*

1498. *De Nominum Analogia (De Nom. Anal.)*, P. N. Zammit (ed.), 1934, *The Analogy of Names*, Bushenski and Koren (trans.), 1953, Pittsburgh: Duquesne University Press.

1507–22. *Commentary on Summa Theologiae of St Thomas (Comm. in S.T.).*

1509 'The Concept of Being', Appendix to *De Nom. Anal.*

Calahan, J. C. 1970. 'Analogy and the disrepute of metaphysics', *The*

Thomist **23,** 3, 387–422.

Carnap, R. 1955. 'Meaning and synonymy in natural languages', *Philosophical Studies* 33–47.

Cartwright, R. 1962. 'Propositions', in R. Butler (ed.) *Analytical Philosophy*, pp. 82–103 (first series). Oxford: Basil Blackwell.

Caton, C. E. 1971. 'Overview', in D. D. Steinberg and L. Jakobovits (eds), *Semantics*. Cambridge: Cambridge University Press.

Chapman, T. 1975. 'Analogy', *The Thomist* **34,** 127–41.

Chisholm, R. M. 1966. *Theory of Knowledge* (2nd ed. 1977). Englewood Cliffs: Prentice Hall.

1976. *Person and Object*. La Salle: Open Court.

Chomsky, N. 1972. *Language and Mind* (enlarged ed.). New York: Harcourt Brace Jovanovich, Inc.

Christian, W. A., 1964. *Meaning and Truth in Religion*. Princeton: Princeton University Press.

Churchland, P. 1979. *Scientific Realism and The Plasticity of Mind*. Cambridge: Cambridge University Press.

Clarke, N. 1976. 'Analogy and the meaningfulness of language about God. A reply to Kai Nielsen', *The Thomist* **40,** 1, 61–95.

Coady, C. A. J. 1976. 'Review of *Meaning*, by Stephen Schiffer' *Philosophy*, 102–9.

Cohen, E. 1976. 'Notes on metaphor', *Journal of Aesthetics and Art Criticism* **34,** 249–59.

Cornman, J. 1975. 'Chisholm on sensing and perceiving', in Keith Lehrer (ed.) *Analysis and Metaphysics*. Boston: Reidel.

Crombie, I. M. 1955. 'Theology and falsification', in A. Flew and A. McIntyre (eds.), *New Essays in Philosophical Theology*. New York: Macmillan.

1968. 'The possibility of theological statements', in R. E. Santoni (ed.) 1968:83–116, (excerpted from Crombie's *Faith and Logic*, 1958:31–67). London: George Allen and Unwin.

Davidson, D. 1965. 'Theories of meaning and learnable languages', in Bar Hillel (ed.), *Proceedings of the 1964 International Congress for Logic, Methodology and Philosophy of Science*. Amsterdam: North Holland Publishing Co.

1967. 'Truth and meaning', *Synthese* **17,** 304–23.

Derwood, E. 1955. 'Shelter', in O. Williams (ed.), *The New Pocket Anthology of American Verse*. New York: Washington Square Press.

Dilley, F. 1964. *Metaphysics and Religious Language*. New York: Columbia University Press.

Donnelly R. C., Goldstein J. and Schwartz R. D. (eds.) 1962. *Criminal Law*. New York: The Free Press, Collier-Macmillan.

Downing, F. G. 1964. *Has Christianity a Revelation?* London: SCM Press.

Drange, T. 1966. *Type Crossing*. The Hague: Mouton and Company.

Dubaile, D. 1969. 'La doctrine Aristotelicienne de l'analogie et sa nomalization rationelle', *Revue des Sciences Philosophiques et Theologiques* **53,** 1, 3–40, and **53,** 2, 212–32.

Duff-Forbes, D. R. 1961. 'Theology and falsification again', *Australasian Journal of Philosophy* **29**, 143–154.

Dummett, M. A. 1958–9. 'Truth'. *Proceedings of the Aristotelean Society* **59**, 141–62. Reprinted in George Pitcher (ed.), *Truth*, 1964. Englewood Cliffs: Prentice Hall.

1973. *Frege: Philosophy of Language*. London: Duckworth.

1975. 'What is a theory of meaning?' Part I, in S. Guttenplan (ed.), *Mind and Language*. London: Oxford University Press. Part II in Evans and J. McDowell (eds.), *Essays in Semantics*. Oxford: Clarendon Press.

1978. *Truth and Other Enigmas*. Cambridge, Mass: Harvard University Press.

Dworkin, R. M. 1977. *Taking Rights Seriously*. Cambridge, Mass: Harvard University Press.

Edwards, S. 1974. *Medieval Theories of Distinction*. Ann Arbor: University Microfilms.

Emmet, D. 1946. *The Nature of Metaphysical Thinking*. London: Macmillan.

Erwin, E. 1970. *The Concept of Meaninglessness*. Baltimore: Johns Hopkins University Press.

Fain, K. T. (ed). 1967. *Ludwig Wittgenstein. The Man and His Philosophy*. New York: Dell.

Ferre, F. 1961. *Language, Logic and God*. New York: Harper and Row.

1963. 'Mapping the logic of models in science and theology', *The Christian Scholar*, **46**, 9–39.

1967. *Basic Modern Philosophy of Religion*. New York: Charles Scribner and Sons.

Field, H. 1978. 'Mental representation', *Erkenntnis*, **13**, 9–61.

Fitch, F. B. 1948. 'On God and immortality', *Philosophy and Phenomenological Research* **8**, 688–93.

Fitzpatrick, N. A. 1971. 'Walter Chatton on the univocity of being: A reaction to Peter Aureoli and William Ockham', *Franciscan Studies*. **31**, 88–177.

Flew, A. G. N. 1966. *God and Philosophy*, New York: Harcourt, Brace and World.

Flew, A. G. N. and MacIntyre, A. (eds). 1955. *New Essays in Philosophical Theology*. New York: MacMillan.

Fodor, J. A. 1975. *The Language of Thought*. New York: Crowell.

1977. *Semantics*. New York: Crowell.

Fodor, J. A. and Katz, J. 1964. *The Structure of Language: Readings in the Philosophy of Language*. Englewood Cliffs: Prentice Hall.

Fowles, John. 1977. *Daniel Martin*. New York: Little Brown and Co.

Frege, G. 1952. *On Sense and Reference, Translations from the Philosophical Writings of Gottlob Frege*. P. T. Geach and M. Black (eds). Oxford.

Fries, C. 1961. 'Advances in linguistics', *College English* **25**, 30–7. Reprinted in H. B. Allen (ed.), *Readings in Applied Linguistics*. New York: Appleton-Century-Crofts.

1966. *Merrill Linguistic Readers*. New York: Merrill Publishing Co.

Garrigou-Lagrange, R. 1947–8. *God: His Existence and Nature*. 2 vols, 5th ed., Dom Bede Rose (trans.). St. Louis: Herder.

Geiger, L. B. 1942. *La participation dans la Philosophie de S. Thomas d'Aquin*. (Bibliothèque Thomiste XXIII) Paris: Vrin.

Gibson, A. B. 1956. 'Empirical evidence and religious faith', *Journal of Religion*, **36**, 24–35.

Gilson, E. 1955. *History of Christian Philosophy in the Middle Ages*. New York: Random House.

Goodman, N. 1949. 'On likeness of meaning', *Analysis* **10**, 1, 1–7.

1953. 'On some differences about meaning', *Analysis* **13**, 4, 90–6.

1965. *Fact, Fiction and Forecast* (2nd ed.). Indianapolis: Bobbs-Merrill.

1968. *Languages of Art*. Indianapolis: Bobbs-Merrill.

Grassi, J. 1930. *Dictionary of Italian and English*, edition by Albert de Beaux, Leipzig.

Grenet, P. 1948. *Les origines de l'analogie philosophique dans les Dialogues de Platon*. Paris: Bovin.

Grice, H. P. 1957. 'Meaning', *Philosophical Review* **66**, 377–88.

1968. 'Utterer's meaning, sentence-meaning and word-meaning', *Foundations of Language* **4**, 1–18.

1969. 'Utterer's meaning and intentions', *Philosophical Review* **78**, 147–77.

Gruber, E. G. 1969. *Miller's Analogies Test, Analogy Questions*. New York: ARCO.

Haack, S. 1968. 'Equivocality: a discussion of Sommers views', *Analysis* **28**, 125, 159–65.

Hardy, Thomas. 1898. *Wessex Poems and Other Verses*.

Harman, G. 1974a. 'Comment on Michael Dummett', *Synthese* **27**, 401–4.

1974b. *Thought*. Princeton: Princeton University Press.

1975. 'Language, thought and communication', in K. Gunderson (ed.), *Language Mind and Knowledge*. Minneapolis: University of Minnesota Press.

Hart, H. L. A. 1953. *Definition and Theory in Jurisprudence*. Oxford: Clarendon Press.

Heaney, J. J. 1971. 'Analogy of kinds of things', *The Thomist* **35**, 2, 291–304.

Heimbeck, R. S. 1969. *Theology and Meaning*. Stanford: Stanford University Press.

Hempel, C. 1948. 'Review of Lewis', *An Analysis of Knowledge and Valuation*', *Journal of Symbolic Logic* **13**, 40–5.

1950. 'Problems and changes in the empiricist criterion of meaning', in L. Linsky (ed.), *Semantics and the Philosophy of Language*. Urbana: University of Illinois Press.

1966. 'Recent problems of induction', in *Mind and Cosmos*. Pittsburgh: University of Pittsburgh Press. Cited from Goodman, 1968, p.225.

Henry, D. P. 1967. *The Logic of Saint Anselm*. Oxford: Oxford University Press.

1972. *Medieval Logic and Metaphysics*. London: Hutchinson University Library.

Hepburn, R. 1958. *Christianity and Paradox*. London.

Hesse, M. B. 1963. *Models and Analogies in Science*. London: Sheed and Ward. Notre Dame Indiana: University of Notre Dame Press, 1966.

1959–60. 'On Defining Analogy'. *Proceedings of the Aristotelean Society* **60.**

Hick, J. 1957. *Faith and Knowledge.* Ithaca, NY: Cornell University Press.

1960. 'Theology and Verification', *Theology Today* **17,** 12–31.

1963. *Philosophy of Religion.* Englewood Cliffs: Prentice Hall.

1964, (ed). *Classical and Contemporary Readings in the Philosophy of Religion.* Englewood Cliffs: Prentice Hall.

High, D. M. 1967. *Language, Persons and Belief: Studies in Wittgenstein's 'Philosophical Investigations', and Religious Uses of Language.* New York: Oxford University Press.

Hill, T. 1974. *The Concept of Meaning.* London: Allen and Unwin.

Hiz, H. 1967. 'Methodological Aspects of the Theory of Syntax, a review of Noam Chomsky's *Aspects of the Theory of Syntax*', *Journal of Philosophy* **64,** 67–74.

Hoenigswald, H. 1965. 'Review of John Lyons's *Structural Semantics: An Analysis of the Vocabulary of Plato*', *Journal of Linguistics* **1,** 2, 191–6.

Hohfeld, W. N. 1923. *Fundamental Legal Conceptions.* W. W. Cook (ed.). New Haven: Yale University Press.

Holdcroft, D. 1976. 'Review of *The Concept of Meaning* by Thomas Hill', *Philosophy* **51.**

Hook, S. (ed.) 1961. *Experience and Truth.* New York: NYU Press.

John of Dacia. 1280. *Summa Gramatica*, Alfredus Otto (ed.). Haunias, 1955.

John of St Thomas (Jean Pinsot). *The Material Logic of John of St Thomas*, Simon, Glanville & Hollenhorst (trans). Chicago: University of Chicago Press, 1955.

Johnson, W. E. 1921. *Logic.* Cambridge.

Katz, J. J. 1966. *The Philosophy of Language.* New York: Harper and Row.

1972. *Semantic Theory.* New York: Harper and Row.

Katz, J. J. and Fodor, J. A. 1963. 'The Structure of a Semantic Theory', *Language* **39,** 170–210. Reprinted in Fodor and Katz, 1964; 479–518.

1964, (eds.). *The Structure of Language: Readings in the Philosophy of Language.* Englewood Cliffs: Prentice Hall.

Klubertanz, G. P. 1960. *St. Thomas on Analogy.* Chicago: Loyola University Press.

Kneale, W. and Kneale, M. 1962. *The Development of Logic.* Oxford: Clarendon Press.

Kretzmann, N. 1967. 'Semantics, History of', in P. Edwards (ed.), *Encyclopedia of Philosophy*, vol. 7, pp. 358–406. New York: Crowell Collier and MacMillan.

Kurylowicz, J. 1955. 'Zametki o značenii slova', *Voprosy iazykoznanija* **3,** 71–81, as cited by Weinreich 1971: 323 and 328.

Lakoff, G. & Johnson, M. 1980. *Metaphors We Live By.* Chicago: University of Chicago Press.

LeBlanc, H. 1969. 'A Rationale for Analogical Inference', *Philosophical Studies* **20.**

Lehrer, A. 1974a. *Semantic Fields and Lexical Structures.* North Holland and New York: Elsevier.

1974b. 'Homonymy and Polysemy: Measuring similarity of meaning', *Language Sciences* **3,** 33–9.

228

Lenneberg, E. H. 1971. 'Language and Cognition', in D. D. Steinberg and L. Jakobovits (eds.), *Semantics*, pp. 536–67. Cambridge.

Lewis, C. I. 1946. *An Analysis of Knowledge and Valuation*. La Salle: Open Court. Reissue 1962.

Lewis, D. 1969. *Convention*. Cambridge, Mass: Harvard University Press.

Lewy, C. 1976. *Meaning and Modality*. Cambridge: Cambridge University Press.

Linsky, L. (ed.) 1952. *Semantics and the Philosophy of Language*. Urbana: University of Illinois Press.

Locke, J. 1706. *An Essay Concerning Human Understanding (Essay)* 5th ed., 2 vols. John W. Yolton (ed.), 1961. London: Dent, Everyman's.

Lonergan, B. 1967. *Verbum, Word and Idea in Aquinas*, David Burrell (ed.). Notre Dame: University of Notre Dame Press.

Long E. (ed.) 1980. *Experience, Reason and God*. Washington: The Catholic University of America Press.

Lyons, J. 1963. *Structural Semantics*. London: Basil Blackwell.

1968. *Introduction to Theoretical Linguistics*. New York: Cambridge University Press.

1977. *Semantics*, 2 vols. New York: Cambridge University Press.

Lyttkens, H. 1952. *The Analogy between God and the World*. Uppsala.

McCawley, J. D. 1971. 'Where do noun phrases come from?', in D. D. Steinberg and L. Jakobovits (eds.), *Semantics*, pp 217–231. Cambridge.

MacDonald, M. 1937–8. 'The philosophers' use of analogy', *Proceedings of the Aristotelean Society*. Reprinted in A. G. Flew (ed.), 1951. *Essays in Logic and Language*. New York: Philosophical Library.

McInerny, R. M. 1957. 'The Logic of Analogy', *The New Scholasticism* **31**, 149–71.

1961. *The Logic of Analogy*. The Hague: M. Nijhoff.

1964. 'Metaphor and Analogy', *Sciences Ecclesiastiques* 273–289. Reprinted in J. F. Ross (ed.), *Inquiries into Medieval Philosophy* 1971, pp. 76–96. Westport, Conn: Greenwood.

1968. *Studies in Analogy*. The Hague: Nijhoff.

MacIntyre, A. 1957. 'The Logical Status of Religious Belief', in A. MacIntyre (ed.), *Metaphysical Beliefs*. London: SCM Press.

Maclay, H. M. 1971. 'Overview', in D. D. Steinberg and L. Jakobovits (eds.), *Semantics*, pp. 157–82. Cambridge.

Martin, C. B. 1959. *Religious Belief*. Ithaca, N. Y.: Cornell University Press.

Martin of Dacia. 'Modi Significandi', *Martini Dacia Opera*, Henricus Roos (ed.), 1961. Haunias.

Mascall, E. L. 1949. *Existence and Analogy*. New York: Longmans, Green and Company.

Maurer, A. 1955. 'St. Thomas and the Analogy of Genus', *The New Scholasticism* **29**, 2, 127–44.

Mavrodes, G. I. 1970. 'On Ross' theory of analogy'. *Journal of Philosophy* **67**, 20, 747–55.

229

Meagher, R. E. 1970. 'Thomas Aquinas–Analogy: A textual analysis', *The Thomist* **34**, 2, 230–53.

Menges, M. C. 1952. *The Concept of Univocity of Being Regarding Predication of God and Creature According to William of Occam*. New York: St. Bonaventure.

Menne, A. 1962. *Logico-Philosophical Studies*. Dordrecht, Holland: D. Reidel.

Miles, T. R. 1959. *Religion and the Scientific Outlook*. London: G. Allen and Unwin.

Miller, G. M. 1971. 'Empirical Methods in the Study of Semantics', in D. D. Steinberg and L. Jakobovits (eds.), *Semantics*, pp. 569–85. Cambridge: Cambridge University Press.

Morris, C. 1953. *Morris on Torts*. Brooklyn: The Foundation Press, Inc.

Murphy, Richard. 1974. 'The Philosopher and the Birds, in memory of Wittgenstein at Rosroe', *High Island*, pp. 6–7. New York: Harper and Row.

Muskens, G. L. 1943. *De Vocis Analogiae Significatione ac Usu apud Aristotalem*. Louvain.

Naess, A. 1957. 'Synonymity as Revealed by Intuition', *Philosophical Review* **66**, 87–93.

Newman, J. H. 1947. *An Essay in Aid of a Grammar of Assent*. C. F. Harrold (ed.) New York: Longmans, Green.

Nielsen, K. 1963 'Can Faith Validate God Talk', *Theology Today* **20**, 158–73.
1966. 'On Fixing the Reference Range of 'God', *Religious Studies* **2**, 13–36.
1976. 'Talk of God and the Doctrine of Analogy', *The Thomist* **40**, 32–60.

Ockham, William. *Super Quattuor Libros Sententiarum Questiones*. (*In Sent.*)

Owen, G. E. L. 1960. 'Logic and Metaphysics in some Early Works of Aristotle', *Plato and Aristotle in Mid-Fourth Century* Duhring and Owen (eds.). Gothenburg.

Owens, J. 1951. *The Doctrine of Being in the Aristotelian Metaphysics*. Toronto: Pontifical Institute of Medieval Studies.

Palmer, H. 1973. *Analogy; a study of qualification and argument in Theology*. New York: St. Martin's Press.

Penido, M. T. L. 1931. *Le Role de l'analogie en Theologie* (Bibliotheque Thomiste, IV). Paris: Vrin.

Perreial, A. R. 1971. 'Approaches to Supposition Theory', *The New Scholasticism* **34**, 381–408.

Philippe, M. D. 1969. 'Analogon and Analogia in the Philosophy of Aristotle', *The Thomist* **33**, 1, 1–74.

Pitcher, G. 1964. *The Philosophy of Wittgenstein*. Englewood Cliffs: Prentice Hall.

Plato. *The Dialogues of Plato*. Translated by B. Jowett (Oxford, 1953):
Phaedo
Parmenides
Cratylus
Republic

Prado, C. G. 1969. 'Analytical Philosophy of Knowledge', *Dialogue* **8**, 503–7.

1970. 'A note on Analogical Predication', *The New Scholasticism* **44**, 603–4.

Prior, A. N. 1949. 'Determinable, determinates, and determinants', *Mind* **58**, 1–20, 178–94.

Putnam, H. 1975. *Philosophical Papers*, 2 vols. London and New York: Cambridge University Press.

Quine, W. V. 1960. *Word and Object*. New York: Wiley.

1969. 'Natural Kinds', *Ontological Relativity and Other Essays*. New York: Columbia University Press.

Radin, M. 1938. 'A Restatement of Hohfeld', *Harvard Law Review* **51**, 1145–64.

Ramsey, I. T. 1965. *Christian Discourse: Some Logical Explorations*. London: Oxford University Press.

1967. *Religious Language: An Empirical Placing of Theological Phrases*. London: SCM Press.

Reese, W. L. and Freeman, E. (eds.) 1964. *The Hartshorne Festschrift: Process and Divinity*. Lasalle, Ill.: Open Court.

Richards, D. A. J. 1977. *The Moral Criticism of Law*. Encino, Cal.: Dickenson.

Rorty, R., (ed.) 1967. *The Linguistic Turn*. Chicago: University of Chicago Press.

Ross, J. F. 1958. *A Critical Analysis of the Theory of Analogy of St. Thomas Aquinas*. Ann Arbor, Mich: University Microfilms, Inc.

1961. 'Analogy as a rule of meaning for Religious Language'. *International Philosophical Quarterly* **1**, 3, 468–502. Reprinted in *Inquiries into Medieval Philosophy*, J. F. Ross (ed.), 1971. Westport: Greenwood Publishing Company; and *Bobbs-Merrill Reprint Series,* Phil-181; and *Aquinas,* A. Kenny (ed.), 1969. New York: Doubleday.

1962a 'Review: The Logic of Analogy, by Ralph McInerny'. *International Philosophical Quarterly* **2**, 633–42.

1962b 'Reply of Professor Ross', *International Philosophical Quarterly* **2**, 658–62.

1969. *Introduction to the Philosophy of Religion*. London: Macmillan.

1970a. 'A New Theory of Analogy', *Proceedings of American Catholic Philosophical Association* **44**, 70–85. Reprinted in *Logical Analysis and Contemporary Theism* pp. 124–42, John Donnelly (ed.), 1972. New York: Fordham University Press.

1970b. 'Analogy and the Resolution of Some Cognitivity Problems', *Journal of Philosophy* **67**, 20, 725–46. Reprinted in *Readings in Philosophy of Religion,* Baruch Brody (ed.), 1974. Englewood Cliffs: Prentice Hall.

1971. 'A Response to Mr. Henry', *The Thomist* **35**, 2, 305–11.

1971. (ed.). *Inquiries into Medieval Philosophy*. Westport, Conn: Greenwood Publishing Company.

1972. 'Religious Knowledge', *Proceedings of the American Catholic Philosophical Association* **46**, 29–43.

1974. 'Review of Heimbeck's Theology and Meaning', *Journal of the American Academy of Religion*, 370–2.

1977. 'Ways of Religious Knowing', Goodspeed Lecture, Dennison University, Spring 1977, forthcoming in *The Challenge of Religion Today*, F. Ferre, J. Smith and J. Kocklemans (eds.). New York: Seabury.

1980. 'Unless You Believe You Will Not Understand', in E. Long (ed.), *Experience, Reason and God*, pp 113–28. Washington: The Catholic University of America Press.

Ryle, G. 1931–2. 'Systematically Misleading Expressions', *Proceedings of the Aristotelean Society*, **32**, 139–70.

1951. 'Heterologicality', *Analysis* **2**, 3, 61–9.

1957. 'The Theory of Meaning', in C. A. Mace (ed.), *British Philosophy in the Mid-Century*, pp. 239–64. New York: Macmillan.

Sacks, S. (ed.) 1980. *On Metaphor*. Chicago: University of Chicago Press.

Santoni, R. E. (ed.) 1968. *Religious Language and the Problem of Religious Knowledge*. Bloomington: Indiana University Press.

Sayers, Dorothy. 1927, 1944. *Unnatural Death. (The Dawson Pedigree)*. New York: Avon.

Schiffer, S. 1972. *Meaning*. Oxford: Clarendon Press.

Schmidt, F. P. 1969. *Religious Knowledge*. Glencoe, Illinois: The Free Press.

Schmidt, R. W. (trans.). 1954. *Truth*, 3 vols. (*Aquinas Disputationes De Veritate*). Chicago: Regnery.

Searle, J. 1967. 'Determinables and Determinates', *Encyclopedia of Philosophy*. Paul Edwards (ed.), vol. 2, pp. 357–9. New York: Crowell, Collier and Macmillan.

1969. *Speech Acts*. London: Cambridge University Press.

Sherry, P. J. 1976a, 'Analogy Reviewed', *Philosophy* **51**, 337–45.

1976b. 'Analogy Today', *Philosophy* **51**, 431–46.

Shircel, C. L. 1942. *The Univocity of the Concept of Being in the Philosophy of John Duns Scotus*. Washington: The Catholic University of America Press.

Siger of Courtrai. *Summa Modorum Significandi*, cited by N. Kretzman, in 'Semantics, History of', *Encyclopaedia of Philosophy*, P. Edwards (ed.), vol. 7, p. 375. New York: Crowell, Collier and Macmillan.

Simmons, E. D. 1955. 'In Defense of Total and Formal Abstraction', *New Scholasticism* **29**, 427–40.

Simon, I. 1960. 'On Order in Analogical Sets', *The New Scholasticism* **34**, 1–42.

Smart, N. 1958. *Reasons and Faiths: An Investigation of Religious Discourse, Christian and Non-Christian*. London.

1961. *Philosophy and Religion: The Logic of Religious Belief*. Oxford.

Smith, J. E. 1958. 'The Present Status of Natural Theology', *Journal of Philosophy* **55**, 22, 925–36.

Stegmuller, W. 1970. *Main Currents in Contemporary German, British and American Philosophy*. Bloomington: Indiana University Press.

Steinberg, D. D. and Jakobovits, L. (eds). 1971. *Semantics*. Cambridge: Cambridge University Press.

Suarez, Francis, 1597, *Disputationes Metaphysicae*, 28. Sec 3. *Opera Omnia*, Vol. 26. 1877. Paris: Vives.

1597. *On Formal and Universal Unity*. J. F. Ross. (trans.), 1964. *De Unitate Formali et Universali*, Disputation VI of *Metaphysical Disputations*, Milwaukee: Marquette University Press.

Synan, E. A. 1976. 'Latin Philosophy of the Middle Ages', in James M. Powell (ed.), *Medieval Studies*. Syracuse, NY: Syracuse University Press.

Taylor, R. 1954. 'Disputes About Synonymy', *Philosophical Review* **63**, 517–29.

Thomas, Dylan, 1934. 'Altarwise by Owl-Light', in O. Williams (ed.), *Master Poems of the English Language*, pp. 1059–63, 1967. New York: Washington Square Press.

Thomson, J. J. 1969. 'Truth Bearers and the Trouble About Propositions', *The Journal of Philosophy* **66**, 737–47.

Tillich, P. 1951, 1957, 1963. *Systematic Theology*, 3 vols. Chicago: University of Chicago Press.

1957. *Dynamics of Faith*. New York: Harper and Row.

1961a. 'The Religious Symbol', in S. Hook (ed.), *Experience and Truth*. New York: NYU Press.

1961b. 'The Meaning and Justification of Religious Symbols', in S. Hook (ed.), *Experience and Truth*. New York: NYU Press.

1964. 'Existential Analyses and Religious Symbols', in J. Hick (ed.), *Classical and Contemporary Readings in the Philosophy of Religion*, section 31. Englewood Cliffs: Prentice Hall.

1968. 'Symbols of Faith', In Santoni 1968: 136–45.

Tindall, W. 1966. 'Thomas, Altarwise by Owl-Light', in O. Williams (ed.), *Master Poems of the English Language*, pp 1063–72, 1967. New York: Washington Square Press.

Updike, John. 1966. *Picked Up Pieces*. New York: Fawcett.

1980. *Problems and Other Stories*. New York: Knopf.

Urmson, J. O. 1956. *Philosophical Analysis*. Oxford.

Von Wright, G. 1967. 'A Biographical Sketch', in K. T. Fain, (ed.) (1967:13–29).

Webster, W. E. 1971a, *A Theory of Diatonic Musical Scores*. Ann Arbor: University Microfilms.

1971b. 'A Theory of the Compositional Work of Music', *The Journal of Aesthetics and Art Criticism* **33.**

Weinreich, U. 1971. 'Explorations in Semantic Theory', in D. D. Steinberg and L. Jakobovits (eds.), *Semantics*, pp. 308–28. Cambridge: Cambridge University Press.

Wettstein, H. K. 1976. 'Can what is asserted be a sentence?', *The Philosophical Review* **85**, 2, 196–207.

White, Patrick. 1957. *Voss*. New York: Viking Press.

Wiggins, D. 1971a. 'On sentence-sense, word-sense, and difference of word sense. Towards a philosophical theory of dictionaries', in D. D. Steinberg and L. Jakobovits (eds.), *Semantics*, pp. 14–34. Cambridge: Cambridge University Press.

1971b. 'A Reply to Mr. Alston', in D. D. Steinberg and L. Jakobovits (eds.), *Semantics*, pp. 48–52. Cambridge: Cambridge University Press.

Williams, O. (ed.) 1955. *The New Pocket Anthology of American Verse*. New York: Washington Square Press.

(ed.) 1967. *Master Poems of the English Language*. New York: Washington Square Press.

Wisdom, John. 1944–5. 'Gods', *Proceedings of the Aristotelian Society*, **45**, 185–206.

Wittgenstein, Ludwig. 1953, 1958. *Philosophical Investigations* (*P.I.*). Oxford: Blackwell.

Wolfson, H. 1977. 'St Thomas on Divine Attributes', in Twersky and Williams (eds.), *Studies in the History of Philosophy and Religion*, vol. 2, pp. 497–524. Cambridge, Mass: Harvard University Press.

Ziff, P. 1960. *Semantic Analysis*. Ithaca: Cornell University Press.

1966. 'Nonsynonymy of Active and Passive Sentences', *Philosophical Review* **75**, 226–32.

Name index

236

Subject index

absolute meaning, 9, 14–15; distinguished from relative, 14–15

abstraction, 107–8; denominative, 121; difference from metaphor, 108; by exclusion of determinables, 108

abstractive analogy, 174; of proportionality, 107–8; 121; (see abstraction)

acceptability, conditions in craftbound discourse, 166; environmentally limited, 56–7; Lyons on, 55; preservation of, 35, 62; theoretically primitive, 58; unacceptability (q.v.) caused by blocking, 75

acquiring presuppositions, 57

adaptation, 3; adjustment and fit, 48; atomic adaptations, 147; caused by dominance (q.v.), 48–51; is explanatory, 49; 'generates' meanings, 147; hypothetical sequence of, 15, 115

ambiguity, 80–1; multiple-scheme membership, 77, 80–1; not *double-entendre*, 77

analogia entis, 17, 18–22; Aquinas and Aristotle, 165, 213 n1, 214 n6

analogia nominum, 17–22; analogous terms, 93–109; analogy (q.v.) of meaning (q.v.), 214 n6, 7 & 8

analogia rationis, 17–22

analogous definitions, xi, 2, 206, 220 n5

analogous words, cannot be defined disjunctively, 199–201; cluster, 97; within clusters, 100–7; clusters the result of analogy, 103; form chains, 96; mutations of presupposition, 99; relatedness of, 97–108; thought efficiency, 99

analogy, 14, 22, of the analogy predicates themselves, 138; another test for, 174; explaining its extension to paronyms, 141; extension of

classifications by analogy, 8–9, 138–41; and figurative discourse, 142–57; paronymy, 8, 136–41; and participation, 136; (see also: analogy of attribution, analogy of proportionality, denominative analogy, and analogy of meaning); and functionally equivalent conditions, 197; cannot be replaced by disjunctive definition, 199–201; with respect to truth conditions, 197–8; analogous definitions, xi, 2, 206–7, 220 n5

analogy of attribution; Aquinas, 121–36; ascriptive attribution, 135; broad reconception, 133–4; Cajetan, 121–36; kinds of, 133–4; Locke, 122–3; relation to denomination (q.v.), 121–31

analogy of inequality, 216 n3

analogy of meaning, 93–109; another test for, 174; atributional analogy, 133–6; functionally equivalent conditions, 197; and paronymy, 136–41

analogy of proportionality, based on relations of relations, 95; and categorial difference, 119–20; defined, 7, 95–6; distinguished from improper proportionality, 95; relations to attribution, 132–3

analysis, philosophical: analogous definitions, xi, 2, 206, 220 n5; analogy in law, 202–11; analytically equivalent truth conditions, 141, 208; antecedent linguistic meaning, 195; articulated conditions, 195; articulated restatement, 191–8; articulation device, 179; capacity of, 2; counterexamples, 201–2; not by disjunctive definition, 199–201; functionally equivalent, 197;

238

meaning-relevent conditions, 195; no
substitutability requirement, 195;
Wiggins critique, 192–3
analytically equivalent truth-conditions,
141, 198; functionally equivalent
conditions, 197–8, 208–11
antecedent linguistic meaning, affects
analysis, 179–85; affects truth-
conditions, 180–5; is basis of
expressive capacity, 184;
characterized, 182; is locus for
analogy, 180; is locus for
equivocation, 180; not same
regardless of environment, 220 n4;
relation to truth conditions, 195; not
same as truth conditions, 184
argumentum ad ignorantiam, 177–8, 219
articulate classification, 60–3
articulation, by analysis, 179, 191–8;
requires decomposition, 191; of
thought, 191
artificial languages vs. natural, 13, 17, 51
ascriptive analogy, 134–5; ascription,
contrasts of, 33
ascriptive attribution, 134–5
asymmetry of metaphors,
superimposed, 91

benchmark sentences, defined, 212 n3,
185–91; benchmark occurrences, 186–
7; need be justified, 189–91;
required, 187; rigidly designate facts,
206
benchmark situations (stereotypes), def.
212 n3, 158; fact stereotypes, 175;
needing to justify, 189–91
blocking, 75

categorial contrasts, 15; and analogy,
119–20, 216 n2
categorial differences, 119–20; analogy,
119, 216 n2
characterization problems, 207–11
classifications, 60–3; articulate, 60;
differentiated analogously, 194;
disjoint, 60; exhaustive, 60; extended
analogically, 138; finite, 60; fixed, 60;
linguistically objective vs. craft
objective, 60
classical analogy theory, xi, 5–6;
compared to new theory, 132–3;
described, 17–19, 164–5; its false
premises, xi; its heart, 22, 28; its

limitations, 19–27
clusters, analogy within, 100–2; mere
equivocation among, 103–4;
overlapping foci, 101–2, 105; result
from analogy, 103; specified by
meaning-relevant near synonyms,
102, 104
co-applicable words, conditions for, 59;
effects of differences of, 67–70; lower
boundary (schemes), 77
cognitive evacuation, 172–8
cognitivity attacks, 218 n1;
representative writers, 218 nn2 & 3
combinatorial possibility, contrasting,
13; relation to same word meanings,
14
community of meaning, by analogy,
165–72; in Aquinas, 164–5; by
embedding, 171
comparative meaning relationships
(univocal, equivocal, analogous,
denominative, paronymous), 50–1
completion words, frame elements, 48;
vs. frame words, 48; sentence
completions, 48
conceptual adjustment, 4
conceptual sets, 218 n3
consequent sentential meaning, 182–3;
antecedent sentential meaning, 182–3;
(see also linguistic meaning)
conflict of dominance, results of, 83
contagion, see semantic contagion
contradictions, and entrenchment, 79;
semantic, 79; not unacceptable, 82
contrast-dependent words, 62; applied
analogously, 62, 67; conditions for,
130; predicate modes, 128–30
continuity, see linguistic continuity
craftbound discourse, 15, 158–78, esp.
167–8; connotes skill, 158;
distinguished from unbound, 165–7;
predicates differentiate, 204; requires
equivocation, 163
craft-conscious hearers, 63

denomination, 4, 6, 8, 122–41;
aliorelative, 124; Anselm, 122;
Aquinas, 122–30; Aristotle, 122;
contrasting, 121; defined, 123;
denominative analogy (q.v.), 121–32;
Locke, 122; productive vs. resultant
properties, 125; relational naming,
123; utility of division, 95

239

denominative analogy, 7–8, 52–3, 95;
Aquinas, 124–30, and 216 n3;
Aquinas' and Cajetan's notion of, 126,
216 n5, 216 n8; and attribution as
Cajetan defined it, 133; contrasting
denominations (q.v.), 121;
contrasting predicate modes (q.v.),
121, 128–32; definition, 131; and
figurative discourse, 142–57; includes
broad reconception of attribution,
133; Locke, 123–4; nature and history,
121–31, 132, 216–7, notes, required in
some figures of speech, 150–3; has
species, 121–2; subdivisions of, 134
determinable, applied analogously, 62;
defined, 60
determinate, applied analogously, 62;
defined, 60
diachronic manifestation, of analogy
structures, 11, 50–1; constructions
(hypothetical constructions, q.v.), 51;
and expressive capacity (q.v.), 51; of
linguistic force (q.v.), 10; of
'software', 6

differences of meaning, Aristotle's 15
tests, 40–7; not result of intention, 213
n4; sense meaning vs. linguistic, 41–2;
same words vs. different words, 13,
38–9; words vs. sentences, 37–8
differentiating elements (conditions) in
analysis, 196
differentiation (of meaning), 6; ch. 2 and
passim; by cancelling presuppositions,
57; caused by dominance, 49; causes
expressive capacity to evolve 50;
defeasible presuppositions, 56;
defined 50, 212 n1; diachronic effects
50–1, generic phenomenon, 6, 33–53;
important to explain 21; involves
exclusion, 50; laws of, listed, 213 n4;
laws of (q.v.), and figures of speech,
148–53; is observable 25, 50; operates
inexorably 62; overlooked 21;
structure, 212 n2; underlying
phenomenon 20
different meanings, of different words,
13; not the same as different ways of
being something, 217 n13; of same
words, 13
discourse context, 37
discourse environment, 1, 37; defined,
59; extent of, 59 (see also
environment)
disjunctive analysis (definitions),
excluded, 198–201, 220 n7
divine attribute words, 170–2
dominated, every word, 78; same words
have to be, 120
dominance, 3, 6, 9, 81–3; capture, 78; is
caused, 49; causes analogy
phenomena, 9; causes 'fit', 48;
conditions for, 82, 215 n5; is
contextually induced, 50–1; defined,
82; displayed, 49; by exclusion, 81; is
explanatory, 49, 73, 151 (proof of);
and indifference (q.v.), 78–83;
intransigence, 78; is law-like, 49;
multivalent (reciprocal), 51–2; and
nonsense, 11; is observable, 25, 50;
principle of, 78; and resistance, 78;
scheme selection, 78–9; suppresses
presupposition, 156
dominating expressions, 76; create
zeugma, 151; exclusion, blocking,
scheme resistance, 77, 81–3; selecting
schemes, 76–7
double differentiation, in figurative
discourse, 15, 42–57, 152–5; in poetry,
154–6; in prose, 155; semantic
signature, 153
double (iterated) homonymy, 92

embedded discourse, 107, 170–1; legal
discourse, 204; matrices, 107
entrenchment, and contradictions, 79–
80; of contrast-dependent relations,
136, 215 n4; of modes, 132; of
schemes, 79–80
environments, alien, 77–8; discourse, 1,
37; extent of, 59; hospitable, 77, 106;
inhospitable (linguistic nonsense), 78
epistemic attitude, 159
equivocation, Aristotle, 215 n1;
Boethius, 215 n1; conditions for, 87;
and dominance, 78; kinds of, 52–3,
87 ff
evacuated content, by mere
equivocation, 160
exclusion of words, 76; blocking, 75–7;
mechanisms for dominance, 81–3;
resistance, 77
experience, 159–61, 163, 167–71
explanatory portrayal, 3–4
expressive capacity, actuality, 13;
affected by analogy and equivocation,

240

180, 184; contrasting, 12; defeasible, 182; evolving, 13, 50–1; limitations of, 11–14; linguistic meaning determines, 65–6; medium of thought, 183; relation to analogy, 157; relation to infinite polysemy, 49; restricted, 183–4 n4; meaning differences are of scheme or mode, 129; meaning-related paronyms are analogous, 138; meaning relevant synonyms specify clusters, 104; of mere equivocation, 92; metaphors can just happen, 113; modes of metaphor, 116–17; operates inexorably, 62; paronymy correlates with analogy, 137; same words substitutable *salva veritate*, 39; synchronic manifestations of inertia and resistance, 11; universally quantified propositions that hold counterfactually, 213 n4

linguistic continuity, 161–3, 165, 218–9 nn1–6 and 7

linguistic discontinuity hypothesis, 161–3; collapses, 163; 'linguistic turn', 219 n4; writers on, 219 n4

linguistic force, 3, 9–11; defined, 10; generates new meanings, 14; principle of, 78, 80; resistance, dominance, capture, fit, 78–82

linguistic inertia, 3, 9–11; see also inertia

linguistic meaning; controls expressive capacity (q.v.), 12; determines expressive capacity, 65–6; difference of (explained), 66; distinguished from sense meaning, 41–2; evolving, 11–15; evolving expressive capacity, 50–1; expansion of, 10; governed, 73; intrinsic, 2; limits analysis, 12, 182–3; and nonsense (q.v.), 77–8; prior to statement, 220 n4; prior to use, 12; related to antecedent meaning, 195; relation to infinite polysemy, 49; sufficient conditions for, 82

linguistic nonsense, 82, 172; alien environments, 77; inhospitable environment, 78; relative to environment, 81–2; 172–3; sufficient conditions for, 82

literal, vs. non-literal, 111; difference from Goodman, 111

logical positivism, see positivism

material supposition (mere mention), 36

meaning, absolute and relative, 9, 14–15; antecedent, 180, 182–3; belief elements of, 11; consequent, 182–3

meaning, classical account of, xi, 2, 17–18, 164–5; Kretzman's statement of, 213 n3

meaning matrices, 107; similarity and analogy, 107, 170–1

meaning related, 7, 170–1

meaning relevance, 7, 63–70; defined, 67–8; intra-theoretical choice, 66; meaning-relevant truth conditions, defined, 16, 180, 195; predicate scheme boundaries, 77–80; representing word meanings, 73

meaninglessness (cf. nonsense), 172–8; conflict of dominance, 172; environmental prevention, 172; exsanguinated sentences, 173–5; not from inconsistency, 57; has to be induced, 172; lack of dominance, 172

media of thought, 11–14; antecedent linguistic meaning, 183; conditions of contrast, 65; language thinks for us, 99–100, 213 n4; linguistic meaning as, 65; vs. media of expression, 13; others, 65; restricted expressive capacity, 183

mere equivocation, 4, 6, 14; among clusters, 103–4; among paronyms, 139; no analogous synonyms, 91; conditions for, 52–3, 87–8; defined, 88; diachronic fallout of differentiation, 99; disparity of schemes, 89–90; induced differentiation, 92–3; iterated disparity, 87–8; iterated homonymy, 92; non-substitutability 90–2, 94

metaphor, 7; Aristotle, 3; can just happen, 113; complex metaphors, 115; exclusion relations, 113–114; false, 114; and figures of speech, 147–53; improper proportionality, 30; in proportionalities, 30–2; a kind of analogy, 109; objective, 117; presuppositions, 111–14; relation to improper proportionality, 95; senses of, 109; simple metaphor (q.v.), 109–19; superimposed asymmetry, 91; thinking, 116–17; with types, 118

Miller's Analogies test, 27–32

modes of metaphor, 116; how generated, 116

musical note (character), 70–2; contrast relationships, 70

near synonyms, 83–5; definition, 84, 215 n2; disparity of, 87; relation to mere equivocation, 87; relation to

243